Teaching Science to English Language Learners

JOYCE W. NUTTA, NAZAN U. BAUTISTA,
MALCOLM B. BUTLER

Routledge
Taylor & Francis Group

NEW YORK AND LONDON

First published 2011
by Routledge
270 Madison Avenue, New York, NY 10016

Simultaneously published in the UK
by Routledge
2 Park Square, Milton Park, Abingdon, Oxon OX14 4RN

Routledge is an imprint of the Taylor & Francis Group, an informa business

© 2011 Taylor & Francis

Typeset in Minion by Prepress Projects Ltd, Perth, UK
Index: Indexing Specialists (UK) Ltd.
Printed and bound in the United States of America on acid-free paper by Edwards Brothers, Inc.

Library of Congress Cataloging in Publication Data
Teaching science to English language learners / Joyce W. Nutta, Nazan U. Bautista, Malcolm B. Butler.
p. cm. -- (Teaching english language learners across the curriculum)
Includes bibliographical references and index.
1. Science--Study and teaching (Elementary) 2. Science--Study and teaching (Secondary) 3. English language--Study and teaching (Elementary)--Foreign speak-ers. 4. English language--Study and teaching (Secondary)--Foreign speakers. I. Bautista, Nazan U. II. Butler, Malcolm B. III. Title.
LB1585.N87 2010
507.1--dc22
2010019908

ISBN 13: 978-0-415-99624-2 (hbk)
ISBN 13: 978-0-415-99625-9 (pbk)
ISBN 13: 978-0-203-85057-2 (ebk)

Teaching Science to English Language Learners

Teaching Science to English Language Learners offers science teachers and teacher educators a straightforward approach for engaging ELLs learning science, offering examples of easy ways to adapt existing lesson plans to be more inclusive. The practical, teacher-friendly strategies and techniques included here are proven effective with ELLs, and many are also effective with all students. The book provides context-specific strategies for the full range of the secondary sciences curriculum, including physical science, life science, earth and space science, science as inquiry, and history and nature of science and more. A fully annotated list of web and print resources completes the book, making this a one-volume reference to help science teachers meet the challenges of including all learners in effective instruction.

Special features:

- Practical examples of science exercises make applying theory to practice simple when teaching science to ELLs
- An overview of the National Science Education Standards offers useful guidelines for effective instructional and assessment practices for ELLs in secondary grades
- Graphs, tables, and illustrations provide additional access points to the text in clear, meaningful ways

Joyce W. Nutta is an Associate Professor of English for Speakers of Other Languages (ESOL) Education and the ESOL Co-ordinator of the College of Education at the University of Central Florida.

Nazan U. Bautista is an Assistant Professor of Science Education in the Department of Teacher Education at Miami University.

Malcolm B. Butler is an Associate Professor of Science Education at the University of South Florida in St. Petersburg, Florida.

Teaching English Language Learners Across the Curriculum

Series Editors: Tony Erben, Bárbara C. Cruz, Stephen J. Thornton

Teaching Mathematics to English Language Learners
Gladis Kersaint, Denisse R. Thompson, Mariana Petkova

Teaching English Language Learners in Career and Technical Education Programs
Victor M. Hernández-Gantes and William Blank

Teaching English Language Learners through Technology
Tony Erben, Ruth Ban, Martha Castañeda

Teaching Social Studies to English Language Learners
Bárbara C. Cruz and Stephen J. Thornton

Teaching Language Arts to English Language Learners
Anete Vásquez, Angela L. Hansen, Philip C. Smith

Teaching Science to English Language Learners
Joyce W. Nutta, Nazan U. Bautista, Malcolm B. Butler

Contents

Figures

Tables

Series
Introduction

No educational issue has proven more controversial than how to teach linguistically diverse students. Intertwined issues of ethnic and cultural differences are often compounded. What is more, at the time of writing, December 2007, how immigrants and their heritages *ought* to fit with the dominant culture is the subject of rancorous debate in the United States and a number of other nations.

However thorny these issues may be to some, both legally and ethically, schools need to accommodate the millions of English language learners (ELLs) who need to be educated. Although the number of ELLs in the United States has burgeoned in recent decades, school programs generally remain organized via traditional subjects, which are delivered in English. Many ELLs are insufficiently fluent in academic English, however, to succeed in these programs. Since policymakers have increasingly insisted that ELLs, regardless of their fluency in English, be mainstreamed into standard courses with all other students, both classroom enactment of the curriculum and teacher education need considerable rethinking.

Language scholars have generally taken the lead in this rethinking. As is evident in Part 1 of the volumes in this series, language scholars have developed a substantial body of research to inform the mainstreaming of ELLs. The primary interest of these language scholars, however, is almost by definition the processes and principles of second language acquisition. Until recently, subject matter has typically been a secondary consideration, used to illustrate language concerns. Perhaps not surprisingly, content-area teachers sometimes have seen this as reducing their subjects to little more than isolated bits of information, such as a list of explorers and dates in history or sundry geological formations in science.

In contrast, secondary school teachers see their charge as effectively conveying a principled understanding of, and interest in, a subject. They look for relationships, seek to develop concepts, search for powerful examples and analogies, and try to explicate principles. By the same token, they strive to make meaningful connections among the subject matter, students' experience, and life outside of school. In our observations, teacher education programs bifurcate courses on content-area methods and (if there are any) courses designed to instill principles of teaching ELLs. One result of this bifurcation seems to be that prospective and in-service teachers are daunted by the challenge of using language principles to inform their teaching of subject matter.

For example, Gloria Ladson-Billings (2001) has experimented with how to prepare new teachers for diverse classrooms through a teacher education program focused on "diversity, equity, and social justice" (p. xiii). Teachers in her program are expected, for instance, to confront rather than become resigned to low academic expectations for children in urban schools. From Ladson-Billings's perspective, "no matter what else the schools find themselves doing, promoting students' academic achievement is among their primary functions" (p. 56).

The authors in this series extend this perspective to teaching ELLs in the content areas. For example, how might ELLs be included in a literature lesson on Hardy's use of landscape imagery in *The Mayor of Casterbridge*, or an economics lesson on the principle of comparative advantage, or a biology lesson on the ecosystem of a pond? Such topics, experienced educators quickly recognize, are often difficult for native speakers of English. How can teachers break down these subjects into topics in a way that is educationally significant for ELLs?

The purpose of this series is to assist current and prospective educators to plan and implement lessons that do justice to the goals of the curriculum and make sense to and interest ELLs. If the needs of diverse learners are to be met, Ladson-Billings (2001) underscores that innovation is demanded, not that teachers merely pine for how things once were. The most obvious innovation in this series is to bring language scholars and specialists in the methods of teaching particular school subjects together. Although this approach is scarcely unique, it remains relatively uncommon. Combining the two groups brings more to addressing the problems of instruction than could be obtained by the two groups working separately. Even so, these volumes hardly tell the reader "everything there is to know" about the problems addressed. But we do know that our teacher education students report that even modest training to teach ELLs can make a significant difference in the classroom. We hope this series extends those successes to all the content areas of the curriculum.

Part 1
Your English Language Learner
Tony Erben
University of Tampa

1.1
Orientation

English language learners (ELLs) represent the fastest growing group throughout all levels of schooling in the United States. For example, between the 1990–1991 school year and the 2000–2001 school year, the ELL population grew approximately 105 percent nationally, while the general school population grew only 12 percent (Kindler, 2002). In several states (including Texas, California, New Mexico, Florida, Arizona, North Carolina, and New York), the percentage of ELLs within school districts ranges anywhere between 10 and 50 percent of the school population. In sum, there are over 10 million ELLs in U.S. schools today. According to the U.S. Department of Education, one out of seven students in our nation's classrooms speaks a language other than English at home. Although many of these students are heritage language learners and are proficient in English, many others are recent immigrants with barely a working knowledge of the language let alone a command of academic English. Meeting the needs of such students can be particularly challenging for all teachers given the often text-dependent nature of content areas. The language of the curriculum is often abstract and includes complex concepts calling for higher-order thinking skills. Additionally, many ELLs do not have a working knowledge of American culture that can serve as a schema for new learning.

But let's now look at these English language learners. Who are they and how do they come to be in our classrooms?

ELL is the term used for any student in an American school setting whose native language is not English. Their English ability lies anywhere on a continuum from knowing only a few words to being able to get by using everyday English, but still in need of acquiring more English so that they can succeed educationally at school. All students enrolled in an American school, including ELLs, have the right to an equitable and quality education. Traditionally, many ELLs are placed in stand-alone English for speakers of other languages (ESOL) classes and learn English until they are deemed capable of following the regular curriculum in English. However, with the introduction of federal and state legislation such as *No Child Left Behind* (2002), Proposition 227 in California, and other English-only legislation in other states, many school systems now require ELLs to receive their English instruction not through stand-alone ESOL classes, but directly through their curriculum content classes.[1] Today "mainstreaming" is the most frequently used method of language instruction for ELL students in U.S. schools. Mainstreaming involves placing ELLs in content-area classrooms where the curriculum is delivered through English; curricula and instruction are typically not modified in these classrooms for non-native English speakers (Carrasquillo & Rodriguez, 2002). According to Meltzer and Hamann (2005), placement of ELLs in mainstream classes occurs for a number of reasons including assumptions by non-educators about what ELLs need, the scarcity of ESOL-trained teachers relative to demand, the growth of ELL populations, the dispersal of ELLs into more districts across the country, and restrictions in a growing number of states regarding the time ELLs can stay in ESOL programs. They predict that, unless these conditions change, ELLs will spend their time in school (1) with teachers not adequately trained to work with ELLs, (2) with teachers who do not see it as a priority to meet the needs of their ELLs, and (3) with curricula and classroom practices that are not designed to target ELL needs (Coady *et al.*, 2003). As we shall later see, of all possible instructional options to help ELLs learn English, placing an ELL in a mainstreamed English-medium classroom where no accommodations are made by the teacher is the least effective approach. It may even be detrimental to the educational progress of ELLs.

This then raises the question of whether or not the thousands of curriculum content teachers across the United States, who now have the collective lion's share of responsibility in providing English language instruction to ELLs, have had preservice or in-service education to modify, adapt, and make the appropriate pedagogical accommodations within their lessons for this special group of students. This is important: ELLs should remain included in the cycle of everyday learning and make academic progress commensurate with grade-level expectations. It is also important that teachers feel competent and effective in their professional duties.

The aim of Part 1 of this book is to provide you the reader with an overview of the linguistic mechanics of second language development. Specifically, as teachers you will learn what to expect in the language abilities of ELLs as their proficiency in English develops over time. Although the rate of language development among ELLs depends on the particular instructional and social circumstances of each ELL, general patterns and expectations will be discussed. We will also outline for teachers the learning outcomes that ELLs typically accomplish in differing ESOL programs and the importance of the maintenance of first language development. School systems differ across the United States in the ways in which they try to deal with ELL populations. Therefore, we describe the pedagogical pros and cons of an array of ESOL programs as well as clarify terminology used in the field. Part 1 will also profile various ELL populations that enter U.S. schools (e.g. refugees vs. migrants, special needs) and share how teachers can make their pedagogy more culturally responsive. Finally, we will also survey what teachers can expect from the cultural practices that ELLs may engage in in the classroom as well as present a myriad of ways in which both school systems and teachers can better foster home–school communication links.

1.2
The Process of English Language Learning and What to Expect

It is generally accepted that anybody who endeavors to learn a second language will go through specific stages of language development. According to some second language acquisition theorists (e.g. Pienemann, 2007), the way in which language is produced under natural time constraints is very regular and systematic. For example, just as a baby needs to learn how to crawl before it can walk, so too a second language learner will produce language structures only in a predetermined psychological order of complexity. What this means is that an ELL will utter "homework do" before being able to utter "tonight I homework do" before ultimately being able to produce a target-like structure such as "I will do my homework tonight." Of course, with regard to being communicatively effective, the first example is as successful as the last example. The main difference is that one is less English-like than the other. Pienemann's work has centered on one subsystem of language, namely morphosyntactic structures. It gives us an interesting glimpse into how an ELL's language may progress (see Table 1.1).

Researchers such as Pienemann (1989; 2007) and Krashen (1981) assert that there is an immutable language acquisition order and, regardless of what the teacher tries to teach to the ELL in terms of English skills, the learner will acquire new language structures only when (s)he is cognitively and psychologically ready to do so.

What can a teacher do if an ELL will only learn English in a set path? Much research has been conducted over the past 20 years on this very question and the upshot is that, although teachers cannot change the route of development for ELLs, they *can* very much affect the rate of development. The way in which teachers can stimulate the language development of ELLs is by providing what is known as an acquisition-rich classroom. Ellis (2005), among others, provides useful research generalizations that constitute a broad basis for "evidence-based practice." Rather

TABLE 1.1. Generalized patterns of ESOL development stages

Stage	Main features	Example
1	Single words; formulas	My name is_____. How are you
2	Subject–verb object word order; plural marking	I see school I buy books
3	"Do"-fronting; adverb preposing; negation + verb	Do you understand me? Yesterday I go to school. She no coming today.
4	Pseudo-inversion; yes/no inversion; verb + to + verb	Where is my purse? Have you a car? I want to go.
5	3rd person –s; do-2nd position	He works in a factory. He did not understand.
6	Question-tag; adverb–verb phrase	He's Polish, isn't he? I can always go.

Source: Pienemann (1988).

than repeat them verbatim here, we have synthesized them into *five principles for creating effective second language learning environments*. They are presented and summarized below.

Principle 1: Give ELLs Many Opportunities to Read, to Write, to Listen to, and to Discuss Oral and Written English Texts Expressed in a Variety of Ways

Camilla had only recently arrived at the school. She was a good student and was making steady progress. She had learned some English in Argentina and used every opportunity to learn new words at school. Just before Thanksgiving her science teacher commenced a new unit of work on the periodic table and elements. During the introductory lesson, the teacher projected a periodic table on the whiteboard. She began asking the students some probing questions about the table. One of her first questions was directed to Camilla. The teacher asked, "Camilla, tell me what you see on the right hand side of the table." Camilla answered, "I see books, Bunsen burner, also pencils."

Of course the teacher was referring not to the table standing in front of the whiteboard, but to the table projected onto the whiteboard. Though a simple mistake, the example above is illustrative of the fact that Camilla has yet to develop academic literacy.

In 2001, Meltzer defined academic literacy as the ability of a person to "use reading, writing, speaking, listening and thinking to learn what they want/need to learn AND [to] communicate/demonstrate that learning to others who need/want to know" (p. 16). The definition is useful in that it rejects literacy as something static and implies agency on the part of a learner who develops an ability to successfully put her/his knowledge and skills to use in new situations. Being proficient in academic literacy requires knowledge of a type of language used predominantly in classrooms and tied very much to learning. However, even though it is extremely important for ELLs to master, not many content teachers take the time to provide explicit instruction in it. Moreover, many content teachers do not necessarily know the discipline-specific discourse features or text structures of their own subject areas.

Currently, there is much research to suggest that both the discussion of texts and the production of texts are important practices in the development of content-area literacy and learning. For ELLs this means that opportunities to create, discuss, share, revise, and edit a variety of texts will help them develop content-area understanding and also recognition and familiarity with the types of texts found in particular content areas (Boscolo & Mason, 2001). Classroom practices that are found to improve academic literacy development include teachers improving reading comprehension through modeling, explicit strategy instruction in context, spending more time giving reading and writing instruction as well as having students spend more time with reading and writing assignments, providing more time for ELLs to talk explicitly about texts as they are trying to process and/or create them, and helping to develop critical thinking skills as well as being responsive to individual learner needs (Meltzer & Hamann, 2005).

The importance of classroom talk in conjunction with learning from and creating texts cannot be underestimated in the development of academic literacy in ELLs. In the case above, rather than smiling at the error and moving on with the lesson, the teacher could have further developed Camilla's vocabulary knowledge by easily taking a two-minute digression from the lesson to brainstorm with the class all the ways the word *table* can be used at school—in math, social studies, language arts, etc.

Principle 2: Draw Attention to Patterns of English Language Structure

In order to ride a bike well, a child needs to actually practice riding the bike. Sometimes, training wheels are fitted to the back of the bike to help the younger child maintain his/her balance. In time, the training wheels are taken away as the child gains more confidence. As this process unfolds, parents also teach kids the rules of the road: how to read road signs, to be attentive to cars, to ride defensively, etc. Although knowing the rules of the road won't help a child learn to ride the bike better in a physical sense, it will help the child avoid being involved in a road accident. Knowing the rules of the road—when and where to ride a bike, etc.—will make the child a more accomplished bike rider. Why use this example? Well, it is a good metaphor to explain that language learning needs to unfold in the same way. An ELL, without much formal schooling, will develop the means to communicate in English. However, it will most likely be only very basic English. Unfortunately, tens of thousands of adult ELLs across this country never progress past this stage. School-age ELLs have an opportunity to move beyond a basic command of English—to become accomplished communicators in English. However, this won't happen on its own. To do so requires the ELL to get actively involved in classroom activities, ones in which an ELL is required to practice speaking.

As mentioned above, early research into naturalistic second language acquisition has evidenced that learners follow a "natural" order and sequence of acquisition. What this means is that grammatical structures emerge in the communicative utterances of second language learners in a relatively fixed, regular, systematic, and universal order. The ways in which teachers can take advantage of this "built-in syllabus" are to implement an activity-centered approach that sets out to provide ELLs with language-rich instructional opportunities and offer ELLs explicit exposure and instruction related to language structures that they are trying to utter but with which they still have trouble.

Principle 3: Give ELLs Classroom Time to Use their English Productively

A theoretical approach within the field of second language acquisition (SLA) called the interaction hypothesis and developed primarily by Long (1996; 2006) posits that acquisition is facilitated through interaction when second language learners are engaged in negotiating for meaning. What this means is that, when ELLs are engaged in talk, they make communication modifications that help language become more comprehensible, they more readily solicit corrective feedback, and they adjust their own use of English.

The discrepancy in the rate of acquisition shown by ELLs can be attributed to the amount and the quality of input they receive as well as the opportunities they have for output. Output means having opportunities to use language. Second language acquisition researchers agree that the opportunity for output plays an important part in facilitating second language development. Skehan (1998) drawing on Swain (1995) summarizes the contributions that output can make: (1) by using language with others, ELLs will obtain a richer language contribution from those around them, (2) ELLs will be forced to pay attention to the structure of language they listen to, (3) ELLs will be able to test out their language assumptions and confirm them through the types of language input they receive, (4) ELLs can better internalize their current language knowledge, (5) by engaging in interaction, ELLs can work towards better discourse fluency, and (6) ELLs will be able to find space to develop their own linguistic style and voice.

It behooves teachers to plan for and incorporate ELLs in all language activities in the classroom. Of course an ELL will engage with an activity based on the level of proficiency (s)he has at any given time and the teacher should take this into account when planning for instruction. Under no circumstances should ELLs be left at the "back of the classroom" to linguistically or pedagogically fend for themselves.

Principle 4: Give ELLs Opportunities to Notice their Errors and to Correct their English

Throughout the day, teachers prepare activities for students that have the sole intent of getting them to learn subject matter. Less often do teachers think about the language learning potential that the same activity may generate. This can be applied to ELLs: Teachers encourage them to notice their errors, to reflect on how they use English, and to think about how English works, which plays a very important role in their language development. In a series of seminal studies, Lyster and his colleagues (Lyster, 1998; 2001; 2004; 2007; Lyster & Ranta, 1997; Lyster & Mori, 2006) outline six feedback moves that teachers can use to direct ELLs' attention to their language output and in doing so help them correct their English.

Example 1

Student: "The heart hits blood to se body. . ."
Teacher: "The heart pumps blood to the body."

In the above example, an ELL's utterance is incorrect, and the teacher provides the correct form. Often teachers gloss over explicitly correcting an ELL's language for fear of singling out the student in class. However, *explicit correction* is a very easy way to help ELLs notice the way they use language.

Example 2

Student: "I can experimenting with Bunsen burner."
Teacher: "What? Can you say that again?"

By using phrases such as "Excuse me?", "I don't understand," or "Can you repeat that?", the teacher shows that the communication has not been understood or that the ELL's utterance contained some kind of error. *Requesting clarification* indicates to the ELL that a repetition or reformulation of the utterance is required.

Example 3

Student: "After today I go to sport."
Teacher: "So, tomorrow you are going to play sports?"
Student: "Yes, tomorrow I am going to play sport."

Without directly showing that the student's utterance was incorrect, the teacher implicitly *recasts* the ELL's error, or provides the correction.

Example 4

Teacher: "Is that how it is said?" or "Is that English?" or "Does that sound right to you?"

Without providing the correct form, the teacher provides a *metalinguistic clue.* This may take the form of asking a question or making a comment related to the formation of the ELL's utterance.

Example 5

Teacher: "So, then it will be a . . ." (with long stress on "a")

The teacher directly gets the correct form from the ELL by pausing to allow the student to complete the teacher's utterance. *Elicitation* questions differ from questions that are defined as metalinguistic clues in that they require more than a yes/no response.

Example 6

Student: "The two boy go to town tomorrow."
Teacher: "The two boys go to town tomorrow." (with teacher making a prolonged stress on "boy"

Repetitions are probably one of the most frequent forms of error correction carried out by teachers. Here a teacher repeats the ELL's error and adjusts intonation to draw an ELL's attention to it.

Using these corrective feedback strategies helps to raise an ELL's awareness and understanding of language conventions used in and across content areas.

Principle 5: Construct Activities that Maximize Opportunities for ELLs to Interact with Others in English

One day, when we had visitors from up north, our daughter came home very excited and said that the teacher had announced that the class would be learning Spanish from the beginning of the month. Our friend, ever the pessimist, said, "I learned Spanish for four years at high school, and look at me now, I can't even string a sentence together in Spanish." What comes to mind is the old saying, "use it or lose it." Of course, my friend and I remember our foreign language learning days being spent listening to the teacher, usually in English. We were lucky if we even got the chance to say anything in Spanish. Since we never used Spanish in class, our hopes of retaining any Spanish diminished with each passing year since graduation. My daughter's 20-year-old brother, on the other hand, had the same Spanish teacher that my daughter will have. He remembers a lot of his Spanish, but also that his Spanish classes were very engaging. A lesson would never pass in which he didn't speak, listen to, read, and write in Spanish. He was always involved in some learning activity and he always expressed how great it was to converse during the class with his friends in Spanish by way of the activities that the teacher had planned.

I use this analogy as it applies to ELLs as well. In order for ELLs to progress with their English language development, a teacher needs to vary the types of instructional tasks that the ELL will engage in. Student involvement during instruction is the key to academic success whereas constant passive learning, mostly through lecture-driven lessons, will greatly impede any language learning efforts by an ELL.

Our five principles provide a framework with which to construct a curriculum that is sensitive to the language developmental needs of ELLs. However, to further solidify our understanding of an ELL's language progress, it is necessary to have a clear picture of what ELLs can do with their language at different levels of proficiency and what implications this has for instruction. Although many taxonomies exist that seek to categorize the developmental stages of second language learners, many education systems throughout the United States have adopted a four-tier description.

The four stages are called Preproduction, Early Production, Speech Emergence, and Intermediate Fluency (Krashen & Terrell, 1983).

The **preproduction stage** applies to ELLs who are unfamiliar with English. They may have had anything from one day to three months of exposure to English. ELLs at this level are trying to absorb the language, and they can find this process overwhelming. In a school context, they are often linguistically overloaded, and get tired quickly because of the need for constant and intense concentration. An ELL's language skills are at the receptive level, and they enter a "silent period" of listening. ELLs at this stage are able to comprehend more English than they can produce. Their attention is focused on developing everyday social English. At the preproduction stage, an ELL can engage in nonverbal responses; follow simple commands; point and respond with movement; and utter simple formulaic structures in English such as "yes," "no," "thank you," or use names. ELLs may develop a receptive vocabulary of up to 500 words.

By the time an ELL enters the **early production stage**, (s)he will have had many opportunities to encounter meaningful and comprehensible English. They will begin to respond with one- or two-word answers or short utterances. ELLs may now have internalized up to 1,000 words in their receptive vocabulary and anything from 100 to 500 words in their active vocabulary. In order for ELLs to begin to speak, teachers should create a low-anxiety environment in their classrooms.

At this stage, ELLs are experimenting and taking risks with English. Errors in grammar and pronunciation are to be expected. Pragmatic errors are also common. Teachers need to model/ demonstrate with correct language responses in context. Redundancies, repetitions, circumlocu- tions, and language enhancement strategies are important for teachers to use when interacting with ELLs at this level.

At the **speech emergence stage**, an ELL will begin to use the language to interact more freely. At this stage, ELLs have a 7,000-word receptive vocabulary. They may have an active vocabulary of up to 2,000 words. By this time, ELLs may have had between one and three years' exposure to English. It is possible that they have a receptive understanding of academic English; however, in order to make content-area subject matter comprehensible, teachers are advised to make great use of advance organizers. Teachers should make explicit attempts to modify the delivery of subject matter, to model language use, and to teach metacognitive strategies in order to help ELLs predict, describe, demonstrate, and problem solve. Because awareness of English is growing, it is also important for teachers to provide ELLs at this stage with opportunities to work in structured small groups so that they can reflect and experiment with their language output.

At the stage of **intermediate fluency**, ELLs may demonstrate near-native or native-like fluency in everyday social English, but not in academic English. Often teachers become acutely aware that, even though an ELL can speak English fluently in social settings (the playground, at sport functions, etc.), they will experience difficulties in understanding and verbalizing cognitively demanding, abstract concepts taught and discussed in the classroom. At this stage ELLs may have developed up to a 12,000-word receptive vocabulary and a 4,000-word active vocabulary. Teachers of ELLs at the intermediate fluency level need to proactively provide relevant content- based literacy experiences such as brainstorming, clustering, synthesizing, categorizing, charting, evaluating, journaling, or log writing, including essay writing and peer critiquing, in order to foster academic proficiency in English.

At the University of South Florida, we have developed online ELL databases that have been created to provide pre- and in-service teachers with annotated audio and video samples of lan- guage use by ELLs who are at each of the four different levels of language proficiency. The video and audio files act as instructional tools that allow teachers to familiarize themselves with the language ability (speaking, reading, writing) of ELLs who are at different stages of development. For example, teachers may have ELLs in classes and not be sure of their level of English language development, nor be sure what to expect the ELL to be able to do with English in terms of pro- duction and comprehension. This naturally impacts how a teacher may plan for instruction. By looking through the databases, a teacher can listen to and watch representations of ELL language production abilities at all four levels (preproduction, early production, speech emergence, and intermediate fluency). In addition, the databases feature interviews with expert ESOL teachers, examples of tests used to evaluate the proficiency levels of ELLs, and selected readings and les- son plans written for ELLs at different levels of proficiency. Lastly, they provide case studies that troubleshoot pedagogical problem areas when teaching ELLs.

There are three databases: one that features ELLs at the elementary school level, one featuring ELLs at the middle school level, and one featuring ELLs at high school.

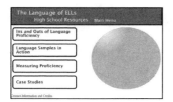 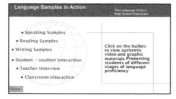 

The three ELL databases can be found at:

- http://esol.coedu.usf.edu/elementary/index.htm (elementary school language samples);
- http://esol.coedu.usf.edu/middleschool/index.htm (middle school language samples);
- http://esol.coedu.usf.edu/highschool/index.htm (high school language samples).

It is important to remember that a lack of language ability does not mean a lack of concept development or a lack of ability to learn. Teachers should continue to ask inferential and higher-order questions (questions requiring reasoning ability, hypothesizing, inferring, analyzing, justifying, and predicting) that challenge an ELL to think.

Teaching Help

For two good websites that outline ways to enhance questioning using Bloom's taxonomy see www.teachers.ash.org.au/researchskills/dalton.htm (Dalton & Smith, 1986) and www.nwlink.com/~donclark/hrd/bloom.html (Clark, 1999). The latter gives a further detailed breakdown of Bloom's Learning Domains in terms of cognitive, affective, and psychomotor key words and how these can be used to foster an ELL's language learning.

Zehler (1994) provides a list of further strategies that teachers can use to engage ELLs at every stage. These include:

- asking questions that require new or extended responses;
- creating opportunities for sustained dialogue and substantive language use;
- providing opportunities for language use in multiple settings;
- restating complex sentences as a sequence of simple sentences;
- avoiding or explaining use of idiomatic expressions;
- restating at a slower rate when needed, but making sure that the pace is not so slow that normal intonation and stress patterns become distorted;
- pausing often to allow students to process what they hear;
- providing specific explanations of key words and special or technical vocabulary, using examples and non-linguistic props when possible;
- using everyday language;
- providing explanations for the indirect use of language (for example, an ELL student may understand the statement, "I like the way Mary is sitting" merely as a simple statement rather than as a reference to an example of good behavior).

1.3
Deciding on the Best ESOL Program

This section outlines the learning outcomes that ELLs typically accomplish in differing ESOL programs and the importance of the maintenance of first language development. Although school systems differ across America in the ways in which they try to deal with ELL populations, this section describes the pedagogical pros and cons of an array of ESOL programs and clarifies terminology used in the field.

There are several factors that influence the design of an effective ELL program. These include considerations regarding the nature of the ELL student demographics to be served, district resources, and individual student characteristics. The MLA Language Map at www.mla.org/map_main provides an interactive look into the distribution of languages spoken in the United States. The online maps are able to show numbers as well as percentages by state, district, and zip code. Over 30 languages may be geographically represented and compared. The MLA Language Map shows graphically that not all districts are the same. ELL populations differ across the country. Some areas may have an overwhelming majority of Spanish speaking ELLs whereas other districts may have an equally large number of ELL students but speaking 50–100 different languages. On the other hand, some districts may have very few ELLs while other districts experience an influx of ELLs of whose language and culture the area's schools have little knowledge (for example, Hmong in Marathon County in Wisconsin, Haitian Creole in Palm Beach, Broward, and Dade counties in Florida, and Somali/Ethiopian in Hennepin and Ramsey counties in Minnesota). Cultural and linguistic differences, as well as factors such as size, age, and mobility of community members, very much influence the types of ESOL instructional programs that school districts choose to develop. Refer to *English Language Learner Programs at the Secondary Level in Relation to Student Performance* (www.nwrel.org/re-eng/products/ELLSynthesis.pdf) for a wonderful research-based yet easy-to-read outline of how the implementation of different ELL programs in schools affects the language learning gains of ELLs.

As mentioned above, not all ELLs are the same. ELLs may enter a school with vastly different educational backgrounds. Some enter U.S. schools with a strong foundational knowledge in their first language. This means that they may have had schooling in their first language, have literacy skills in their first language, and/or have developed social everyday language competency as well as academic proficiency in their first language. Other ELLs may have had less or even no academic schooling in their first language. Many ELLs, especially refugees, may have attended school in their homeland only for it to have been interrupted by famine or war, or for other socioeconomic or political reasons. Some ELLs arrive in the United States with their families at a very young age and, although they speak their first language at home, they may have never developed reading or writing proficiency in it. As will be discussed in the next chapter, it is of great importance to uncover the nature of an ELL's first language development since this has a profound bearing on how an ELL manages to acquire English.

A third factor, according to the Center for Applied Linguistics (CAL, 1987, at www.cal.org), is the resources that a district has at its disposal. Some districts may have a cadre of qualified ESOL specialists working in schools, whereas other districts may only be able to use paraprofessionals and yet others draw on the surrounding community for help. Based on these constraints, one can classify different ESOL programs into what Baker (2001) terms strong and weak forms of bilingual education. Table 1.2 provides an overview of the merits of the many types of ESOL programs operating across the United States.

According to a report submitted to the San Diego County Office of Education (Gold, 2006), "there is no widely accepted definition of a bilingual school in published research in this country" (p. 37). As a rule of thumb, they are widely understood to be schools that promote bilingualism and literacy in two or more languages as goals for students (Baker, 2001; Crawford, 2004).

TABLE 1.2. Types of ESOL programs in the United States

Type of program	Target ELLs and expectations	Program description	What research says
Submersion	All ELLs regardless of proficiency level or length of time since arrival. No accommodations are made. The goal is to reach full English proficiency and assimilation	ELLs remain in their home classroom and learn with native speakers of English. The teacher makes no modifications or accommodations for the ELL in terms of the curriculum content or in teaching English	States such as Florida have in the past faced potential litigation because of not training teachers to work with ELLs or modifying curriculum and/or establishing ELL programs. In order to avoid submersion models, Florida has established specific ELL instructional guidelines (Consent Decree, 1990)
ESL class period	As above, though usually in school districts with higher concentrations of ELLs	Groups ELLs together, to teach English skills and instruct them in a manner similar to that used in foreign language classes. The focus is primarily linguistic and ELLs visit these classes typically 2 or 3 times per week	This model does not necessarily help ELLs with academic content. The effect is that these programs can tend to create "ESL ghettos." Being placed in such programs can preclude ELLs from gaining college-entrance applicable credits (Diaz-Rico & Weed, 2006)
ESL-plus (sometimes called submersion with primary language)	ELLs who are usually at speech emergence and/or intermediate fluency stage. The aim is to hasten ELLs' ability to integrate and follow content classroom instruction	Includes instruction in English (similar to ESL class period and pull-out) but generally goes beyond the language to focus on content-area instruction. This may be given in the ELL's native language or in English. Often these programs may incorporate the ELL for the majority or all of the school day	According to Ovando & Collier (1998) the most effective ESL-plus and content-based ESL instruction is where the ESL teacher collaborates closely with the content teacher
Content-based ESL	As above	ELLs are still separated from mainstream content classes, but content is organized around an academic curriculum with grade-level objectives. There is no explicit English instruction	See above

continued overleaf

TABLE 1.2. *(continued)* Types of ESOL programs in the United States

Type of program	Target ELLs and expectations	Program description	What research says
Pull-out ESL	Early arrival ELLs. Usually in school districts with limited resources. Achieving proficiency in English fast is a priority so that the ELL can follow the regular curriculum	ELLs leave their home room for specific instruction in English: grammar, vocabulary, spelling, oral communication, etc. ELLs are not taught the curriculum when they are removed from their classrooms, which may be anything from 30 minutes to 1 hour every day	This model has been the most implemented though the least effective program for the instruction of ELLs (Collier & Thomas, 1997)
Sheltered instruction or SDAIE (specifically designed academic instruction in English). Sometimes called structured immersion	Targets all ELLs regardless of proficiency level or age. ELLs remain in their classrooms	This is an approach used in multilinguistic classrooms to provide principled language support to ELLs while they are learning content. Has same curriculum objectives as mainstream classroom in addition to specific language and learning strategy objectives	ELLs are able to improve their English language skills while learning content. Exposure to higher-level language through content materials and explicit focus on language fosters successful language acquisition (Brinton, 2003)
Transitional bilingual	Usually present in communities with a single large ELL population. Geared towards grades K–3. Initial instruction in home language and then switching to English by grade 2 or 3	ELLs enter school in kindergarten and the medium of instruction is in the home language. The reasoning behind this is to allow the ELL to develop full proficiency in the home language so that the benefits of this solid linguistic foundation may transfer over to and aid in the acquisition of English. Intended to move ELL students along relatively quickly (2–3 years)	Of all forms of traditional bilingual programs, the transitional model entails the least benefit to the ELL in terms of maintaining and building cognitive academic language proficiency (CALP) in their home language

TABLE 1.2. *(continued)* Types of ESOL programs in the United States

Type of program	Target ELLs and expectations	Program description	What research says
Maintenance bilingual	As above, but the ELL continues to receive language and content instruction in the home language along with English	As above, but are geared to the more gradual mastering of English and native language skills (5–7 years)	ELLs compare favorably on state standardized tests when measured against achievement grades of ELLs in transitional bilingual programs or ESL pull-out, ESL class period and ESL-plus programs (Hakuta *et al.*, 2000)
Dual language/ Two-way immersion	This model targets native speakers of English as well as native speakers of other languages, depending on which group predominates in the community	The aim of this program is for both English native speakers and ELLs to maintain their home language as well as acquire another language. Curriculum is delivered in English as well as in the ELL's language. Instructional time is usually split between the two languages, depending on the subject area and the expertise of the teachers	Dual language programs have shown the most promise in terms of first and second language proficiency attainment. Research results from standardized assessments across the United States indicated that ELLs can outperform monolingual English children in English literacy, mathematics, and other content curriculum areas. Has also many positive social and individual affective benefits for the ELL (Genesee, 1999)
Heritage language	Targets communities with high native population numbers, e.g. Hawai'i, Native Americans in New Mexico. Community heritage language maintenance is the goal	In heritage language programs, the aim can be to help revitalize the language of a community. Sometimes English is offered as the medium of instruction in only a few courses. Usually the majority of the curriculum is delivered in the home language	Language diversity can be seen as a problem, as a right, or as a resource. Heritage language programs are operationalized through local, state, and federal language policies as emancipatory (Cummins, 2001)

1.4
Teaching for English Language Development

This section explains the very practical implications of research in the phenomenon of bilingualism for classroom teachers as it relates to a context where many ELLs are learning English as their second, third, or even fourth language. One very important objective of this section is to help teachers understand how they can positively and purposefully mediate an ELL's language development in English.

A very prevalent concept of academic English that has been advanced and refined over the years is based on the work of Jim Cummins (1979; 1980; 1986; 1992; 2001). Cummins analyzed the characteristics of children growing up in two language environments. He found that the level of language proficiency attained in both languages, regardless of what they may be, has an enormous influence on and implications for an ELL's educational success. One situation that teachers often discover about their ELLs is that they arrived in the United States at an early age or were born in the United States but did not learn English until commencing school. Once they begin attending school, their chances for developing their home language are limited, and this home language is eventually superseded by English. This phenomenon is often referred to as limited bilingualism or subtractive bilingualism. Very often ELLs in this situation do not develop high levels of proficiency in either language. Cummins has found that ELLs with limited bilingual ability are overwhelmingly disadvantaged cognitively and academically from this linguistic condition. However, ELLs who develop language proficiency in at least one of the two languages derive neither benefit nor detriment. Only in ELLs who are able to develop high levels of proficiency in both languages did Cummins find positive cognitive outcomes.

The upshot of this line of research in bilingualism seems counterintuitive for the lay person, but it does conclusively show that, rather than providing ELLs with more English instruction, it is important to provide ELLs with instruction in their home language. By reaching higher levels of proficiency in their first language, an ELL will be able to transfer the cognitive benefits to learn English more effectively.

Of course, we don't live in a perfect world, and it is not always feasible to provide instruction in an ELL's home language, so it behooves all teachers to be cognizant of the types of language development processes that ELLs undergo. Cummins (1981) also posited two different types of English language skills. These he called BICS and CALP. The former, basic interpersonal communication skills (BICS), correspond to the social, everyday language and skills that an ELL develops. BICS is very much context-embedded in that it is always used in real-life situations that have real-world connections for the ELL, for example in the playground, at home, shopping, playing sports, and interacting with friends. Cognitive academic language proficiency (CALP), by contrast, is very different from BICS in that it is abstract, decontextualized, and scholarly in nature. This is the type of language required to succeed at school or in a professional setting. CALP, however, is the type of language that most ELLs have the hardest time mastering exactly because it is not everyday language.

Even after being in the United States for years, an ELL may appear fluent in English but still have significant gaps in their CALP. Teachers can be easily fooled by this phenomenon. What is needed is for teachers in all content areas to pay particular attention to an ELL's development in the subject-specific language of a school discipline. Many researchers (Hakuta *et al.*, 2000) agree that an ELL may easily achieve native-like conversational proficiency within two years, but it may take anywhere between five and ten years for an ELL to reach native-like proficiency in CALP.

Since Cummins's groundbreaking research, there has been a lot of work carried out in the area of academic literacy. An alternative view of what constitutes literacy is provided by Valdez (2000), who supports the notion of *multiple literacies*. Scholars holding this perspective suggest that efforts to teach academic language to ELLs are counterproductive since it comprises multiple dynamic and ever-evolving literacies. In their view, school systems should accept multiple ways of communicating and not marginalize students when they use a variety of English that is not accepted in academic contexts (Zamel & Spack, 1998).

However, one very important fact remains. As it stands now, in order to be successful in a school, all students need to become proficient in academic literacy.

A third view is one that sees academic literacy as a dynamic interrelated process (Scarcella, 2003), one in which cultural, social, and psychological factors play an equally important role. Scarcella provides a description of academic English that includes a phonological, lexical (vocabulary), grammatical (syntax, morphology), sociolinguistic, and discourse (rhetorical) component.

Regardless of how one defines academic literacy, many have criticized teacher education programs for failing to train content-area teachers to recognize the language specificity of their own discipline and thus being unable to help their students recognize it and adequately acquire proficiency in it (Bailey *et al.*, 2002; Kern, 2000).

Ragan (2005) provides a simple framework to help teachers better understand the academic language of their content area. He proposes that teachers ask themselves three questions:

- What do you expect ELLs to know after reading a text?
- What language in the text may be difficult for ELLs to understand?
- What specific academic language should be taught?

Another very useful instructional heuristic to consider when creating materials to help ELLs acquire academic literacy was developed by Cummins and is called Cummins' Quadrants. In the Quadrants, Cummins (2001) successfully aligns the pedagogical imperative with an ELL's linguistic requirements. The four quadrants represent a sequence of instructional choices that teachers can make based on the degree of contextual support given to an ELL and the degree of cognitive demand placed on an ELL during any given instructional activity. The resulting quadrants are illustrated in Table 1.3.

TABLE 1.3. Cummins' Quadrants

Quadrant I: High context embeddedness, and Low cognitive demand (easiest)	Quadrant III: High context embeddedness, and High cognitive demand
Quadrant II: Low context embeddedness, and Low cognitive demand	Quadrant IV: Low context embeddedness, and High cognitive demand (most difficult)

Quadrant I corresponds to pedagogic activities that require an ELL to use language that is easy to acquire. This may involve everyday social English and strategies that have a high degree of contextual support (i.e. lots of scaffolding, visual clues and manipulatives to aid understanding, language redundancies, repetitions, and reinforcements) or this may include experiential learning techniques, task-based learning, and already familiarized computer programs. Activities in this quadrant also have a low degree of cognitive demand (i.e. are context embedded). In other words, they are centered on topics that are familiar to the ELL or that the ELL has already mastered and do not require abstract thought in and of themselves.

Quadrant IV corresponds to pedagogic activities that require the ELL to use language that is highly decontextualized, abstract, subject-specific, and/or technical/specialized. Examples of these include lectures, subject-specific texts, and how-to manuals. The topics within this quadrant may be unfamiliar to the ELL and impose a greater cognitive demand on the ELL. Academic language associated with Quadrant IV is difficult for ELLs to internalize because it is usually supported by a very low ratio of context-embedded clues to meaning (low contextual support). At the same time, it is often centered on difficult topics that require abstract thought (high cognitive demand). It is important for the teacher to (1) elaborate language, as well as (2) provide opportunities for the ELL to reflect on, talk through, discuss, and engage with decontextualized oral or written texts. By doing this the teacher provides linguistic scaffolds for the ELL to grasp academically.

Quadrants II and III are pedagogic "go-between" categories. In Quadrant II, the amount of context embeddedness is lessened, and so related development increases the complexity of the language while maintaining a focus on topics that are easy and familiar for the ELL. In Quadrant III, language is again made easier through the escalation of the level of context embeddedness to support and facilitate comprehension. However, Quadrant III instruction allows the teacher to introduce more difficult content-area topics.

When a teacher develops lesson plans and activities that are situated within the framework of Quadrant I and II, the ELL engages in work that is not usually overwhelming. In low-anxiety classrooms, ELLs feel more comfortable to experiment with their language to learn more content. As an ELL moves from level 1 of English language development (preproduction) to level 3 (speech emergence), a teacher may feel that the time is right to progress to creating lesson plans and activities that fit pedagogically into Quadrants III and IV. A gradual progression to Quadrant III reinforces language learning and promotes comprehension of academic content. According to Collier (1995):

> A major problem arising from the failure of educators to understand the implications of these continuums is that ELLs are frequently moved from ESOL classrooms and activities represented by Quadrant I to classrooms represented by Quadrant IV, with little opportunity for transitional language experiences characterized by Quadrants II and III. Such a move may well set the stage for school failure. By attending to both language

dimensions (level of contextual support and degree of cognitive demand) and planning accordingly, schools and teachers can provide more effective instruction and sounder assistance to second-language learners. (p. 35)

The degree of cognitive demand for any given activity will differ for each ELL, depending on the ELL's prior knowledge of the topic.

1.5
Not All ELLs are the Same

The United States continues to be enriched by immigrants from countries the world over. Many cities have ethnic enclaves of language minority and immigrant groups and these populations are reflected in school classrooms. This section outlines the background characteristics of ELLs that teachers need to be aware of when planning or delivering instruction. Certainly, ELLs bring their own strengths to the task of learning but they also face many challenges. Equally, these diverse backgrounds impact classroom practices culturally in terms of how ELLs behave in classrooms, how they come to understand curriculum content, and how their interactions with others are affected (Zehler, 1994). The following affords a glimpse of their diversity:

María is seven years old and is a well-adjusted girl in second grade. She was born in Colombia, but came to the United States when she was four. Spanish is the medium of communication at home. When she entered kindergarten, she knew only a smattering of English. By grade 2 she had developed good basic interpersonal communication skills (BICS). These are the language skills needed to get by in social situations. María sounded proficient in English; she had the day-to-day communication skills to interact socially with other people on the playground, in the lunchroom, and on the school bus. Of course, all these situations are very much context-embedded and not cognitively demanding. In the classroom, however, María had problems with her cognitive academic language proficiency (CALP). This included speaking, reading, and writing about subject-area content material. It was obvious to her teacher that Maria needed extra time and support to become proficient in academic areas but, because she had come to the United States as a four-year-old and had already been three years in the school, she was not eligible for direct ESOL support. Collier and Thomas (1997) have shown that, if young ELLs have no prior schooling or have no support in native language development, it may take seven to ten years for them to catch up to their peers.

Ismael Abudullahi Adan is from Somalia. He is 13 and was resettled in Florida as a refugee through the Office of the United Nations High Commissioner for Refugees (UNHCR; see www.unhcr.org/home.html). As is the case with all refugees in the USA, Ismael's family was matched with an American resettlement organization (see www.refugees.org/). No one in his family knew any English. They were subsistence farmers in Somalia and, because of the civil war in Somalia, Ismael had never attended school. The resettlement organization helped the family find a place to live, but financial aid was forthcoming for only six months. While all members of the family were suffering degrees of war-related trauma, culture shock, and emotional upheaval, as well as the stress and anxiety of forced migration, Ismael had to attend the local school. Everything was foreign to him. He had no idea how to act as a student and all the rules of the school made no sense to him. All Ismael wanted to do was work and help his family financially; he knew that at the end of six months financial aid from the government would stop and he worried about how his family was going to feed itself. He is currently placed in a sheltered English instruction class at school.

José came to the United States from Honduras with his parents two years ago. He is now 14. His parents work as farm laborers and throughout the year move interstate depending where crops are being harvested. This usually involves spending the beginning of the calendar year in Florida for strawberry picking, late spring in Georgia for the peach harvest, early fall in North Carolina for the cotton harvest, and then late fall in Illinois for the pumpkin harvest. When the family first came to the United States from Honduras as undocumented immigrants, José followed his parents around the country. His itinerancy did not afford him any consistency with schooling. Last year, his parents decided to leave José with his uncle and aunt in North Carolina so that he would have more chances at school. Now he doesn't see his parents for eight months out of the year. He misses them very much. At school José has low grades and has been retained in grade 8 because he did not pass the North Carolina High School Comprehensive Test. He goes to an ESOL pull-out class once a day at his school.

Andrzej is 17 years old. He arrived with his father, mother, and 12-year-old sister from Poland. They live in Baltimore where his father is a civil engineer. The family immigrated the year before so that Andrzej's mother could be closer to her sister (who had married an American and had been living in the United States for the past 10 years). Andrzej always wanted to be an engineer like has father, but now he isn't sure what he wants to do. His grades at school have slipped since leaving Poland. He suspects that this is because of his English. Even though he studied English at school in Poland, he never became proficient at writing. Because he has been in the United States for more than a year, he no longer receives ESOL support at school. His parents, however, pay for an English tutor to come to his house once a week.

The above cases reflect the very wide differences in the ELL population in schools today. One cannot assume that every ELL speaks Spanish or that all ELLs entered the country illegally. The ELL population in a school may include permanent residents, naturalized citizens, legal immigrants, undocumented immigrants, refugees, and asylees. Of this foreign-born population, 4.8 million originate from Europe, 9.5 million from Asia, 19 million from Latin America, 1.2 million from Africa, and 1 million from other areas including Oceania and the Caribbean (U.S. Census Bureau, 2005).

Stages of Cultural Adjustment

What the above cases of María, Ismael, José, and Andrzej also identify is that since the nation's founding immigrants have come to the United States for a wide variety of reasons. These may include one or any combination of economic, political, religious, and family reunification reasons. Depending on the reason for coming to the United States, an ELL might be very eager to learn English since they might see having English proficiency as the single best means to "get ahead" economically in their new life, or they might resist learning English because they see this as an erosion of their cultural and linguistic identity. A teacher may find an ELL swaying between these two extremes simply because they are displaying the characteristics and stages of *cultural adjustment*.

The notion of cultural adjustment or, as it is sometimes called, "culture shock" was first introduced by anthropologist Kalvero Oberg in 1954. The emotional and behavioral symptoms of each stage of this process can manifest themselves constantly or only appear at disparate times.

Honeymoon Stage

The first stage is called the "honeymoon" stage and is marked by enthusiasm and excitement by the ELL. At this stage, ELLs may be very positive about the culture and express being overwhelmed with their impressions particularly because they find American culture exotic and are fascinated by it. Conversely, an ELL may be largely passive and not confront the culture even though (s)he finds everything in the new culture wonderful, exciting, and novel. After a few days, weeks, or months, ELLs typically enter the second stage.

Hostility Stage

At this stage, differences between the ELL's old and new cultures become aggravatingly stark. An ELL may begin to find anything and everything in the new culture annoying and/or tiresome. An ELL will most likely find the behavior of those around him/her unusual and unpredictable and thus begin to dislike American culture as well as Americans. They may begin to stereotype Americans and idealize their own culture. They may experience cultural confusion and communication difficulties. At this stage, feelings of boredom, lethargy, restlessness, irritation, antagonism, depression, and feelings of ineptitude are very common. This occurs when an ELL is trying to acclimatize to the new culture, which may be very dissimilar to the culture of origin. Shifting between former cultural discourse practices and those of the new country is a problematic process and can take a very long time to overcome. If it is prolonged, an ELL may withdraw because of feelings of loneliness and anxiety.

Home Stage

The third stage is typified by the ELL achieving a sense of understanding of the new culture. The ELL may feel more comfortable living in the new country and experiencing the new culture. They may regain their sense of humor. In psychological terms, an ELL may start to feel a certain emotional balance. Although feelings of isolation may persist, the ELL may stop feeling lost and even begin to have a feeling of direction. The ELL re-emerges more culturally stable, being more familiar with the environment and wanting to belong. For the ELL, this period of new adjustment could initiate an evaluation of old cultural practices versus new ones.

Assimilation Stage

In the fourth stage, the ELL realizes that the new culture has positives as well as negatives to offer. Integration patterns and practices displayed by the ELL become apparent. It is accompanied by a more solid feeling of belonging. The ELL enjoys being in the new culture, functions easily in the new environment (even though they might already have been in the new culture for a few years) and may even adopt cultural practices of the new culture. This stage may be seen as one of amalgamation and assimilation.

Re-Entry Shock Stage

This happens when an ELL returns to the old culture for a visit and notices how many things have changed in the country as well as how they themselves have changed. Upon returning from the home country, an ELL will have developed a new sense of appreciation and of belonging to the new culture.

Worthy of note is the fact that the length of time an ELL spends in each of these stages varies considerably. The stages are neither discrete nor sequential and some ELLs may completely skip stages. They may even exhibit affective behaviors characteristic of more than one stage.

Cultural Practices at School

Whenever an ELL steps into a new school environment, the ELL will be sure to go through a process of cultural adjustment. For an ELL, the countless arrays of unspoken rules acquired in his/her culture of origin may not be suitable in the new school and a new set of practices needs to be discovered and internalized. These include, but are of course not limited to, school rules, what it means to be a "good" student, how to interact with fellow students and teachers, eating practices, bathroom practices, and even ways of learning. It would be fairly easy to learn new rules for living if such were made explicit and one were provided with lists of things to learn. However, most cultural rules operate at a level below conscious awareness and are not easily relayed to students.

Often ELLs find themselves in the position of having to discover these rules on their own. Shared cultural discourse practices can be seen as the oil that lubricates social interaction; however, what a community's cultural practices are, as well as the meanings that group members attach to their shared repertoire of cultural practices, are not always made explicit. Unfamiliarity with these cultural rules on the part of an ELL can cause a great deal of stress.

Many definitions regarding what culture is or is not abound. Diaz-Rico and Weed (2006) provide a very nice overview of the characteristics of culture. For them, culture is an adaptive mechanism, culture is learned, cultures change, culture is universal, culture provides a set of rules for living and a range of permissible behavior patterns, culture is a process of deep conditioning, culture is demonstrated in values, people usually are not aware of their culture, people do not know all of their own culture, culture is expressed verbally and non-verbally, culture no longer exists in isolation, and, last but very poignantly, culture affects people's attitudes toward schooling and it governs the way they learn. It can affect how they come to understand curriculum content and how they interact with fellow students.

Diaz-Rico and Weed (2006) offer a number of strategies to promote cultural pluralism and assuage potential exclusionary practices such as stereotyping, prejudice, and racism in the classroom. Ways to acknowledge different values, beliefs, and practices include accommodating different concepts of time and work rhythms, as well as different concepts of work space. Being open to culturally sensitive dress codes and inclusive of culture in school rituals are effective ways of promoting cultural pluralism. Considering different notions about work and play and maintaining an inclusive understanding of different health and hygiene practices as well as being tolerant of different religious practices and food and eating practices are critical in teaching acceptance. Most important to remember in relation to your ELL students are culturally based educational expectations (roles, status, gender), different discourse patterns, and your need to foster cultural pride and home–school communication.

One way to ease your ELL's cultural adjustment while demonstrating inclusiveness is to get to know where your ELLs come from and then incorporate aspects of their culture into your lessons. You could overtly ask your ELL about their home country, but this tactic may not provide you with the type of information you want since your ELL may not have the language proficiency in English to express abstract cultural concepts. Therefore, you should observe your ELL and how they behave, interview people from the same country, conduct a home visit, or visit the community in which the ELL lives. Of course, teachers are often constrained by time, so an alternative is to conduct internet research or buy appropriate books.

1.6
Culturally Responsive Pedagogy

As more and more students from diverse backgrounds populate 21st century class-rooms, and efforts mount to identify effective methods to teach these students, the need for pedagogical approaches that are culturally responsive intensifies. Today's classrooms require teachers to educate students varying in culture, language, abilities, and many other characteristics.

(Gollnick & Chinn, 2002: 21)

The question is: How does a teacher adequately respond to the multicultural classroom?

In 2000 Gay wrote that culturally responsive pedagogy is validating, comprehensive, multidimensional, empowering, transformative, and emancipatory. In other words, culturally responsive pedagogy necessitates that teachers tread outside their comfort circles. It is only natural for humans to see, understand, judge, make sense of, and canonize the world around them through their own discursive norms of practice. What this means in the context of education is that teachers make choices every day about what they will and will not teach. More importantly, teachers make choices as to how they will present and frame their curriculum choices. Of course this sends a subtle message to students: What curriculum matter is taught and how it is framed tends to legitimatize, validate, and endorse it over other potential curricular perspectives, which by default are marginalized.

Thus, teachers instruct in ways and about things that are familiar to them. They usually adopt and transmit the dominant voice in society, namely that of white middle-class America. The problem is, if a student is an ELL, (s)he is usually not white, middle-class, or American. This is where the practice of culturally responsive pedagogy can help. Look at the reflection vignette below. It

Reflection Vignette

I was driving my 12-year-old son to school in the fall of 2003 when over the radio we heard a commercial for the movie *Alamo*. Coincidently, the previous day we had been to the movies and one of the trailers was for the same movie. Kevin Costner was one of the Texan heroes in the movie, and every time the movie trailer showed the Texans the screen was bright and full of smiling people. The music was light and they were obviously the "good guys." However, when the screen shot showed the Mexican antagonists, the screen was dark, with hues of blue and red, the background images were full of cannon sounds, and the faces were "mean-looking."

Back in the car, I asked my son, who at the time was focused on playing his Gameboy, "You're doing American history now in your social studies class, right?"

My son, recognizing that another of dad's teachable moments was upon him, just rolled his eyes and disgruntledly put down his Gameboy.

"Yes, why?" he said.

"What aspect of U.S. history are you learning about now?" I asked.

"We're learning about the westward colonization of North America."

"Did you hear that ad?" I asked.

"Sure."

"Let me ask you something. What do you think would happen if a bunch of Cubans came into the middle of Florida, bought up a cluster of farms, and then told the government they were not going to pay taxes?"

"I suppose the government would fine them," he said.

"Well, what would happen if those same Cubans then told the government that they were going to create their own country?"

"The government would send in the army and kick 'em all out and probably send them back to Cuba."

At that point, I could see a flash of realization cross my son's face. "Oh, I get it," he said, "the Cubans are the Texans."

shows how the media can tend to reinforce dominant societal perspectives, perspectives that are reinforced and repeated in school curricula and textbooks across the country.

In the United States the Alamo is usually constructed as part of a righteous war of independence against an autocratic foreign government, namely Mexico. Yet in Mexican schools the war surrounding the Alamo is constructed as an aggressive grab for land by non-Spanish speaking settlers. Who is right? Perhaps the question should be: Am I teaching curriculum matter in a way that alienates and inadvertently marginalizes my students? How would a Mexican ELL feel in your classroom if you taught a unit on the Alamo, or on the westward European settlement of North America, and Mexico and the Mexicans were portrayed as the baddies? At the very least it marginalizes an ELL's voice in the classroom and indirectly discredits his/her potential contribution of another perspective for the class to think about.

Using Gay's (2000) principles of culturally responsive pedagogy, how does a teacher make the curriculum more validating, comprehensive, multidimensional, empowering, transformative, and emancipatory?

The first step is to be conscious of our choice of language. Language is never neutral. What and how we say things in the classroom affects the way our students perceive curriculum matter.

The second step is to be conscious of the images we present to the students. The third step is to engage in critical and reflexive thinking and writing tasks. By getting teachers to reflect critically on the language, images, and content of their teaching, we begin to open the door on *other* ways to think about teaching that are less ethnocentric. The fourth step is to learn the history and culture of the ELL groups in your classroom. The fifth step is to try and visit teachers who are successful at implementing culturally responsive pedagogy and, last, become an advocate in your own educational institution to reform ethnocentric discursive practices so that it becomes more inclusive. Richards, Brown, and Forde (2004) suggest the following activities to become more culturally responsive:

1. acknowledge students' differences as well as their commonalities;
2. validate students' cultural identity in classroom practices and instructional materials;
3. educate students about the diversity of the world around them;
4. promote equity and mutual respect among students;
5. assess students' ability and achievement validly;
6. foster a positive interrelationship among students, their families, the community, and school;
7. motivate students to become active participants in their learning;
8. encourage students to think critically;
9. challenge students to strive for excellence as defined by their potential;
10. assist students in becoming socially and politically conscious.

1.7
Not All Parents are the Same
Home–School Communication

Any school administrator and teacher will readily admit that the key to a school's success and indeed the key to a child's learning success is the active involvement of parents in the learning process. In the case of ELLs, parents are often at a loss because of barriers that prevent them from fully participating in the school community. Parents' hesitancy to involve themselves in their child's school arises from barriers such as the frustration they feel because of their own limited knowledge of English, their own possible lack of schooling, perceptions about power and status roles, or the anxiety they have because of different cultural norms such that they do not readily understand American school cultures or the cultural expectations, rights, roles, and responsibilities of teachers, parents, and students.

Schools can greatly enhance the effectiveness of ELL home–school communication and involvement by taking active steps to reduce these barriers. Careful planning is required to meet these challenges, though it can be done.

1. *Knowledge is King!* Get as much background information as is possible. Information useful to schools and teachers includes home language, home cultural/ethnic values, parental attitudes towards education, work schedules of parents, English proficiency, and the circumstances under which they have come to be in the United States (e.g. are they refugees, itinerant migrants, political asylees, second or third generation heritage speakers?). Depending on the information a school receives, a classroom teacher may make informed decisions about bilingual aide support, translation support, and changing school cultural practices that raise rather than bring down barriers to ELL home–school communication and parental involvement.

2. *Communicate as if it is going out of style!* The importance of fostering ELL parental involvement centers foremost on fostering and maintaining good lines of communication between the school/teacher and the home/parents. An important facet that frames parents' participation

in schools is their perceptions of school personnel. Is the school inviting and welcoming? Are teachers and the administration approachable? Are teachers empathetic to ELL parental concerns, wishes, contributions, values, and cultural practices? How often are they invited to attend school functions? Do teachers follow through on their communications? Do teachers make an effort to talk directly and in person with parents? Are parents allowed to visit often and learn what goes on in the classroom? Do teachers take the time to explain the whats, whys, and hows of their teaching and the ELL child's learning?

3. *It's not just about educating the ELL!* If schools want to enlist the support and help of ELL parents, then both the administration of a school and its teachers need to be prepared to extend their instruction beyond the ELL student to the ELL parent—beyond the classroom and into the ELL home. In other words, in order to break down the types of barriers that inhibit ELL parents from school involvement, steps need to be taken to educate the parents in matters concerning English language, as well as U.S. school customs. What would such steps look like? In an article published in *Essential Teacher* (2004), Bassoff says it centers solely on *access, approachability,* and *follow-through*.

Ideas: On Fostering Access

- Create, endorse, and implement an ELL parent–school participation program/policy.
- Have an ELL parent representative on school committees.
- Make the school a place to foster ELL community events.
- Provide access to the school library to aid ELL parents' learning of English.
- Translate all school communications into the home language.
- Make sure all written communication reaches the ELL parent.
- Foster in-school support groups for ELL parents.
- Advocate that your school district establish an "Intake Center" for new arrivals that will help ELL newcomers with school registrations, placement, testing, and information services.
- Allow ELL parents to come to school professional development opportunities.
- Provide ELL parent education workshops and orientation opportunities.
- Advertise the contact information of bilingual school staff.

Ideas: On Fostering Approachability

- Use ELL parents as sources of information.
- Invite ELL parents to school.
- Use parents to raise multicultural awareness in the school and classroom; multiculturalism is a two-way street—foster inclusion through the provision of multicultural workshops, presentations, and events to mainstream monolingual school personnel and students.
- Multicultural appreciation events could include ethnic music and dance performances, art displays, drama shows, science fairs, and festival evenings, all accompanied by talks from ELL parents or ELL community leaders.
- Be amenable and open to different ways about thinking about education—show this through inclusive classroom practices, activities, realia, and visuals.
- Embed multicultural routines in everything and all the time.
- Foster ELL literacy family evenings.
- Establish native language parent groups.

Ideas: On Achieving Good Follow-Through

- Give mainstream students service-learning opportunities to help ELL parents/families adjust to U.S. life.
- Foster ELL parent network circles.
- Provide classes that help ELL parents to meet their children's education needs.
- Have the school library purchase a wide range of fiction and non-fiction bilingual books.
- Take the time to learn about the culture, language, and education system of the ELLs' home countries and apply what you learn in your classroom.
- Create virtual spaces to post ongoing information for ELL parents as well as WWW links to useful websites.[1]

1.8
English Language Learners with Special Needs

We want to highlight an important subset of the ELL population that is often disadvantaged because its members fall simultaneously into two underrepresented groups: special needs and ELL. They are underprivileged because many teachers within these separate discipline areas have not been trained to work with this population of students—ESOL teachers with special needs students, or special needs teachers with ELLs.

In 1984 the National Office for Educational Statistics reported that 500,000 students in the United States were English language learners with exceptionalities. Today, more than 20 years later, it is projected that there are more than 1 million ELLs with special needs in the United States (Baca & Cervantes, 2004).

Despite an abundance of legislative initiatives (*Civil Rights Act—Title VI* in 1963, *Title VII of the Elementary and Secondary Education Act* (ESEA) reauthorized in 1974, 1978, 1984, and 1998, *Lau v. Nichols* in 1974, and the *Equal Educational Opportunity Act*, extending the Lau decision to all schools, *President's Committee on Mental Retardation* in 1970, the *Education for All Handicapped Children Act* in 1975, the *Bilingual Education Act* in 1984, reauthorization of the ESEA in 1994 coupled with a Presidential Executive Order in 2000, the *Individuals with Disability Education Act* (IDEA) of 1997 and *Title II* of the *No Child Left Behind* (NCLB) *Act* 2002), inappropriate referrals, assessments, and the institutionalization of inappropriate instructional processes remain crucial issues in the education of ELL special needs children.

A colleague of ours once told the story of when he first came to the United States. His son was seven years old and at the end of the summer in 2005 was ready to be placed in grade 2. In Florida, the parents of every newly enrolled student are obliged to fill out a home language survey form. Our colleague was raising his children bilingually and both his children were equally fluent in English and German. When asked on the form what languages were spoken at home, he wrote German and English. A week later, his son innocuously said at the dinner table that he enjoyed being pulled out of the classroom, whereupon both parents asked the son what he meant. "Why I love being in the ESOL class with all the kids who speak other languages." Little did my colleague know that, because he had written German on the home language survey, the school was legally bound to place his son in ESOL classes. The upshot of the story was that our colleague went to the school and explained to the administration that his son was a balanced bilingual speaker and having him in ESOL classes was unnecessary. The administration told him that there was nothing they could do because the home survey was filled out as it was. Ultimately, my colleague had to disenroll his son, re-enroll him in the same school, and fill out the home survey again (this time just putting English as the home language) to finally have him pulled from the ESOL classes. The reason this story is related is because parents and teachers are all too familiar with the fact that, within education environments, rule-driven practices, acronyms, and terminologies abound that more often than not pigeon-hole students into predetermined roles and assign these students to inevitable and predictable expectations. Unfortunately, ELLs with special needs have fallen prey to this stereotyping. There is, however, an ever-increasing but incomplete body of research that spotlights instructional strategies for ELLs with special needs that teachers may draw upon to help them in their efforts to identify, instruct, and assess. The following section summarizes some of the more important aspects of this research. The following two points may act as instructional guides:

- Students with mild to severe disability levels benefit from native language instruction (de Valenzuela & Niccolai, 2004).
- Instruction needs to be enriching and not remedial, empower language learners, recognize the learners' culture and background, provide learners with authentic and meaningful activities, connect students to real-life experiences, begin with context-embedded material that leads to the use of context-reduced material, and provide a literacy/language-rich environment (Echeverria and McDonough, 1993).

But how can we translate the above into effective classroom practice?

There are various pedagogic models that have been developed based on theoretical frameworks, research findings, and recommended practices appropriate for ELLs with special needs (Ruiz, 1995a, b). Ortiz (1984) describes four basic types of pedagogic models that offer structured institutional support for ELLs with special needs to achieve more accomplished social and academic skill levels. These models are:

1. *Coordinated services model*—assists the ELL with special needs with a monolingual English speaking special education teacher and a bilingual educator.
2. *Bilingual support model*—bilingual paraprofessionals are teamed with monolingual English speaking special educators and assist with the individualized education plans of ELLs with special needs. Wherever noted on the individualized education program (IEP), the bilingual paraprofessional provides home language instruction concurrently with the teacher providing content expertise.
3. *Integrated bilingual special education model*—consists of one teacher who is certified in both bilingual education and special education, where the teacher is able to assist with level-appropriate English language instruction as the learner develops in proficiency.
4. *Bilingual special education model*—in this model all professionals interacting with the ELL special needs student have received bilingual special education training and are qualified to provide services that meet the goals outlined in any IEP.

Another model, the Optimal Learning Environment (OLE) Project (Ruiz, 1989), is based on a constructivist philosophy and works within a holistic–constructivist paradigm, focusing on the extensive use of interactive journals, writers' workshops, shared reading practices, literature conversations, response journals, patterned writing, as well as the provision of extended assessment time. The aim of the strategies is to build on a student's schema and interest.

The benefits of such models highlight the individualized and diverse needs of language learning students with special needs. As yet, guaranteeing unambiguous benefits across the board is not possible precisely because of the dearth of empirical research on instructional planning and curriculum design in this area. A very real consequence of this situation is the paucity of curricular materials available specifically geared to bilingual special education. Both fields of education have propagated methods on preparing either English language learners or special needs students. The main point to be internalized here is that materials must be integrated and specifically designed for English language learners *with* special needs. It is not enough that they receive "half of each curriculum" (Collier, 1995). Lack of curricular materials and trained personnel is still cited as the greatest barrier to providing services to English language learners with special needs.

So, what can teachers do to facilitate language learning for ELL students with a special need?

Of course, implementing well-informed instructional practices is one thing, but awareness raising, understanding of difficulties, and knowledge of differences and disorders are also an integral part of assisting the English language learner with disabilities.

In conclusion, we offer Hoover and Collier's (1989) recommendations as a point of departure to think about teaching ELLs with special needs:

1. Know the specific language abilities of each student.

2. Include appropriate cultural experiences in material adapted or developed.

3. Ensure that material progresses at a rate commensurate with student needs and abilities.

4. Document the success of selected materials.

5. Adapt only specific materials requiring modifications, and do not attempt to change too much at one time.

6. Try out different materials and adaptations until an appropriate education for each student is achieved.

7. Strategically implement materials adaptations to ensure smooth transitions into the new materials.

8. Follow some consistent format or guide when evaluating materials.

9. Be knowledgeable about particular cultures and heritages and their compatibility with selected materials.

10. Follow a well-developed process for evaluating the success of adapted or developed materials as the individual language and cultural needs of students are addressed. (Hoover & Collier, 1989: 253)

Conclusion

Understanding your English language learners can be daunting. They are different; they probably come from very different home environments from you, their teachers. Some of your students may be third-generation American and yet others may be newly arrived undocumented immigrants.

After reading Part 1, we don't expect you to now know everything there is to know about ELLs. We did not set out to provide you in these few short pages with an all-inclusive research-informed, all-encompassing treatise on ELLs in education. We have been circumspect, to be sure, in trying to introduce you to ELLs. There are plenty of ELL-specific books for that. It *was* our intent, however, to raise your awareness about the educational implications of having ELLs in your classroom. Our goal with this is to start drawing a picture of who an English language learner is and from this position help you think about the educational possibilities for your class.

Parts 2, 3, and 4 of this book are devoted exclusively to completing this picture. Not in a global sense, but finely etched within the parameters of your own content area.

What will be introduced to you in the pages to come will undoubtedly refer back to some of the points raised in Part 1. We have no intention of offering you static teaching recipes; instead we offer something akin to ideas, understandings, and skills that you can transfer to your own classrooms. Last, we refer you to Part 4 of this book, which offers you avenues for future professional development.

Part 2
What We Know From Research

Analysis of the intersection of ELL research and science content-based research is in its infancy. We will consider the research that has explored precisely this nexus and what teachers can learn from it, but first we would like to present the principles that support science teaching and learning in our middle and high schools.

2.1
Principles of Science Teaching and Learning

Teaching and learning should be inseparable, in that learning is a criterion and product of effective teaching. In essence, learning is the goal of teaching. However, teaching is no longer considered as something done to students in order for learning to occur. Rather, both teaching and learning happen at the same time, and both processes are completed by learners. This constructivist view promotes the idea that learners best learn when they build their own understanding of the concepts in hand. Thus, the teacher's role in this process is to facilitate students' active involvement in their own learning. (Committee on Undergraduate Science Education, National Research Council, 1997: 2)

This quote from an august body of individuals clearly links teaching and learning, and explicates their interdependence. Thus, as teachers, we cannot focus on teaching without considering its impact on learning, and vice versa. In our attempt to support this notion, we will weave the two ideas into one, as they must co-exist in the secondary science classroom.

The research that supports science as a subject in secondary schools continues to evolve, as scholars and educators seek to identify those strategies and techniques that afford every student the best opportunity to learn the science needed to be successful in life. This way of thinking about science teaching and learning is consistent with the National Research Council's (NRC) National Science Education Standards (NSES) (1996). In fact, the prestigious group charged with developing the national science standards in the mid-1990s not only forged a set of science content standards (i.e., what is supposed to be *learned*), but also identified standards for science teaching, assessment, professional development, school-level science programs, and district-level programs. These are the standards most state and local educational agencies in the United States use in the development of statewide and district or local science standards. As delineated and discussed in the NRC document (National Research Council, 1996), the six sets of standards focus on:

- Science Teaching— "what teachers should know and be able to do."
- Professional Development for Teachers of Science—"the development of professional knowledge and skills among teachers."
- Assessment in Science Education—"criteria against which to judge the quality of assessment practices."
- Science Content—"what students should know, understand and be able to do in the natural sciences over the course of a K–12 education."
- Science Education Programs—"the conditions necessary for quality school science programs."
- Education Systems—"criteria for judging the performance of the overall science education system."

With all six sections of the national standards as a backdrop, we will focus on the teaching and content standards, especially as they relate to ELLs.

The main principles that guide our recommendations for instruction will be discussed in this section. While we believe these principles are consistent with research about effective science instruction, we also realize that no amount of research can prove we should teach one way rather than another. According to this line of reasoning, we can posit that for educating ELLs:

> There will probably never be a formula for educating ELLs, just as there is no formula for educating students who already know English. What we can do is provide guidelines based on our strongest research about effective practices for teaching ELLs. (Goldenberg, 2008)

Thus we use research to support teaching science that matters, which we believe means productively engaging all learners with significant subject matter and supporting scientific skill development. Some of the principles that underpin our work in this book are:

1. Learners make sense of new phenomena within their existing understanding (Driver, 1983; Hsin-Kai, 2003; Morrison & Lederman, 2003; Osborne & Freyberg, 1985; Scott, Dyson & Gater, 1987).
2. Teachers should provide opportunities for learners to challenge their understanding of science concepts to help learners restructure their ideas (Driver & Oldham, 1986; Lee & Fradd, 1998; Savinainen, Scott, & Viiri, 2004).
3. Active learning is critical to student success, as it can enliven instruction and positively impact student motivation to learn (Rodgers & Withrow-Thorton, 2005).
4. Students' interests and aptitudes vary, making it desirable to make available more than one way to reach instructional goals (Noddings, 2005).
5. Learners must practice those skills that are important in science (e.g., making observations, measuring, classifying, inferring, etc.) while learning new science concepts (National Research Council, 1996).
6. Science is best learned when it is understood as a natural and important component of learners' lived experiences (National Research Council, 2000).

Let's take a look at each of these six principles in a bit more detail. The first principle focuses on the widely held belief (which is supported by research and successful measures acknowledged by the professional community) that students will better understand new scientific concepts if those phenomena are linked to students' prior knowledge. For ELLs, the idea that what they already know is valued in the science classroom can be a significant factor in their eagerness to understand new concepts. Science teachers can tap into this prior knowledge in multiple ways, some of which will be shared in upcoming sections of this book.

The second principle is a corollary to the first, for if a secondary teacher is to value ELLs' prior knowledge, the teacher must also be prepared to address scientific misconceptions ELLs may harbor. An effective and well-documented strategy that can be used to challenge ELLs' misconceptions incorporates hands-on, minds-on activities. Discrepant events are activities or teacher demonstrations where the outcome is unexpected by the students (Misiti, 2000). Psychologists refer to this "disequilibrium in thought" as cognitive dissonance (Festinger, Schachter, & Back, 1950). The students are typically surprised by the outcome and are motivated to figure out what happened. Using discrepant events encourages teachers to use activities that may go against commonly held beliefs about scientific concepts to ascertain students' depth of understanding of a "new" phenomenon (Eick, Meadows, & Balkcom, 2005; Haines, 2001; McCarthy, 2005).

The third principle reinforces the antithesis of passive learning. Brophy (2004) suggests that our work as teachers should include motivational techniques. Few subjects taught in middle and high schools can compare with science when it comes to opportunities to have students engage in their learning in tactile and kinesthetic ways that increase motivation and, subsequently, learning. Engaging ELLs in what is to be studied can increase the odds that learning will take place and understanding will occur.

The fourth principle draws upon our knowledge of how students come to understandings about science concepts. For ELLs, it is important that teachers provide multiple avenues for achieving success (Jarrett, 1999). To show how one knows something is very different from showing that one knows something. In the former, the learner is given some flexibility in demonstrating understanding. In the latter, the opportunity to demonstrate understanding is more restrictive. Of course, the caveat here is that, in this current era of accountability, teachers must prepare ELLs to be successful on standardized tests. Good teachers are savvy at doing both (Jarrett, 1999).

The penultimate principle serves as a reminder that science is not just a body of facts, but also encompasses the ways by which scientists go about their work. The scientific skills are so important to the teaching and learning of science that, in many states, secondary science teachers must not only identify a content standard for every lesson that is taught—they must also match a skill-related standard that comes from the nature of science standards portion of the respective state standards.

The sixth and final principle aligns the rest of this book with the concept of culturally relevant teaching, where teachers connect what happens in the science classroom with the lives of their ELLs. The relevancy of the science to the ELLs' lived experiences increases the possibility that true learning and conceptual understanding will take place. Rarely should a science teacher engage students in a lesson without considering how the topic can be understood within the context of the students' daily lives.

Hopefully, it will be apparent that these principles are not meant to be considered in isolation when it comes to their application in the classroom with ELLs. There are overlaps, parallels, and intersections aplenty. At the expense of being prescriptive, we leave it to the reader to consider the examples in this book as opportunities to further explore, discuss, and consider the various ways these principles come into play in planning effective science instruction.

2.2
Science-Focused ESOL Research

There is a growing body of research on teaching science to English language learners. Both qualitative and quantitative studies have attempted to identify what aspects of science instruction are especially challenging and which methods of instruction lead to greater scientific understanding for ELLs. While some of the studies have been inconclusive or contradictory, a number of recommendations for science teachers can be culled from the research.

Overview of Research on Science Instruction for ELLs from 1982–2005

Most notable among recent research in science education with ELLs is the scholarly work of Okhee Lee. In addition to conducting a series of studies with science students from different cultural and linguistic backgrounds, Lee (2005) surveyed and summarized findings from published research on teaching science to ELLs over the past two decades. In a synthesis of studies published from 1982 to 2004, she offers insights into effective practices. This section presents an overview of the major findings from Lee's research review, organized into five areas: science learning, curriculum, instruction, assessment, and teacher education.

In science learning, Lee categorized studies into cultural beliefs and practices, scientific reasoning and argumentation, and linguistic influences on science learning. In a line of research entitled Science for All, Lee and Fradd (1996a; 1996b) and Lee, Fradd, and Sutman (1995) examined African American, Haitian, Hispanic, and White elementary students and found that the communication and interaction behaviors of the minority students were not consistent with school science practices. Certain cultures do not encourage students to ask questions and work autonomously, which is a hallmark of scientific inquiry. Unlike the discontinuities found in the Science for All research, the Chèche Konnen Project (Ballenger, 1997; Rosebery, Warren, & Conant, 1992;

Warren, Ballenger, Ogonowski, Rosebery, & Hudicourt-Barnes, 2001) found that students from language minority backgrounds were able to use their background experiences to make inferences for scientific argumentation when instruction supports this connection.

It is not surprising that there are linguistic influences on science learning and that they have a marked effect on ELLs' achievement in science. A study conducted by Torres and Zeidler (2002) found that ELLs' level of English proficiency and their scientific reasoning skills had significant effects on their scientific content knowledge. The use of the native language for science instruction has shown benefits for students with limited English proficiency, such as in the case of the qualitative research conducted by Tobin and McRobbie (1996). Cantonese-speaking ELLs in Australia who used their native language to discuss and write about chemistry showed more effort, commitment, and task orientation. Lee (2005) concludes that, in settings where English is the medium of instruction, ELLs' science learning is directly affected by their proficiency level in English.

In regards to science curriculum, Lee reports that there is a lack of culturally and linguistically relevant science materials for ELLs. In a study addressing this issue, Lee and colleagues found that providing materials that integrate home language and culture led to statistically significant improvement in science knowledge and inquiry (Fradd, Lee, Sutman, & Saxton, 2002). However, due to the small number of studies in this area, Lee urges caution in forming conclusions.

The major area of focus in Lee's research review, science instruction, divides the research into three categories, culturally congruent science instruction, cognitively based science instruction, and linguistic processes in science instruction.

Along with Sandra Fradd, Lee proposes a variation on the concepts of cultural congruence and culturally relevant pedagogy (Ladson-Billings, 1994, 1995a, b; Osborne, 1996), termed "instructional congruence" (Lee, 2002, 2003; Lee & Fradd, 1998). This concept emphasizes congruence between ELLs' language and culture backgrounds and science fields and instruction. Lee posits that students who come from language and culture backgrounds other than the culture of power need explicit instruction regarding expected behavior in school. In a study of third and fourth grade students from diverse cultural and linguistic backgrounds, Cuevas, Lee, Hart, and Deaktor (2005) found that implementing their framework of instructional congruence led to improved science and literacy achievement and inquiry abilities and narrowed science and literacy gaps.

The second line of inquiry regarding science instruction pertains to cognitively based science instruction. The previously mentioned Chèche Konnen Project (Rosebery, Warren, & Conant, 1992) has demonstrated how science instruction can be generated from students' beliefs, observations, and questions. Teachers used students' informal knowledge and linguistic and cultural experiences as a basis for scientific inquiry.

Students' development of English proficiency and use of language constitute the third category of science instruction. Inquiry-based instruction to promote language acquisition has been studied in various contexts. Merino and Hammond (2001) found that ELLs who participated in integrated writing during inquiry lessons improved in writing and showed scientific understanding. A comparative study conducted by Rodriguez and Bethel (1983) showed the third grade ELLs taught in inquiry-based lessons performed significantly better in classification and oral communication than those taught in traditional lessons.

Science assessment is the fourth area of the research synthesis, and Lee found few studies about this topic. There is controversy about how to ensure valid and reliable assessments of ELLs' science knowledge given that language proficiency is so intertwined with science assessment. In other words, when students who are not fully proficient in English are given tests in English, it is difficult to determine whether the tests are measuring language proficiency or scientific knowledge. Some scholars assert that for the sake of fairness all tests be administered in English and students' native languages, yet others point out that doing so presents problems, both of cost as well as psychometric validity (Abedi, 2004).

The last area of the research synthesis focuses on science teacher education and calls for improved preparation. In a number of studies (Hart & Lee, 2003; Lee, 2004), Lee and colleagues found that professional development can impact teachers' beliefs and practices regarding teaching science to ELLs. One study found that professional development led to improved science and literacy achievement of ELLs (Amaral, Garrison, & Klentschy, 2002).

Lee (2005) summarizes the practical implications of the studies she surveyed into three key findings about science instruction for ELLs. First, while all students should be challenged with exploring scientific phenomena and constructing scientific meanings based on their personal linguistic and cultural experiences, some students need explicit guidance in linking their own exploratory and constructivist experiences with scientific knowledge and practices. This means that teacher-directed activities may be more appropriate than student-directed activities for English language learners if their linguistic and cultural experiences lack congruity with the science content. Teachers should therefore bridge those gaps with explicit guidance and scaffolding for ELLs whose cultures' educational practices may not promote direct inquiry and questioning or whose English proficiency may preclude meaningful discussions with peers in student-directed activities.

The second practical implication pertains to the benefits of hands-on, inquiry-based instruction for ELLs. Because they are less language dependent, hands-on activities reduce the linguistic burden for comprehension and expression of information. For example, a demonstration of condensation forming in soda bottles presents a clearer explanation of the process than assigning a reading passage about condensation for ELLs at beginning or intermediate levels of proficiency. In addition, pair and group work allow for authentic communication about science. Authentic communication, a necessary element for language development, entails using language to comprehend and express meaning for a real purpose, as opposed to some types of instructed language development that analyze language or promote rote memorization of terms and phrases. Moreover, inquiry-based learning provides a variety of communication formats, including spoken, print, and non-verbal (gestures and graphics). Lastly, science inquiry offers opportunities for ELLs to acquire grammar and vocabulary in English.

Lee's third practical implication relates to the knowledge and skills that science teachers should have regarding educating English language learners. Pointing to an essay by Fillmore and Snow (2000), Lee asserts that teachers should foster development of general and academic language functions, including describing, explaining, comparing, and concluding. In addition, Lee suggests that teachers need to understand second language development so their expectations about students' language comprehension and production are appropriate. Finally, educators should apply their knowledge to teaching general and specific academic language. If teachers possess these skills and knowledge, they will be capable of involving students at all levels of English proficiency with multiple entry points and provide multiple modes for communicating learning, both of which lead to optimal language development.

The following section addresses practical aspects of the issues that Lee (2005) and other scholars researched regarding teaching science to ELLs. It also examines related research on teaching and assessing English language learners' achievement in other academic subjects. The section is divided into two areas: 1) adapting direct instruction, inquiry-based learning, and assessment according to ELLs' linguistic and cultural backgrounds; and 2) supporting ELLs' academic language development in science.

2.3
Supporting Communication in Content Instruction for ELLs

As a group, English language learners are diverse. An ELL can be from a rich or poor family, live in a single parent or extended family household, speak any one (or more) of hundreds of possible native languages, come from cultural backgrounds from any place on the globe, and can be United States born or a recent immigrant. The common element that all English language learners share is their developing proficiency in English.

When considering how instruction and assessment should be planned and implemented for maximum comprehensibility and participation, it is important to understand how communication can be hindered or furthered for English language learners. English language learners who began schooling in another language may understand scientific concepts they were previously taught, but they just don't understand them in English. On the other hand, many English language learners are learning concepts in their science classes that are completely new to them, and they need to comprehend the concepts via their teachers' and classmates' communication, both verbal and non-verbal, about the concepts.

Classroom communication is key to ELLs' academic success. Effective teachers are effective communicators (Fillmore & Snow, 2000), and this is even more true for teachers of ELLs. When teachers consider how their classroom communication supports ELLs, it is important to include three essential elements for second language development: input, interaction, and output.

According to Stephen Krashen (1985), comprehensible input is crucial to second language acquisition. Krashen's definition of comprehensible input is verbal input that is provided at a level slightly above the learner's current level of language proficiency and that is supported by non-verbal cues. By connecting meaning to new vocabulary and structures, learners expand their language proficiency. What this means for teaching science is that any verbal input (teacher talk or text) directed to students should be adjusted, to the extent possible, to ELLs' level of proficiency and non-verbal input should be increased to the maximum amount possible. For example, when teaching about the structure of the atom, in addition to the explanation and readings directed to the native speakers in class, a handout or other individualized instructional material using simple language and highlighting keywords can be provided. In addition, graphics, props, hands-on experiences, and diagrams can be used in providing input to all students, which benefits not only ELLs, but also students with diverse learning preferences or special needs. Consider the explanation of the structure of an atom available at http://www.vtaide.com/png/atom.htm. While accurate, the text is filled with problematic terms and structures for ELLs, hence for most ELLs it does not provide comprehensible input without adaptations such as text simplification/elaboration and visual support:

> All matter is made up of[1] atoms. An atom is like a[2] tiny solar system. In the center of the atom is the nucleus, which is a cluster of protons and neutrons.[3] The protons have a positive electric charge while[4] the neutrons are electrically neutral. The nucleus makes up[5] almost all of an atom's mass or weight.[6] Whirling[7] at fantastic[8] speeds around the nucleus[9] are smaller and lighter particles called electrons, which have a negative electric charge.[10]

Note text can be found on pp. 172–173.

To improve comprehensibility, in addition to simplifying or elaborating (providing glossaries or background information) the explanatory text, science teachers can focus on the diagram that is included on the website. The website graphic enables the viewer to move the mouse over each element for a definition and explanation. This is a very helpful feature for ELLs because it connects visual and linguistic information.

Interaction with the teacher or with other students, which requires ELLs' input and output, is an equally important condition for second language acquisition (Gass, 1997; Long, 2006). Interaction is crucial to second language acquisition because it requires learners to comprehend language input and produce language output to exchange information and enables them to negotiate meaning with another communicator. Negotiation of meaning involves establishing and clarifying meaning, using communication strategies such as circumlocution (describing a concept when unfamiliar with the term in the second language) when communication breaks down. Through having opportunities to negotiate meaning in the area of science, ELLs not only develop skills in talking about science but also clarify their understanding with classmates who are more proficient in English. Because of the importance of interaction, pair and group activities such as co-operative learning are effective strategies for promoting ELLs' comprehension of science. However, pairing or grouping students is not enough. Their communication must be supported and their roles must be carefully assigned according to their English proficiency. We will discuss proficiency levels in more detail in this chapter as well as in Chapter 3.

The counterpart of input is output. For ELLs, expressing meaning in presenting information or displaying knowledge on assessments is output. Requiring students to produce output is important to their language development (Swain, 1985), but this must be mediated by appropriate scaffolding in order for ELLs to be successful. For example, simplifying the directions on a performance assessment for ELLs can be an effective scaffold for output.

2.4
Stages of Second Language Acquisition

Students learning a second language move across a continuum from no listening, speaking, reading, or writing ability in the language to near-native or native-like proficiency. Along this continuum they progress through predictable stages, from uttering one word or short, simple phrases, to producing complete sentences with complex grammatical forms. At each stage students take in more complex vocabulary and grammatical structures and attempt to use them for real communication. When a structure is new, students often go through a process of producing it with errors before it becomes part of the individual's working grammar. For example, students at the beginning stages may say, "I no go," which precedes "I don't go" at a later point on the continuum. These types of erroneous utterances are called *interlanguage*, and for most middle and high-school students the errors will be replaced by the correct form over time and with more opportunities to communicate.

Science teachers need to understand what ELLs can do at different stages of second language acquisition to differentiate instruction appropriately. One model that describes stages of second language acquisition is called the Natural Approach (Krashen & Terrell, 1983). The Natural Approach divides the process of second language acquisition into four stages for teaching purposes: pre-production, early production, speech emergence, and intermediate fluency. Science teachers can adjust their instruction based on their ELLs' stages to promote comprehension.

The Oral Language Acquisition Grid by Virginia Collier (http://www.neboces.com/SRIT/ORAL%20LANGUAGE%20ACQUISITION%20GRID.pdf) summarizes a variety of learner behaviors and types of tasks by stage of second language acquisition, extending Krashen and Terrell's approach to six stages. Stages five and six represent what Cummins (1999) terms academic language or Cognitive Academic Language Proficiency (CALP), a more complicated type of language comprehension and production that is required for performing academic tasks on par with (or close to on par with) native speakers. When preparing a lesson, teachers can consult this table for ideas targeted to ELLs at different stages of English proficiency. Examples of science lesson plans differentiated by stage of second language acquisition are presented in Part 3.

Providing scaffolding of input, interaction, and output is a hallmark of the teaching and instruction approach known as sheltered instruction. In the next section, we will explore the most noted method of sheltered instruction, the SIOP Model.

2.5
Adapting Direct Instruction, Inquiry-Based Learning, and Assessment

At one time educators thought that students had to learn English before they could learn a subject, such as science, in English. Through "content-based" approaches to teaching English as a second language such as the Cognitive Academic Language Learning Approach (CALLA) (Chamot & O'Malley, 1994) and the Sheltered Instruction Observation Protocol (SIOP) (Echevarria, Vogt, & Short, 2008), educators have learned that the concurrent processes of developing English proficiency and learning academic content are in fact mutually beneficial, given the right circumstances. This means that if we teach students an academic subject in a way that they can understand, and if we support students' demonstration of their understanding of the subject, by the act of comprehension and expression, their English skills will grow. Conversely, as the students' English communication skills grow, their mastery of academic content increases.

Sheltered Instruction Observation Protocol (SIOP)

Teaching ELLs through making subject area content comprehensible has two aims for students: 1) to learn the subject matter concepts and/or skills; 2) to develop English language proficiency, especially the vocabulary and discourse of the subject matter. The SIOP is an approach to teaching ELLs subject matter content that has been researched and developed since the early 1990s (Echevarria, Vogt, & Short, 2008). Two research studies on the SIOP have demonstrated its effectiveness in supporting language growth. In a 1997–1998 study of middle-school ELLs (Echevarria, Vogt, & Short, 2008), two groups' performance on the Illinois Measure of Annual Growth in English (IMAGE) writing test were compared, English language learners whose teachers were training in using the SIOP and ELLs whose teachers were not. Both groups of ELLs were composed of mixed levels of English proficiency. Students in the classes whose teachers were SIOP trained to a high degree had statistically significant differences in their writing scores in the second semester of the academic year. A similar study in 1998–1999 showed essentially the same results.

Given the SIOP's increasing national profile, it is worthwhile to explore its characteristics. It is divided into three main phases: 1) preparation; 2) instruction; and 3) review assessment. Each of these phases contains segments and/or items. The following provides an overview of the SIOP's elements:

I.   Preparation
    a.   Content objectives
    b.   Language objectives
    c.   Content concepts
    d.   Supplementary materials
    e.   Adaptation of content
    f.   Meaningful activities

II. Instruction
    a.   Building background
        i.   Link concepts to experiences
        ii. Link concepts to past learning
        iii. Key vocabulary highlighted
    b.   Comprehensible input
        i.   Appropriate speech
        ii. Clear explanation of tasks
        iii. Comprehensibility techniques
    c.   Strategies
        i.   Opportunities for strategies
        ii. Scaffolding
        iii. Higher order questions
    d.   Interaction
        i.   Opportunities for interaction
        ii. Supportive grouping
        iii. Wait time
        iv. Clarification of key concepts
    e.   Practice/Application
        i.   Hands-on
        ii. Apply content and language knowledge
        iii. Integrate language skills
    f.   Lesson delivery
        i.   Supports content objectives
        ii. Supports language objectives
        iii. Students engaged >90% of time
        iv. Appropriate pacing

III. Review/Assessment
    a.   Review vocabulary
    b.   Review key concepts
    c.   Provide feedback
    d.   Assess comprehension and learning

Phase I, Preparation, emphasizes planning the lesson focus, including subject matter (content) and language objectives. By linking the content objectives to the TESOL science standards and performance indicators (Teachers of English to Speakers of Other Languages, 2006) appropriate to the subject of instruction (science) and the ELLs' level of English proficiency (see Part 3 for more information on the TESOL Science Standards), science teachers can set reasonable expectations for their ELLs' performance in a given lesson. For example, for a lesson on nuclear structures and functions, an ELL at level three can "draw or build models of elements from oral descriptions in small groups" (Teachers of English to Speakers of Other Languages, 2006: 94). Language objectives, in contrast, focus on the specific vocabulary, grammatical, rhetorical, and discourse structures of the language required to learn and demonstrate learning of the science content. In conducting a scientific experiment, for example, a language objective might be to "comprehend and express the simple command form" used in the sequence of steps in an experiment—1) *Measure* 50 grams of salt; 2) *Dissolve* the salt in a cup of water, etc. Content concepts, supplementary materials, adaptation of content, and meaningful activities, the remaining components of the planning phase, focus on the special preparation needed to improve comprehension and develop language skills for ELLs.

The instruction phase provides rich details to guide science teachers during the lesson. The first segment connects concepts to students' background, a key finding of Lee's (2005) research review. Key terms are also emphasized during this segment. Krashen's (1985) notion of comprehensible input is the third segment, stressing techniques such as slower, simplified speech, modeling, and visuals. Learning strategies are next, which focus on individual learner mental processes. O'Malley & Chamot (1990) identified three categories of strategies, metacognitive, cognitive, and social/affective. Metacognitive strategies involve monitoring thinking, for example a reader who questions her understanding of the text while reading. Cognitive strategies are directly connected to the specific task a learner is completing, such as note-taking while listening to an explanation. Social/affective strategies involve human interaction and motivation and emotional aspects of learning. Understanding how to interact in small group discussion is one example of social/affective strategies. Including strategy development in lessons empowers individual learners to reflect upon and improve the way they approach a task. Explicit strategy instruction is important for ELLs because, in K–12 schools in the United States, students are expected to employ many of these strategies as part of normal classroom behavior (e.g., know how to interact in small groups).

The fifth area of instruction is interaction, which as we have seen in the previous section, is a key element in second-language acquisition. Ensuring ample interaction improves opportunities for language development as well as subject matter learning. Interaction can be between teacher and student(s) or between student(s) and student(s). Following interaction, practice/application involves using hands-on experiences, developing content knowledge, and integrating language skills. Lesson delivery, the seventh area, evaluates whether the instruction supports the content and language objectives, promotes student engagement, and properly paces the delivery.

The third phase, review/assessment, encompasses review of vocabulary and concepts, providing feedback, and assessing lesson objectives. Assessment must provide a variety of means for students to show their mastery of the topic, avoiding the trap of assessing language proficiency instead of meeting the lesson objectives. For example, when assessing comprehension of a process such as the water cycle, ELLs can draw or complete a diagram with keywords and pictures rather than write a paragraph explaining the process or select the best answer for multiple choice questions in English.

The SIOP model can be applied successfully to the teaching of science. Many of its principles are compatible with best practices for scientific teaching. In Part 3 we present two science lesson plans that have been revised to follow key principles of the SIOP.

Assessment and Accommodations for Teaching Academic Subjects to ELLs

Just as with teaching science, assessing ELLs' mastery of science content requires language support and accommodations. Jamal Abedi and Ron Dietel (2004) of the National Center for Research on Evaluation, Standards, and Student Testing (CRESST) surveyed the research on various types of test modifications and accommodations for ELLs. Their findings show that modifying test items' language by simplifying sentence structures can increase ELL performance by 10% to 20%. Hence, any test assesses not only knowledge of the subject matter but also of the language used in the evaluation.

Modifying test items' language requires a basic understanding of English sentence structure. A good place to start is to count the number of verb phrases in a sentence. Sentences with multiple verb phrases can often be broken down into smaller sentences. For example, "Although copper is a good conductor, gold exceeds its conductivity," could be broken down to "Copper is a good conductor. Gold is a better conductor than copper." Complex sentences using *that* or *which* can also be simplified. For example, "Place the cylinder that has been heated to 220° in the red receptacle," has two verb phrases separated by a relative clause (that …). This could be rephrased in simpler form as, "Put the 220° cylinder in the red receptacle." Passive verb construction can be revised to active, such as "Liquid was drawn from the container with a syringe," to "The experimenter removed liquid from the container with a syringe."

In addition to modifying the language used in assessing English language learners' knowledge and skills in academic subjects such as science, Abedi and Dietel found that accommodations, such as allowing extra time to complete the assessment or a glossary of key terms in conjunction with additional time, have promoted ELLs' improved performance.

Reducing the language demands of an assessment by providing other means to express comprehension and demonstrate mastery is a good option for assessing ELLs' science knowledge and skills. Concept maps are a particularly effective way of showing complex relationships without resorting to lengthy verbal descriptions. Flowcharts can provide explanations of conditional relationships in simple, diagram form. Wherever possible, science teachers should ask themselves if students' knowledge and skills could be demonstrated through primarily graphic rather than primarily linguistic means. Demonstrating understanding of the water cycle can be more easily accomplished by labeling key concepts in Figure 2.1 from the USGS than by writing a lengthy explanation or answering multiple-choice questions.

The United States Geological Survey, a "Federal source for science about the Earth, its natural and living resources, natural hazards, and the environment" (http://www.usgs.gov/), provides this diagram and many other diagrams and visuals that can improve comprehension for ELLs.

The English version of this diagram is available at http://ga.water.usgs.gov/edu/watercyclehi.html. This diagram is also available in over 60 languages at http://ga.water.usgs.gov/edu/watercycle.html.

The software program *Inspiration* is a great tool for creating graphic organizers. Teachers can create concept maps to present when introducing a new topic, or students can document their findings from inquiry-based learning in graphic organizer templates. The templates presented in Figures 2.2 and 2.3 (overleaf) offer a feasible alternative to writing a narrative explanation.

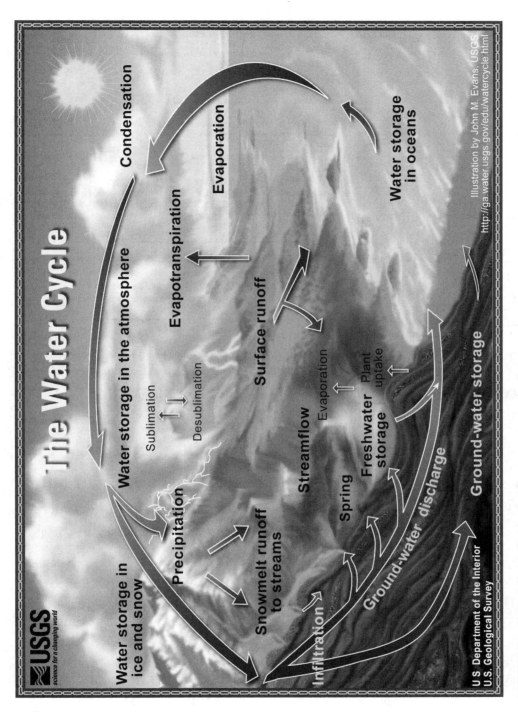

FIGURE 2.1. United States Geological Survey water cycle diagram.

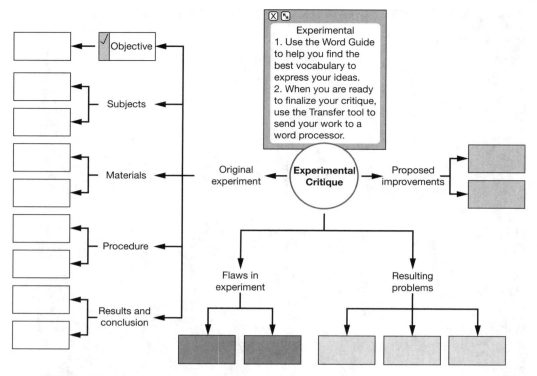

FIGURE 2.2. *Inspiration* template for experimental description/critique.

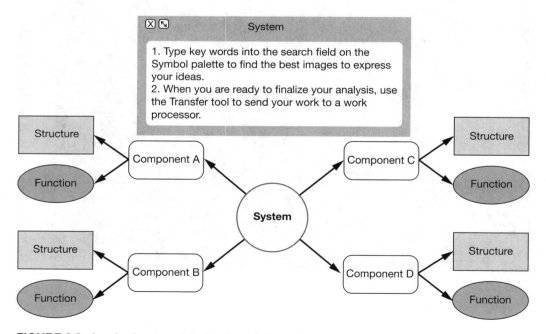

FIGURE 2.3. *Inspiration* template for description of a system.

2.6
Supporting ELLs' Academic Language Development in Science

According to the National Clearinghouse for English Language Education report, *Educating English language learners: building teacher capacity* (Ballantyne, Sanderman, & Levy, 2008), vocabulary development, talking science, and writing science are important areas of focus for science teachers with English language learners in their classes. The importance of talking about and reading science are the primary emphasis of *Essential elements of effective science instruction for English learners* (Dobb, 2004). Both of these reports offer valuable insights on ways science teachers can help build their ELLs' English language proficiency.

Recommendations for building science vocabulary include dedicating a few minutes at the beginning of each class to focus on the lesson's vocabulary. A good resource pointed out in Dobb's report provides ELLs with vocabulary specific to scientific fields through the following two science word list websites: http://www.theinterpretersfriend.com/tech/vocab/vl/science.html and http://www.uefap.com/vocab/select/sp_sci.htm.

In addition to focusing on scientific vocabulary, it is important to build students' general academic vocabulary. Websites such as the Academic Word List (http://www.nottingham. ac.uk/%7Ealzsh3/acvocab/index.htm) provide lists of the most common academic terms in English. English language learners can use these lists to study the words in context (the website offers special functions for identifying these words in text) or to look them up in their bilingual dictionaries. According to the Academic Word List, the 50 most common academic terms in English are: *analysis, approach, area, assessment, assume, authority, available, benefit, concept, consistent, constitutional, context, contract, create, data, definition, derived, distribution, economic, environment, established, estimate, evidence, export, factors, financial, formula, function, identified, income, indicate, individual, interpretation, involved, issues, labor, legal, legislation, major, method, occur, percent, period, policy, principle, procedure, process, required, research, response, role, section, sector, significant, similar, source, specific, structure, theory,* and *variable.* The majority of these terms have applications to scientific discourse and text. For secondary students in particular, providing definitions of these words in context can facilitate academic language development.

Another vocabulary-building strategy is to explicitly address cognates, which are words that sound and/or look similar and mean the same thing in different languages, such as *educación* in Spanish and *education* in English or *biología* in Spanish or *biologie* in Dutch/German/French and *biology* in English. This is particularly important in science, a field that uses many terms derived from Latin, which also was the origin of languages such as Spanish, Italian, French, and Portuguese. Teachers can begin by pointing out examples of cognates and then challenging students to find as many as possible in a science textbook passage. Two excellent websites for Spanish cognates are:

> http://www.esdict.com/English-Spanish-Cognates.html#nouns
> http://kellyjones.netfirms.com/spanish/cognatedoublets.shtml

A site that provides science terms in English and Spanish (cognates or not) is:

> http://www.learninglive.co.uk/teachers/primary/science/teaching/Spanish%20Science%20
>   key%20words.pdf

For information on a lesson plan that shows how to teach cognates in science, see:

> http://seedsofscience.org/PDFs/StrategyGuides/SG_WalkinWoods_single.pdf

To promote optimal opportunities for ELLs to talk about science, Ballantyne, Sanderman, & Levy (2008) recommend small group work with the following characteristics: 1) provide written and oral directions to groups; 2) group students with others who share their native language (L1) and allow them to use their L1 to discuss scientific concepts; 3) for groups with multiple L1s and mixtures of native speakers and ELLs, carefully assign roles according to the ELLs' level of English proficiency, asking beginners to perform tasks that are less language dependent.

Writing about science is perhaps one of the most challenging demands on ELLs, especially those at lower levels of English proficiency. In lieu of requiring narrative reports that answer one or more questions, Ballantyne, Sanderman, and Levy (2008) suggest using "sentence chunks" that provide most of the sentence structure with blanks for ELLs to write one or two words. For example, "This study examines the relationship between _____ and _____," or "Based on _____ I predict that _____."

Science textbooks present special linguistic challenges for ELLs. Haynes (2007) identified challenges for ELLs in science textbooks, including too many concepts addressed in reading passages, confusing explanatory visuals, and complex sentence structure that uses the passive voice. According to Rosenthal (1995), the factual style of scientific writing is harder to understand than the narrative structure of fiction. Moreover, unfamiliar terms are introduced constantly, details typically precede the general concepts to which they pertain, and there is a lack of repetition or paraphrasing of information. Dobb suggests six strategies for addressing these concerns. The first, native language use, involves support including bilingual dictionaries or materials and native language instruction provided by an aide or bilingual teacher. Reading comprehension activities are the second area, which includes previewing information, summarizing, and comprehending visuals and graphs. Building study skills, area three includes helping readers focus on crucial versus extraneous information in textbooks and reviewing strategies that successful science students use to learn the chapter content. Area four, vocabulary development, was discussed in the vocabulary section above. In area five, teaching scientific discourse patterns is presented. Showing the differences between expository versus narrative genres and practice with common sentence structure, such as "if _____, then _____," improve comprehension. Lastly, area six discusses materials to supplement the textbook, offering a resource for science materials at http://www.cde.ca.gov/ci/sc/ll/.

In Part 3, we provide more detail on teaching specific scientific content to ELLs, built on the principles discussed in previous sections.

Part 3
Teaching Science

In Part 2 we explored the research on 1) science teaching and learning, 2) teaching and assessing English language learners in science, and 3) teaching and assessing English language learners in academic content areas.

We began by offering six principles for science instruction derived from the NSES and current research on science education. After reviewing the principles for science instruction, we explored the research on science education for English language learners. Three practical findings on teaching and assessing science emerged from the research: 1) English language learners whose linguistic or cultural backgrounds are not congruent with science instructional methods and techniques commonly used in the US need explicit instruction in developing conceptual knowledge; 2) Hands-on activities, which are a common feature of science instruction, are beneficial for ELLs' comprehension and promote discussion about science, a plus for language development; and 3) Science teachers need to understand the second-language acquisition process, and they must use this knowledge to teach science-related language as a natural part of instruction.

Following the survey of research on science instruction for ELLs, we looked at instructional practices that are conducive to ELLs' subject matter comprehension. Using the constructs of input, interaction, and output, we examined the language demands placed on science students and how to narrow the gap between ELLs' English language proficiency and the level of discourse and literacy necessary to succeed in science education. We then took a closer look at the stages of second language development and at how these stages affect what ELLs can comprehend and express. Table 3.1 provides a summary of the stages.

A current approach to teaching ELLs academic content, the Sheltered Instruction Observation Protocol (SIOP), was presented with a discussion of how it reflects research on best practices in teaching ELLs. Last, we explored research on how formal and informal assessment can be modified to lessen linguistic and cultural bias.

TABLE 3.1. Four stages of second language acquisition

	Preproduction	Early Production	Speech Emergence	Intermediate Fluency
Second Language Communication Ability	"Silent Period" Pointing Responding with movement Following commands Receptive vocabulary up to 500 words	1 or 2 word responses Labeling Listing Receptive vocabulary up to 1,000 words Expressive vocabulary 100–500 words	Short phrases and sentences Comparing and contrasting Descriptions Receptive vocabulary up to 7,000 words Expressive vocabulary 2,000 words	Dialogue Reading academic texts Writing Receptive vocabulary up to 12,000 words Expressive vocabulary 4,000 words
Teaching Strategies	Yes/no questions Simplified speech Gestures Visuals Picture books Word walls Simple cloze activities Realia TPR	Questions that require: yes/no, either/or, 2-word responses, lists of words, definitions, description. Reader's theater Drama Graphic organizers	How and why questions Modeling Demonstrating Cooperative learning Comprehension checks Alternative assessments Simulations	Brainstorming Journal writing Literary analysis Problem solving Role playing Monologues Storytelling Oral reports Interviewing and applications

Adapted from Krahen and Terrell (1982) by Cruz and Thornton, 2009: 67.

Our final topic was promoting ELLs' English language development in science instruction. Promising practices discussed include an explicit focus on vocabulary instruction, including common science and academic terms as well as cognates in the native language of students and English, and ample opportunities for talking and writing about science.

As mentioned previously, the purpose of this book is twofold: 1) how to promote ELLs' English development through science instruction, and 2) how to teach science content to ELLs who are at different levels of English language proficiency. Science teachers do not necessarily use their full repertoire of pedagogical practices wholly to engage and help ELLs in ways consistent with the two purposes of this book. We intend to show, with a varied range of examples, how these two purposes can be achieved by building on the knowledge, skills and strategies teachers already possess and use in their secondary science classrooms. Our book is about mainstreaming and inclusion and reaching out to all students—about using strategies that help ELLs, and do not exclude them from understanding the science curriculum. The ELLs will ultimately have the kind of scientific literacy advocated by the National Research Council (1996) in the NSES that will help them to be informed and productive members of society.

In Part 3, we apply the principles and practices highlighted and explicated in Part 2 to specific learning activities for the eight areas of secondary science contained in the NSES. Beginning with a description of teaching science topics across the K–12 continuum, we focus on how the content of the NSES differs at each grade cluster. We then examine the Teachers of English to Speakers of Other Languages (TESOL) Pre-K–12 English Language Proficiency Standards for Science and how they can guide teachers' expectations of ELLs' performance in science. As an introduction to effective instructional and assessment practices for ELLs learning science, we present a teaching case highlighting a science instructor's approach to teaching the same topic—with and without accommodations for ELLs. We then explore how science instruction can be culturally relevant and how science assessment can be more inclusive. Last, we give concrete examples of effective instructional practices for common science topics in eight areas: 1) physical science; 2) life science; 3) earth and space science; 4) science and technology; 5) history and nature of science; 6) science and inquiry; 7) personal and social perspectives in science; and, 8) unifying concepts and processes.

3.1
Teaching Science to ELLs at Secondary Grade Levels

The NSES (National Research Council, 1996), *Science for all Americans: project 2061* (Rutherford & Ahlgren, 1989), *Benchmarks for science literacy* (American Association for the Advancement of Science, 1993), and *Atlas of science literacy* (American Association for the Advancement of Science, 2001) are the major science education reform documents that influence current science teaching and learning practices in K–12 classrooms in the U.S. Although there are differences between the ways these documents present the science education curriculum, they all advocate for science education that is consistent with how children learn. Each provides a plan to be used by teachers in designing a curriculum appropriate for their particular situation. They do not dictate what to teach. Instead, they are references that describe the levels of understanding all students should reach on the way to becoming scientifically literate. They present the science content in a way that it is continuously re-visited at higher and higher levels of sophistication across the grade levels. This model ensures that the coverage of content knowledge focuses on fewer major topics in depth than on superficial knowledge.

In order to understand how to teach science to ELLs at the secondary grade levels, we must focus on how science content progresses from elementary grades to middle grades and to high school grade levels in these documents. This book discusses science teaching in the light of the NSES,[1] so we will explain the content progression across grade levels by providing specific examples from these standards.

The standards are clustered and grouped for grades K–4, 5–8, and 9–12 based on cognitive development theory (Piaget, 1952), as well as the classroom experiences of teachers and the organization of schools. Piaget suggested that cognitive development in children occurs in a series of four distinct and increasingly sophisticated and abstract levels of thought: *sensorimotor stage* (birth to 24 months), *pre-operational stage* (2 to 6 years), *concrete operational stage* (7 to 11 years), and *formal operational stage* (12 to 15 and to adult years). According to Piaget's theory, children at elementary grade levels are expected to perform logical operations in relation to concrete external objects rather than ideas. They can add, subtract, count, and measure, and they can begin to learn about the conservation of length, mass, area, weight, time, and volume. They can sort items into categories, and think about two variables, such as length and width, simultaneously. While still holding egocentric views, they begin to understand a situation from the viewpoint of another person. At middle and high school, on the other hand, children develop the ability to think logically about abstract concepts, including speculations about what might happen in the future. They start formulating and testing hypotheses, understand cause-and-effect relationships and abstract concepts, such as probability, ratio, proportion, and analogies.

When applied to science education, elementary science curriculum (K–4) targets *pre-operational* and *concrete operational* stages, whereas secondary level science curriculum, including middle (5–8) and high school (9–12) grade levels, targets *concrete operational* and *formal operational* stages. Thus, at elementary grade levels, students learn simple concepts that can be directly investigated in a hands-on manner using simple materials. The activities should be related to children's close environment and involve children through as many senses as possible. At early elementary grades, children should control one variable at a time when engaged in experiments. For example, when studying what plants need to grow, children can study variables such as water, air, temperature, sunlight, and soil separately; it is not appropriate to expect them to understand the relationships among these variables. Toward the end of elementary school, children start to make inferences and are ready to design controlled experiments and to discover the relationships among variables. For instance, when investigating floating objects, they can manipulate the mass of the object or the contact surface area, and determine whether one or both of these variables determine whether an object floats.

As their ability to reason and think abstractly develops during the middle school years, the level of complexity related to understanding the science concepts grows as well. Rather than simply looking at the physical properties of matter that can be investigated directly through observation and classification activities, such as size and shape, middle-school students explore matter and how its properties change and how these changes are related to the transference of energy. Students can classify objects by multiple attributes and start experimenting with different organizational strategies. Thus, teachers should provide science experiences that move students toward higher levels of abstract thinking. Classroom discussions and debates on social and scientific issues will help students become aware of the variety of possible opinions on science-related topics.

Despite the development of abstract thinking, students at the middle school level still rely on concrete instruction. Hence, teachers should continue to use concrete props, visual aids, and three-dimensional models when dealing with concepts that are difficult for children to comprehend.

At the high school years, students are expected to understand more complex and sophisticated levels of science content knowledge, and are involved not only in more extensive investigations but also in concepts that are more abstract and more directly related to the community and the world in which they live. Students can understand highly complex organizational schemes, such as the periodic table and the structure of DNA. They should start thinking more like research scientists, devising plans to solve problems and systematically testing solutions. They should be given opportunities to implement these processes to explore many hypothetical questions. Students at this level look for evidence that supports contemporary models, and ways of understanding how matter is organized and structured. For example, students build upon and go beyond their understanding of the structure of an atom. Understanding the structure of matter as atoms and molecules helps students understand other properties of matter, such as diffusion, heat transference, and changes of state. Although students at this age group are expected to be at the *formal operational* stage of cognitive development according to Piaget, several studies have reported that only 30% to 35% of adolescents and adults have ever achieved this level of thinking (Huitt & Hummel, 2003). Therefore, teachers should still continue to use many of the teaching strategies and materials appropriate for students at the concrete operational stage, like visual aids such as charts and illustrations, as well as simple but somewhat more sophisticated graphs and diagrams, and step-by-step explanations for investigations when necessary.

In order to assist schools and teachers in developing their elementary (K–4), middle (5–8), and high school (9–12) level science curricula, the NSES identify specific concepts and performances for students at different grade levels to accomplish. These concepts and performances indicate what students on the way to scientific literacy should know by the conclusion of each of the grade bands. For example, in dealing with physical science, the following concepts and performances are listed.

Grades K–4. By the end of 4th grade students should know:

Properties of Objects and Materials

- Objects have many observable properties, including size, weight, shape, color, temperature, and the ability to react with other substances. Those properties can be measured using tools, such as rulers, balances, and thermometers.
- Objects are made of one or more materials, such as paper, wood, and metal. Objects can be described by the properties of the materials from which they are made, and those properties can be used to separate or sort a group of objects or materials.
- Materials can exist in different states—solid, liquid, and gas. Some common materials, such as water, can be changed from one state to another by heating or cooling.

Position and Motion of Objects

- The position of an object can be described by locating it relative to another object or the background.
- An object's motion can be described by tracing and measuring its position over time.
- The position and motion of objects can be changed by pushing or pulling. The size of the change is related to the strength of the push or pull.
- Sound is produced by vibrating objects. The pitch of the sound can be varied by changing the rate of vibration.

Light, Heat, Electricity, and Magnetism

- Light travels in a straight line until it strikes an object. Light can be reflected by a mirror, refracted by a lens, or absorbed by the object.
- Heat can be produced in many ways, such as burning, rubbing, or mixing one substance with another. Heat can move from one object to another by conduction.
- Electricity in circuits can produce light, heat, sound, and magnetic effects. Electrical circuits require a complete loop through which an electrical current can pass.
- Magnets attract and repel each other and certain kinds of other materials. (p. 127)

Grades 5–8. By the end of 8th grade students should develop an understanding of:

Properties and Changes of Properties in Matter

- A substance has characteristic properties, such as density, a boiling point, and solubility, all of which are independent of the amount of the sample. A mixture of substances often can be separated into the original substances using one or more of the characteristic properties.
- Substances react chemically in characteristic ways with other substances to form new substances (compounds) with different characteristic properties. In chemical reactions, the total mass is conserved. Substances often are placed in categories or groups if they react in similar ways; an example of such a grouping is metals.
- Chemical elements do not break down during normal laboratory reactions involving such treatments as heating, exposure to electric current, or reaction with acids. There are more than 100 known elements that combine in a multitude of ways to produce compounds, which account for the living and non-living substances that we encounter.

Motions and Forces

- The motion of an object can be described by its position, direction of motion, and speed. That motion can be measured and represented on a graph.
- An object that is not being subjected to a force will continue to move at a constant speed and in a straight line.
- If more than one force acts on an object along a straight line, then the forces will reinforce or cancel one another, depending on their direction and magnitude. Unbalanced forces will cause changes in the speed or direction of an object's motion.

Transfer of Energy

- Energy is a property of many substances and is associated with heat, light, electricity, mechanical motion, sound, nuclei, and the nature of a chemical. Energy is transferred in many ways.
- Heat moves in predictable ways, flowing from warmer objects to cooler ones, until both reach the same temperature.
- Light interacts with matter by transmission (including refraction), absorption, or scattering (including reflection). To see an object, light from that object—emitted by or scattered from it—must enter the eye.
- Electrical circuits provide a means of transferring electrical energy when heat, light, sound, and chemical changes are produced.
- In most chemical and nuclear reactions, energy is transferred into or out of a system. Heat, light, mechanical motion, or electricity might all be involved in such transfers.
- The sun is a major source of energy for changes on the earth's surface. The sun loses energy by emitting light. A tiny fraction of that light reaches the earth, transferring energy from the sun to the earth. The sun's energy arrives as light with a range of wavelengths, consisting of visible light, infrared, and ultraviolet radiation. (pp. 154–155)

Grades 9–12. By the end of 12th grade students should develop an understanding of:

Structure of Atoms

- Matter is made of minute particles called atoms, and atoms are composed of even smaller components. These components have measurable properties, such as mass and electrical charge. Each atom has a positively charged nucleus surrounded by negatively charged electrons. The electric force between the nucleus and electrons holds the atom together.
- The atom's nucleus is composed of protons and neutrons, which are much more massive than electrons. When an element has atoms that differ in the number of neutrons, these atoms are called different isotopes of the element.
- The nuclear forces that hold the nucleus of an atom together, at nuclear distances, are usually stronger than the electric forces that would make it fly apart. Nuclear reactions convert a fraction of the mass of interacting particles into energy, and they can release much greater amounts of energy than atomic interactions. Fission is the splitting of a large nucleus into smaller pieces. Fusion is the joining of two nuclei at extremely high temperature and pressure, and is the process responsible for the energy of the sun and other stars.
- Radioactive isotopes are unstable and undergo spontaneous nuclear reactions, emitting particles and/or wavelike radiation. The decay of any one nucleus cannot be predicted, but a large group of identical nuclei decay at a predictable rate. This predictability can be used to estimate the age of materials that contain radioactive isotopes.

Structure and Properties of Matter

- Atoms interact with one another by transferring or sharing electrons that are furthest from the nucleus. These outer electrons govern the chemical properties of the element.
- An element is composed of a single type of atom. When elements are listed in order according to the number of protons (called the atomic number), repeating patterns of physical and chemical properties identify families of elements with similar properties. This "Periodic Table" is a consequence of the repeating pattern of outermost electrons and their permitted energies.
- Bonds between atoms are created when electrons are paired up by being transferred or shared. A substance composed of a single kind of atom is called an element. The atoms may be bonded together into molecules or crystalline solids. A compound is formed when two or more kinds of atoms bind together chemically.
- The physical properties of compounds reflect the nature of the interactions among its molecules. These interactions are determined by the structure of the molecule, including the constituent atoms and the distances and angles between them.
- Solids, liquids, and gases differ in the distances and angles between molecules or atoms and therefore the energy that binds them together. In solids the structure is nearly rigid; in liquids molecules or atoms move around each other but do not move apart; and in gases molecules or atoms move almost independently of each other and are mostly far apart.
- Carbon atoms can bond to one another in chains, rings, and branching networks

to form a variety of structures, including synthetic polymers, oils, and the large molecules essential to life.

Chemical Reactions

- Chemical reactions occur all around us, for example in health care, cooking, cosmetics, and automobiles. Complex chemical reactions involving carbon-based molecules take place constantly in every cell in our bodies.
- Chemical reactions may release or consume energy. Some reactions such as the burning of fossil fuels release large amounts of energy by losing heat and by emitting light. Light can initiate many chemical reactions such as photosynthesis and the evolution of urban smog.
- A large number of important reactions involve the transfer of either electrons (oxidation/reduction reactions) or hydrogen ions (acid/base reactions) between reacting ions, molecules, or atoms. In other reactions, chemical bonds are broken by heat or light to form very reactive radicals with electrons ready to form new bonds. Radical reactions control many processes such as the presence of ozone and greenhouse gases in the atmosphere, burning and processing of fossil fuels, the formation of polymers, and explosions.
- Chemical reactions can take place in time periods ranging from the few femtoseconds (10–15 seconds) required for an atom to move a fraction of a chemical bond distance to geologic time scales of billions of years. Reaction rates depend on how often the reacting atoms and molecules encounter one another, on the temperature, and on the properties—including shape—of the reacting species.
- Catalysts, such as metal surfaces, accelerate chemical reactions. Chemical reactions in living systems are catalyzed by protein molecules called enzymes.

Motions and Forces

- Objects change their motion only when a net force is applied. Laws of motion are used to calculate precisely the effects of forces on the motion of objects. The magnitude of the change in motion can be calculated using the relationship $F = ma$, which is independent of the nature of the force. Whenever one object exerts force on another, a force equal in magnitude and opposite in direction is exerted on the first object.
- Gravitation is a universal force that each mass exerts on any other mass. The strength of the gravitational attractive force between two masses is proportional to the masses and inversely proportional to the square of the distance between them.
- The electric force is a universal force that exists between any two charged objects. Opposite charges attract while like charges repel. The strength of the force is proportional to the charges, and, as with gravitation, inversely proportional to the square of the distance between them.
- Between any two charged particles, electric force is vastly greater than the gravitational force. Most observable forces such as those exerted by a coiled spring or friction may be traced to electric forces acting between atoms and molecules.
- Electricity and magnetism are two aspects of a single electromagnetic force. Moving electric charges produce magnetic forces, and moving magnets produce electric forces. These effects help students to understand electric motors and generators.

Conservation of Energy and the Increase in Disorder

- The total energy of the universe is constant. Energy can be transferred by collisions in chemical and nuclear reactions, by light waves and other radiations, and in many other ways. However, it can never be destroyed. As these transfers occur, the matter involved becomes steadily less ordered.
- All energy can be considered to be either kinetic energy, which is the energy of motion; potential energy, which depends on relative position; or energy contained by a field, such as electromagnetic waves.
- Heat consists of random motion and the vibrations of atoms, molecules, and ions. The higher the temperature, the greater the atomic or molecular motion.
- Everything tends to become less organized and less orderly over time. Thus, in all energy transfers, the overall effect is that the energy is spread out uniformly. Examples are the transfer of energy from hotter to cooler objects by conduction, radiation, or convection and the warming of our surroundings when we burn fuels.

Interactions of Energy and Matter

- Waves, including sound and seismic waves, waves on water, and light waves, have energy and can transfer energy when they interact with matter.
- Electromagnetic waves result when a charged object is accelerated or decelerated. Electromagnetic waves include radio waves (the longest wavelength), microwaves, infrared radiation (radiant heat), visible light, ultraviolet radiation, x-rays, and gamma rays. The energy of electromagnetic waves is carried in packets whose magnitude is inversely proportional to the wavelength.
- Each kind of atom or molecule can gain or lose energy only in particular discrete amounts and thus can absorb and emit light only at wavelengths corresponding to these amounts. These wavelengths can be used to identify the substance.
- In some materials, such as metals, electrons flow easily, whereas in insulating materials such as glass they can hardly flow at all. Semiconducting materials have intermediate behavior. At low temperatures some materials become superconductors and offer no resistance to the flow of electrons. (pp. 178–181)

The NSES state that science is for *all* students, and all students from all backgrounds should be included in challenging science learning opportunities with specified levels of understanding and abilities that every student should develop. The standards define excellence in science education as achievement of understanding of science by all students if given the opportunity. This means that ELL students that currently make up 5% of the United States' student population (National Center for Education Statistics, 2003) are subject to learning these concepts and performances. This expectation seems reasonable considering that cognitive development theory applies to children from all cultural backgrounds. However, it is not reasonable for teachers to assume that they should use the same instructional strategies that they use for English-speaking students to help ELL students master the necessary science understanding. In a study that examined the effects of English language proficiency and scientific reasoning on the performance of a group of Grade 10 Hispanic English language learners and native English language speaking students on a standardized science test, Torres and Zeidler (2002) reported that there is a strong relationship between English language proficiency, scientific reasoning, and science content learning. More specifically, English language proficiency and scientific reasoning significantly affect the learning of science content knowledge of Hispanic English language learners, and higher levels of English language proficiency and scientific reasoning were shown to predict success in learning science concepts.

Considering the complexity of the science concepts at secondary grade levels, the level of abstract thinking, and the amount of vocabulary required to achieve science understanding, we believe that science learning can be even more difficult for ELL students at these levels.

For ELL students, the opportunity to practice oral communication in the context of actual science activities is a powerful way to develop language fluency (Amaral, Garrison, & Klentschy, 2002; Linik, 2004), which then can help them achieve science learning. English language learners should be involved in inquiry-based hands-on investigations during which they collaborate with others who are fluent in English and communicate their experiences and understanding in verbal and written forms. Both teachers and ELL students should use visual aids, such as charts, drawings, graphs, and models, and other concrete teaching strategies to go along with verbally describing a concept. In addition, providing simple written instructions for ELLs to refer to supports both comprehension and language development. Instead of focusing on students' grammar, or correcting language, teachers should continually model the scientific language and vocabulary appropriate for secondary level science settings and make conscious efforts to incorporate language development, even as scientific ideas are being discussed and science process skills are being performed. Science teachers should actively participate in co-operative groups that involve ELL students so they can monitor and assist them as needed.

When at all possible, instructions for science activities should be presented in both English and, for ELLs at the pre-production and early production levels of English proficiency, in the ELL's own first language. If the school does not have translation services, a parent, college professor, or a teacher can help with translating directions into other languages (Ramirez & Douglas, 1988). Finding access to such services or establishing other community-based resources (e.g., bilingual community members) at the outset of the school year will be an essential component of structuring successful experiences for ELL students. Providing examples from ELLs' own cultures, as well as describing the contributions of scientists from different nations and cultures can also contribute to their success in learning science.

Section 3.2 provides a detailed explanation of the Teachers of English to Speakers of Other Languages (TESOL) Pre-K–12 English Language Proficiency Standards for Science and explains how teachers can use them to understand what ELLs at different levels of English proficiency can understand and express about scientific topics and processes.

Teaching about Motion in High School, Middle School and Elementary School: An Experiential Perspective

Having taught children science in elementary, middle and high school settings, I can attest to the difference in the depth of understanding students can accomplish at the three distinct grade levels. The teaching of motion is an example of how instruction must vary to accommodate the various developmental levels of students as they progress in their cognitive abilities across the grade spectrum.

For example, in my first year of teaching, I taught physics and environmental science. In my physics class, we worked on kinematics—the study of the motion of objects through the use of mental models. These mental models can be used to understand and explain the motion of objects in real life. My 11th and 12th graders were able to grasp this concept after we reviewed their understanding of Newton's Laws of Motion. We developed the necessary formulas, graphs, equations and diagrams to describe various types of motion—circular, angular, projectile, etc. Our culminating activity for this unit was the students' development of activities for their classmates that underscored their learning of kinematics. For example, one student, who was a softball player on the high school team, explained projectile motion by taking the class outside and striking out another classmate who was a member of the boy's baseball team. Another student showed his peers how to tackle someone in football properly. His technique emphasized how to avoid serious neck injuries. Finally, another demonstrated the many variables involved in the tumbling that cheerleaders do at the school's various sporting events.

At the middle school level, I was fortunate to teach 6th and 8th graders. For these students, the topic of motion focused on Newton's Laws of Motion, with special attention paid to Newton's Second Law, the well-known, $F = m \times a$. This formula has two, possibly three, abstract aspects to it, so making the concept graspable for my students involved the use of motion cars, ramps and springs. We attempted to understand how the application of a force to an object caused it to move, with an unequal net force causing the object/car to accelerate. After observing, drawing, graphing, writing and solving, the students moved forward in their thinking about cars. We also discussed why it was important to wear seat belts.

Hot Wheel™ cars came in handy for the elementary students, as we played with them and came to understand that objects travel at different speeds and different distances depending on the size of the force applied to them. We built ramps for our cars, pushed them across the floor and debated about the time and distances the cars traveled. Through the use of their science notebooks, students were able to write, draw and sketch about what they observed during their inquiries.

The three teaching experiences mentioned above highlight how the concept of motion can be taught at the elementary and secondary levels at various depths of conceptual development. It is obvious the same concept must be treated and taught in a "spiral" manner, where students' previous knowledge and experiences are used as the basis for new knowledge and deeper understanding of the motion of objects. For ELLs, the situation is even more critical, as they seek to understand the academic language of science, as well as continue to increase their acquisition of the English language.

Malcolm Butler

3.2
Pre-K–12 English Language Proficiency Standards for Science

The professional organization Teachers of English to Speakers of Other Languages (TESOL) published Pre-K–12 English Language Proficiency Standards in March 2006. For the first time, the standards include academic subject matter content, whereas the previous standards focused primarily on learning English. This represents a shift in theory and practice that had been building over the previous decade. Previously, TESOL was primarily concerned with language development as an end in itself, but research in the field of second language acquisition showed increasing evidence for content-focused language development. This means that, for example, language skills and knowledge such as the future tense (I will go) can be learned in the context of academic subject matter, for instance in predicting the outcome of an experiment (the object will float). This shift has strengthened the partnership of ESOL specialists and content teachers, sharing the responsibility for supporting second language acquisition and content area knowledge and skills development.

The Pre-K–12 English Language Proficiency Standards include five **standards**, which are divided into five **grade level clusters**, four **language domains**, and five **levels of English proficiency**:

Standards

Standard 1: English language learners communicate for social, intercultural, and instructional purposes within the school setting.

Standard 2: English language learners communicate information, ideas, and concepts necessary for academic success in the area of language arts.

Standard 3: English language learners communicate information, ideas, and concepts necessary for academic success in the area of mathematics.

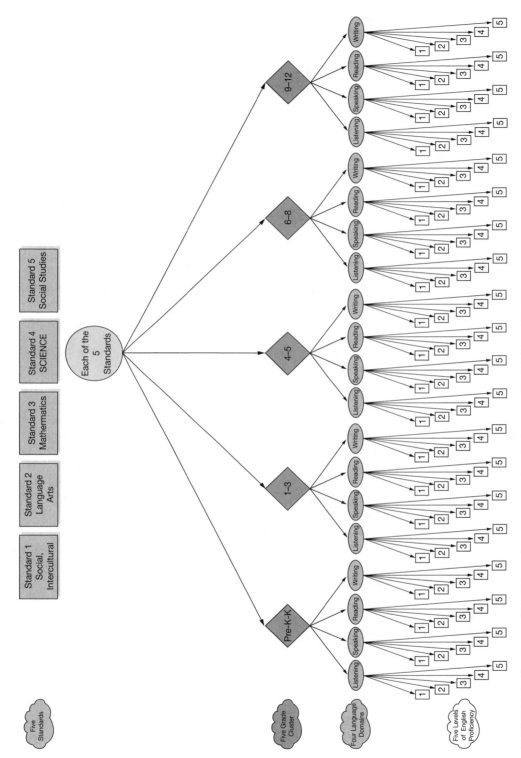

FIGURE 3.1. Teachers of English to Speakers of Other Languages (TESOL) pre-K–12 English language proficiency standards.

Standard 4: English language learners communicate information, ideas, and concepts necessary for academic success in the area of **science**.

Standard 5: English language learners communicate information, ideas, and concepts necessary for academic success in the area of social studies.

Grade Level Clusters

Pre-K–K, 1–3, 4–5, 6–8, 9–12

Language Domains

Listening, Speaking, Reading, Writing

Levels of English Proficiency

Level 1—Starting. Limited or no understanding of English. Respond non-verbally.

Level 2—Emerging. Can understand phrases and short sentences. Use memorized phrases and groups of words.

Level 3—Developing. Can understand more complex speech but require repetition. Use simple sentences.

Level 4—Expanding. Can communicate day-to-day needs. Can read independently but have challenges with comprehension.

Level 5—Bridging. Can express personal or academic topics fluently. Grammatical errors are minimal.

Figure 3.1 provides details on the organization of the PK–12 English Language Proficiency Standards.

Standard 4, the standard that pertains to teaching science to ELLs, has five grade levels, two of which are represented here in tables—grade level 6–8 (Table 3.2) and grade level 9–12 (Table 3.3).

Through referring to the standards when planning lessons, a science teacher can determine tasks for ELLs at different proficiency levels appropriate to the topic of focus. For example, in the grades 6–8 table, as ELLs move from starting-up to bridging over in the topic of nuclear structures and functions, they progress from identifying elements on a diagram to following sequential oral commands and ultimately to constructing diagrams from discourse.

The standards indicate that an ELL can be at any stage of English proficiency regardless of grade level. This means that a kindergartener can be more proficient in English than a tenth grader and vice versa. Depending on their background, English language learners can also be strong in one language domain, such as reading, but weak in another, such as speaking. Another variable is ELLs' previous exposure to the topic of instruction, most likely if they studied the subject in the native language prior to beginning schooling in English.

The TESOL standards can be a helpful resource for science teachers with ELLs in their classes. By viewing what students at each English proficiency level are capable of comprehending, expressing, and doing related to science, teachers can plan their accommodations accordingly.

TABLE 3.2. Standard 4: English language learners communicate information, ideas, and concepts necessary for academic success in the areas of science for Grade Level 6–8

Domain	Topic	Grade Level 6–8				
		Proficiency Level 1	Proficiency Level 2	Proficiency Level 3	Proficiency Level 4	Proficiency Level 5
Listening	Atoms Cells Molecules	Identify elements within models or diagrams according to oral directions	Match oral descriptions of functions of various elements with models or diagrams	Arrange models or diagrams based on sequential oral directions (e.g., stages of mitosis or fission)	Reproduce models or diagrams based on visually supported tapes, CDs, videos, or lectures	Design or construct models or diagrams from decontextualized oral discourse
Speaking	Solar System	Repeat definitions of key objects in the solar system (e.g., planets, asteroids) with a partner	Describe appearance and composition of objects in the solar system with a partner	Compare appearance and composition of objects in the galaxy with a partner	Present or discuss illustrated processes involving planetary objects (e.g., measuring distances or time spans)	Explain, using technical terms, the structure of the universe using examples of planetary components (e.g., stars and galaxies)
Reading	Body systems Organs	Match descriptive phrases or words to diagrams or models	Classify short descriptions of systems (e.g., respiratory or digestive) using visual or graphic support	Find or sort visually or graphically supported information about processes (e.g., veins vs. arteries)	Transform graphically supported, expository text into sequenced steps to illustrate processes (e.g., oxygen exchange)	Make predictions or inferences (e.g., consequences of losing kidney function) from modified grade-level material
Writing	Weather Climate zones Natural disasters	Draw and label charts of features, conditions, or occurrences using information from newspapers or the Internet	Describe features, conditions, or occurrences around the world based on newspapers, the Internet, or illustrated text	Compare features, conditions, or occurrences between two areas (e.g., native country and the United States) using information from multiple sources	Narrate personal impact of features, conditions, or occurrences around the world using multiple sources (e.g., the Internet and family stories)	Interpret global impact of varying features, conditions, or occurrences from modified grade-level source material

From *PreK–12 English Language Proficiency Standards*. (TESOL, 2006: 84–85, 94–95).

TABLE 3.3. Standard 4: English language learners communicate information, ideas, and concepts necessary for academic success in the areas of science for Grade Level 9–12

Domain	Topic	Grade Level 9–12				
		Proficiency Level 1	Proficiency Level 2	Proficiency Level 3	Proficiency Level 4	Proficiency Level 5
Listening	Nuclear structures and functions	Distinguish parts of elements (e.g., atoms, molecules) from oral statement using visuals, models, or manipulatives	Compare the arrangement of elements (e.g., atoms, ionic crystals, polymers) from oral statements using visual or graphic support	Draw or build models of elements from oral descriptions in small groups	Create representations of the properties, features, and uses of elements from oral descriptions in small groups	Evaluate delivery of oral reports about elements presented by peers
Speaking	Chemical or physical change Compounds	Name and describe common mixtures and compounds, and their composition, from visuals, real-life examples, or symbols (e.g., H_2O)	State or predict transformations or exchanges involving chemical or physical reactions with a partner	Outline steps, using sequential language, in transformations or exchanges involving chemical or physical reactions with a partner	Report and exchange information on processes and results from chemical or physical reactions with a partner	Explain changes in matter, the nature of changes, and their real-world applications in extended discourse
Reading	Scientific research and investigation	Match vocabulary associated with scientific inquiry with illustrated examples	Categorize phases and sentences descriptive of processes and products of scientific inquiry using graphic support (e.g., hypotheses, variables, results)	Sequence paragraphs descriptive of the processes and products of scientific inquiry using graphic support	Extract information on the processes and products of scientific inquiry using graphic support (e.g., lab reports)	Analyze, review, and critique explanations and conclusions from scientific inquiry using modified grade-level materials
Writing	Conservation of energy and matter	Label or list everyday ways to preserve or protect the environment using graphic support	Compare results of experiments or readings on ecology (e.g., biodegradability of materials) using visual or graphic support	Summarize experiments, readings, or research on ecology using visual or graphic support	Summarize experiments, readings, or research on ecology using visual or graphic support	Select and defend ecological methods and explain their real-world applications

From *PreK–12 English Language Proficiency Standards.* (TESOL, 2006: 84–85, 94–95).

3.3
Culturally and Linguistically Congruent Instruction and Assessment

Sally London didn't go into teaching the traditional way. She began in her 30s, after a successful career as a geologist, but now she was treading water as a beginning teacher, struggling to teach science to seventh graders. She knew her subject well, and she was developing teaching competence, but Sally was challenged by the different needs of her students. Even though Sally perceived her pupils as equally deserving of the best education, their needs and backgrounds were extremely diverse. Beyond the difference in their ethnicity, race, and socio-economic status, many of them had been assigned labels that set them apart from others. Gifted, ADHD, specific learning disabilities, and ELLs were all mixed among the bunch of awkward adolescents that comprised her fourth-period class.

Sally was getting the hang of teaching students with exceptionalities and filling out the requisite paperwork, but her English language learners presented different challenges. There was Nashida, who just arrived from Algeria; Miguel, who came to the United States from Mexico eight months earlier; and Mariana, who left Puerto Rico for the mainland in fourth grade. All three were classified as ELLs, but their ability to communicate varied greatly.

Sally was a science teacher, not a language arts teacher, and she felt ill-prepared to teach her ELLs, especially Nashida. Nashida could answer only one question, "What is your name?" Anything else went over her head. Miguel spoke broken English and could not understand complex concepts in English. Mariana could hold a conversation in English like a native speaker, but she struggled with reading and writing.

Monday's lesson was on moon phases, and Sally hadn't prepared much because she was so behind in her grading. She decided to start the lesson by connecting students' prior knowledge to the topic. "Who can tell me the phases of the moon and what makes them happen?" she questioned the class. Steve raised his hand and explained hesitatingly. "Good, Steve!" Sally praised. "Everyone, look at the diagram of the moon phases in your textbook and read section

8.3." Nashida looked at her book but appeared lost. "Look at the diagram, Nashida. That explains the process." Nashida dutifully stared at the diagram, but she was confused because she had not previously learned about moon phases in Algeria . Miguel could understand the terms and labels, but he wasn't sure how the process happened. And Mariana was able to understand the diagram but could not fully comprehend the detailed explanation in the text.

When Sally noticed her ELLs' confusion, she began to feel overwhelmed. "How can I balance the needs of my native English speakers with those of my ELLs? Does helping my ELLs comprehend science mean I have to dumb down the curriculum? Do my ELLs bring anything special to the task that I can build on?" She decided to contact Lisa Rodriguez, the ESOL resource teacher, for ideas on teaching common science procedures and concepts to ELLs.

"Do I need to create separate lessons for each of my ELLs?" Sally inquired. "No, that wouldn't be practical, would it?" replied Lisa. "Tell me how you would teach a typical lesson, and I'll tell you what parts of that lesson can be tweaked to help your ELLs." Sally explained how she had taught the moon phase lesson, and Lisa listened intently. "Class discussion, read the textbook, hmm … Those activities require a pretty high level of proficiency in English to participate. Let's start with tweaks we can make that are appropriate for everyone but are especially helpful for ELLs." Ms. Rodriguez was referring to enhancing the non-verbal elements of the lesson. "Now let's look at what is feasible for you to do to reach your ELLs at their individual levels of English proficiency." Those adjustments were specific to linguistic comprehension, expression, and growth.

After about 10 minutes of brainstorming together, Sally and Lisa came up with a greatly improved lesson. Instead of reading, discussing, and viewing information on the topic, Ms. London's students would be actively engaged in experiencing moon phases. She couldn't wait until the next day to re-do the lesson with a more hands-on approach.

In the center of the classroom stood a single light bulb atop a floor lamp. Around the lamp the students assembled in a circle, each holding a ping-pong ball attached to a wooden skewer. Ms. London demonstrated to the class how they should turn and hold their ping-pong balls on a stick. As they turned, they witnessed the shaded impression of a quarter, half, and full moon. Each and every student was trying it out, and even Nashida seemed completely with it. Sally had paired Nashida with a proficient speaker of English who helped her add new vocabulary to her notebook word bank as the experience occurred. Prior to the lesson she prepared a brief list of phrases, which she gave to Miguel to support writing his findings in his science journal. After the experience, Miguel immediately began recording his description. And for all students she followed up the experience with the Science Writing Heuristic (explained in the following section), which was especially helpful for Mariana.

With most of the changes to her lesson, she provided a more engaging learning experience that enabled all students to develop a deeper understanding. And with a few brief preparations, she helped her ELLs comprehend and express essential information about scientific concepts, all of which also led to increased proficiency in English. It was a win-win for everyone.

3.4
Science and Culturally Relevant Teaching

Gloria Ladson-Billings, in her widely acclaimed book, *The dreamkeepers* (Ladson-Billings, 1994) defined culturally relevant teaching (CRT) as:

> "a pedagogy that empowers students intellectually, socially, emotionally, and politically by using cultural referents to impart knowledge, skills, and attitudes. These cultural referents are not merely vehicles for bridging or explaining the dominant culture; they are aspects of the curriculum in their own right." (p. 18)

As a result of her work with the teachers in her study, Ladson-Billings (1994) identified six key aspects of culturally relevant teaching:

1. "Students whose educational, economic, social, political, and cultural futures are most tenuous are helped to become intellectual leaders in the classroom" (p. 117).
2. "Students are apprenticed in a learning community rather than taught in an isolated way" (p. 117).
3. "Students' real life experiences are legitimized as they become part of the 'official' curriculum" (p. 117).
4. "Teachers and students participate in a broad conception of literacy that incorporates both literature and oratory" (p. 117).
5. "Teachers and students engage in a collective struggle against the status quo" (p. 118).
6. "Teachers are cognizant of themselves as political beings" (p. 118).

Over the 15 years since the publication of Ladson-Billings' groundbreaking look at eight teachers of African-American children, there has been a plethora of research and examination of strategies that lend themselves to the original thoughts of Ladson-Billings on what it means to be a culturally relevant teacher. Application of Ladson-Billings' seminal work has contributed to the success of teachers who work with diverse student populations. Yet, much work remains. Multicultural education scholars and educators continue to fine-tune their approaches as they seek to help all populations of students learn. For example, Heather Coffey (2008), a former middle- and high-school English teacher, explicated her understanding of CRT by summarizing her interpretation of the three CRT principles (Ladson-Billings, 1995a, 1995b). Having spent time working with ELLs, Coffey (2008) was able to distill the three principles in terms of what must happen for the students of culturally relevant teachers:

1. "Students must experience success.
2. Students must develop and/or maintain cultural competence.
3. Students must develop a critical consciousness through which they challenge the status quo of the current social order." (p. 2)

So, if someone well versed in the underpinnings of CRT were to observe your science classroom, what might that person witness? According to Craviotto and Heras (1999), that person might expect to observe activities, behaviors, conversations, and interactions that are indicative of the following:

- Families are actively sought as resources for knowledge.
- Multicultural literature is used as a resource for understanding multiple perspectives.
- Students are regarded as active knowledge generators.
- Classroom dialogue is a fundamental aspect of classroom discourse.
- Classrooms are framed as an inviting space for exploration, learning, and dialogue among peers, students and adults.
- Several languages are used in the classroom as resources for communication and learning. (Craviotto & Heras, 1999: 27)

While these six characteristics were not specifically written with secondary science classrooms in mind, they include numerous aspects that have become cornerstones of science teaching and learning in the 21st century. Co-joining with the ideas of inquiry-based instruction and social constructivism, CRT can be the catalyst that ignites the kind of learning that we want for our ELLs. For ELLs in particular, the principles of CRT lead us to practices that attempt to build cultural and linguistic congruence between their background knowledge, experiences, and English language proficiency and the subject and method of instruction and assessment.

3.5
Classroom-Based Science Assessment at the Secondary Level

While the major emphasis in secondary schools seems to be on high-stakes testing, teachers have the most immediate impact in student learning through their use of assessments that are directly linked to the activities of the classroom. These classroom-based assessments can be summative (e.g., end-of-unit tests) or formative (e.g., teacher observations of students as they collaborate on inquiries). Formative assessments of inquiry-based science instruction and learning are most productive in ascertaining the success of student comprehension. In addition to teacher observations, deeper understanding of science concepts can also be attained through the use of writing tasks that require students to articulate their newly acquired knowledge and skills. The NSES highlight how science teachers can be more effective in their use of classroom-based assessments by changing the aspects of the assessments (both summative and formative) that are emphasized.

As secondary science teachers continue to improve as pedagogues, assessment must be a part

TABLE 3.4. Changing emphases in science assessment

Less Emphasis On	More Emphasis On
Assessing what is easily measured	Assessing what is most highly valued
Assessing discrete knowledge	Assessing rich, well-structured knowledge
Assessing scientific knowledge	Assessing scientific understanding and reasoning
Assessing only achievement	Assessing achievement and opportunity to learn
End of term assessments by teachers	Students engaged in ongoing assessment of their work and that of others

Chart adapted from *National Science Education Standards* (NRC, 1996: 100).

of the growth process. The following "five-part plan" would serve them well as they think about what it means to determine the success of their students in science:

- Current research shows, and best practices document, that continuous and high-quality assessment can positively impact student achievement.
- Information collected through assessment must be used to assist the science teacher and her/his students on how they will proceed. Science teaching and learning must improve as a result of the interpretation of the assessment information.
- Students must be included in the assessment process, understanding of what the objective and criteria encompass, being able to self-assess their work and having responsibility in taking action based on the assessment feedback.
- Time and assistance are needed for science teachers to develop reliable and valid classroom assessments.
- Classroom assessments must be aligned with externally developed assessments, e.g., district, state, national and international assessments and tests that are not administered as often as classroom assessments.

Adapted from *Classroom Assessment and the National Science Education Standards* (National Research Council, 2001).

Table 3.5 clearly shows how the role of the science teacher changes based on multiple aspects of the assessment and the type of assessment varies. Assessments that take into account ELLs' level of language proficiency and attempt to evaluate their knowledge and skills of the topic rather than their English language proficiency reflect the principles of the five-part plan.

TABLE 3.5. Assessment formats and procedures

| Formats | On demand ⟶ Over time | | | |
	Multiple choice, true/false matching	Constructed response, essays	Investigations, research reports, projects	Portfolios, journals, lab notebooks
Amount of time	Typically ~ 1 min 2–3 min with justifications	1–2 min short answers 5–15 min open-ended responses	Days, weeks, or months	Months or even years
Whose questions? (audience for the answer)	Anonymous or the teacher's	Anonymous or the teacher's	The teacher's or the student's	The teacher's or the student's
What kind of questions?	Posed narrowly	Posed narrowly	Posed more openly	Varies
Source of answer	Anonymous or the teacher's	The student's	The student's	The student's
What kind of answers?	Right/wrong	Extent of correctness	Standards or criteria for quality	Standards or criteria for quality

TABLE 3.5. *(continued)* Assessment formats and procedures

	On demand ⟶			Over time
Formats	**Multiple choice, true/false matching**	**Constructed response, essays**	**Investigations, research reports, projects**	**Portfolios, journals, lab notebooks**
Resources available during assessment	Usually none	None or some equipment	Equipment, references	Equipment, references
Opportunity for feedback, revision	None	Usually none	Usually some from teachers and peers	Usually some from teachers and peers

From *Inquiry and the National Science Education Standards: A Guide for Teaching and Learning* (NRC, 2000: 82).

We now shift from an overview of teaching and assessing science for ELLs at the secondary level to the eight areas of science addressed in the NSES: life science, physical science, earth and space science, science and technology, history and nature of science, science and inquiry, personal and social perspectives in science, and unifying concepts and processes.

3.6
Life Science

The NSES for the elementary grade levels focus on the characteristics of living organisms (e.g., basic needs of all organisms), their life cycles, and their interaction with other organisms within their environment. Students move from studying individual organisms to the systems that make up the organisms in middle school. They learn about animal and plant cells as well as single-celled organisms, and develop an understanding of reproduction and heredity. They also study the regulation of biological systems and behaviors of animals in these systems, start looking at all organisms as part of ecosystems, and investigate diversity and adaptation of organisms and how these help organisms survive and interact with one another within their ecosystems.

Life science concepts at high-school level are advanced but build upon what students learned at the earlier grade levels. Students study genetics, in which they investigate the molecules that make up the cells and their functions in various biological processes such as heredity and evolution. On a larger scale, they study interdependence of organisms and their behaviors and organizations in biological systems, and flow of matter and energy through these systems.

Among all science concepts, life science is probably the most popular science content area, with most states requiring it in their list of courses for graduation requirements and/or high school graduation examinations. Thus, ELLs will have to be successful in this subject area. However, learning life sciences can be very complex for ELLs because of the large number of scientific terms and vocabulary that need to be learned. One might argue that this is a common challenge for English speaking students as well as ELLs. However, unlike English speaking students, ELLs are constantly learning new vocabulary both in and outside of schools. Thus, science teachers of ELLs must provide additional support for ELL students.

Additionally, acquiring extensive scientific vocabulary is, in some sense, a requirement for success in learning science. Dobb (2004) reports that there is a strong relationship between the amount of scientific vocabulary a student has and his overall academic achievement. Considering the alignment between vocabulary used in standardized science tests and the national as well as local science standards, it is not surprising that students with well-developed scientific vocabulary have better science scores in tests. When applied to ELLs, as their scientific vocabulary expands, they are more likely to be successful in science.

Much of the vocabulary in life sciences include words with Latin roots, such as *photosynthesis* and *biodiversity*, and Latin word roots and prefixes can be a bridge for ELLs whose first language is Latin-based, such as Spanish (*fotosíntesis* and *biodiversidad*), Portuguese (*fotosíntese* and *biodiversidade*), and French (*photosynthèse* and *biodiversité*). However, it is likely that students will not be familiar with the meaning of these words in their first language either. In order to make scientific vocabulary comprehensible to ELLs, Fang (2006) suggests using a definition table (see Table 3.6 for an example), which includes a list of scientific terms along with their meanings described in everyday language. For instance, "nutrient depletion" is defined as "use up nutrients" and "erosion" becomes "soil washed away slowly" (Fang, 2006: 501). Preparing a definition table prior to teaching each unit and sharing it with students can help ELLs become familiar with and practice vocabulary in advance. Teachers can also include visual aids, such as pictures and images of the terms in the table to make vocabulary learning easier. This strategy can help ELLs and English-speaking students alike.

Nevertheless, learning scientific vocabulary and using it appropriately will take time, and students may memorize the vocabulary but may not understand the concept. As they engage in inquiry-based activities and become familiar with the concept, they will come up with their own ways to explain their experiences and what they learned first. Once they become familiar with the concept, remembering vocabulary is so much easier and more meaningful. Teachers then encourage students gradually to use the newly learned vocabulary while communicating their understanding and experiences without paying attention to proper grammar or pronunciation. In the meantime, they should model the use of new vocabulary in context and use simpler sentences and visual aids, such as pictures, to make it understandable to ELLs. This process requires teachers to be patient and more receptive and responsive to ELLs' efforts to develop their language skills.

Engaging strategies such as field trips, simulations, and inquiry-based activities can help ELLs master the terminology and increase their understanding of the concepts. Field trips have been reported to contribute to students' learning of science by increasing their motivation for learning and their attitude toward science and environment (Bitgood, 1989; Kern & Carpenter, 1984; Knapp, 2000). Effective field trips are those that are meaningfully integrated in the science curriculum and aligned with the NSES, and that engage students in exploratory hands-on activities in which students actively construct their knowledge through their interactions with

TABLE 3.6. Example of a definition table

Biology terms	Definitions
Ecosystem	A biological community and its physical/nonliving environment
Bioenergetics	Energy flow and change
Biosphere	The layer of the Earth where life exists /all living things (animals, plants) live
Autotroph	Any organism that produces its own food. Producer (e.g., plants)
Heterotroph	An organism that obtains carbon compounds by eating plants and/or animals. Consumer (e.g., animals)

the environment (Athman & Monroe, 2008). For instance, if students are studying patterns in ecosystems and how populations and communities of species interact with each other and the environment in a middle-school science classroom, they can participate in a bird-watching activity to identify and observe species of birds in an ecosystem, and to investigate their characteristics, behavior, diet, habitat, size, and shape. Then, students can pick their favorite bird to investigate, and keep a more detailed journal about it. They can share their investigation with their teachers, parents, and peers by preparing a poster presentation. Such field trips, which are closely tied in with the concepts ELLs have been learning in class, will help them comprehend the concepts more easily and provide them with opportunities to practice the scientific vocabulary in an authentic environment.

Simulations can also help ELLs see the connection between the concepts learned in the class and their environment by having students actively become a part of some real-life issue. They increase ELLs' motivation to learn science as they reduce ELLs' anxiety level which is important in language development (Lee & Avalos, 2003). As with field trips, effective simulation activities should also be relevant to the science curriculum and engage ELLs in inquiry-based activities in which they actively practice science process skills, such as observation, data collection, and communication. There are several successful curriculum materials, such as Projects WILD, Learning Tree, and WET, which teach life science concepts through simulations and are also aligned with the NSES and promote inquiry-based learning. Projects WILD, Learning Tree, and WET interdisciplinary environmental education programs emphasize concepts related to wildlife, forest, and water, and interdependence of organisms with the natural world. Using hands-on activities that create awareness, appreciation, understanding, and skills, students learn to address environmental issues within the framework of their existing science curriculum. Teachers of ELLs can modify these activities in a way to help them improve their oral and written language skills. In fact, several states, such as Colorado and California, have collaborated with Projects WET, WILD, and Learning Tree in modifying some of the activities for ELL students and published documents called *Using Project WILD and Project Learning Tree materials with second language learners of English* (available at http://wildlife.state.co.us/NR/rdonlyres/9299B084-9078-482F-8FB6-F3413C53B2A0/0/WILDSecondLanguageShelteredLearning.pdf) and *English Language development theory and practices: Background information for "EE" providers* (available at http://www.plt.org/curriculum/eldforee1099.pdf).

The following lesson plan (adapted from lesson plans at http://school.discoveryeducation.com/lessonplans/programs/eb_genetics/) shows a lesson before and after modification for ELLs, using the SIOP principles offered in Part 2.

Life Sciences (Before Modification)

Activity: Genetic Manipulation
Grade level: 9–12
Duration: 90–120 minutes

Objectives
1. Explain how the technology enables scientists to manipulate genes.
2. Identify pros and cons of genetic manipulation for human beings.
3. Debate the ethical implications of the genetic manipulation.

Materials
Elements of biology: genetics, DVD by Discovery School (2006).

Vocabulary
Gene, genetic disorder, genetic manipulation, genetic testing, in vitro fertilization, pre-natal testing.

Procedures
1. Pre-assessment: Ask students to write down what they would do if they found out that some-one they know is pregnant with a child who has a genetic defect. What actions would they take? What ethical concerns might they face during the course of action?
2. Divide students into small groups. Provide them with the following discussion questions and let them know that they will discuss them after they watch a DVD on genetic manipula-tion. Have students watch the "Part 2: Making Babies Genetically Correct" segment of the DVD. What is your reaction to the parents' decision to have another baby to help correct the genetic defects of their daughter? What ethical issues would the couple and scientists face? What technological advances do we need to even consider correcting the genetic defects? How do you react to the second couple's decision to have a child, even though the father has Huntington's chorea? What actions, if any, would you take to prevent the baby from having any birth defects? What are the pros and cons of genetic manipulation? If the ethical issues regarding genetic manipulation were resolved, where else could it be beneficial and considered?
3. Have students discuss the questions provided, and any other questions they may have, within their small groups. Tell them that they will get to share their answers and views on the issue during a debate. By keeping the students in their original groups, create two teams for the debate; one will argue for the genetic manipulation and the other will be against it. Give students some time to prepare and provide the following links to help prepare for the debate. Also, ask each group to prepare written opening and closing statements.

    http://kidshealth.org/parent/system/medical/pre-natal_tests.html
    http://www.genetics.com.au/factsheet/15.htm
    http://www.genome.gov/10002401
    http://www.geocities.com/geneinfo/facts/disabilities.html
    http://www.hejweca.org/benoc/papers/ethicalhgp.doc

4. Before the debate, remind students that each group will get a chance to voice its opinion and that they should not interrupt each other's argument. Allow teams to defend their positions for 30 to 45 minutes. At the end of the debate discuss the results of the debate: Did one group make a better case than the other? Which argument was the strongest? Did any of the students change their views on the issue after the debate?
5. Post-assessment: Ask students to review their answers to the question they were given at the beginning of the lesson. Tell them to write a short paragraph about whether or not their suggestion would be different, based on what they have learned. Why or why not?

Use the following three-point rubric to evaluate students' work during this lesson.

TABLE 3.7a. Evaluation rubric

	3	2	1
Quality of student work	Students described in-depth new technologies that have made genetic manipulation possible; identified a variety of situations in which genetic manipulation could solve a problem; and developed clear and persuasive arguments of the ethical issues surrounding the use of genetic manipulation.	Students satisfactorily described new technologies that have made genetic manipulation possible; identified some situations in which genetic manipulation could solve a problem; and developed adequate arguments of the ethical issues surrounding the use of genetic manipulation.	Students had difficulty describing the new technologies that have made genetic manipulation possible; could not identify situations in which genetic manipulation could solve a problem; and did not develop complete arguments of the ethical issues surrounding the use of genetic manipulation.

Life Sciences (After Modification in bold)

Activity: Genetic Manipulation
Grade level: 9–12
Duration: 90–120 minutes

Content *Objectives*
1. Explain how the technology enables scientists to manipulate genes.
2. Identify pros and cons of genetic manipulation for human beings.
3. Debate the ethical implications of the genetic manipulation.

Language Objectives
Complex sentences using "because": It is unethical to manipulate genes because_____.
or It is ethical to manipulate genes because_____.

Materials
Elements of biology: genetics DVD by Discovery School (2006).

Supplementary Materials
Websites on genetic manipulation in various languages.
Handouts prepared for ELLs.

Vocabulary
Gene, genetic disorder, genetic manipulation, genetic testing, in vitro fertilization, pre-natal testing.

Procedures
1. Pre-Assessment: **Write "genetic defect" on the board. Ask students to think about what they would tell a friend who is pregnant with a baby that has a genetic defect. What would they tell the friend to do? Tell them to write down their ideas to talk about at the end of the lesson.** Ask students to write down what they would do if they found out that someone

they know is pregnant with a baby who has a genetic defect. What actions would they take? What ethical concerns might they face during the course of action?

2. Divide students into small groups. Provide them with the following discussion questions and let them know that they will discuss them after they watch a DVD on genetic manipulation. **Prepare a video preview handout for ELLs. The handout includes the following: Bullet point overview of the video content; words to watch for—a list of key vocabulary from the video; the discussion questions listed below with sentence completion prompts (see below).** Have students watch the "Part 2: Making Babies Genetically Correct" segment of the DVD. **If time permits, stop the video every few minutes and ask students to summarize the issues raised in that segment.**

   Word bank: **moral, immoral, right, wrong, self-centered, altruistic, ethical, unethical**

   What is your reaction to the parents' decision to have another baby to help correct the genetic defects of their daughter? What ethical issues would the couple and scientists face?

   Sentence completion: I think the parents' decision is_____.

   Genetic manipulation can cause these ethical problems:_____.

   Genetic manipulation can help solve these problems_____. **[Have students list problems and solutions.]**

   What technological advances do we need to even consider correcting the genetic defects?

   How do you react to the second couple's decision to have a child, even though the father has Huntington's chorea? What actions, if any, would you take to prevent the baby from having any birth defects?

   Sentence completion: I think the second couple's decision is _____ **because** _____.

   What are the pros and cons of genetic manipulation? If the ethical issues regarding genetic manipulation were resolved, where else could it be beneficial and considered? **[Ask students to make a bullet point list of a situation when genetic manipulation can be used.]**

3. **Pair each ELL within the groups with a classmate who is more proficient in English. Tell groups to make a T diagram on chart paper with "Genetic Manipulation" written at the top, a minus on the left side of the T, and a plus on the right side of the T. Assign an English-proficient student in each group to categorize keywords that represent the group's opinions. While circulating among the groups, work one-on-one with beginning ELLs, checking comprehension with questions and tasks appropriate for their level of proficiency.** Have students discussion questions provided and any other questions they may have within their small groups. Tell them that they will get to share their answers and views on the issue during a debate. By keeping the students in their original groups, create two teams for the debate; one will argue for the genetic manipulation and the other will be against

it. Give students some time to prepare and provide the following links to help prepare for the debate. Also, ask each group to prepare a written opening and closing statements. **Assign an English-proficient student in each group to summarize the main points from their position on T chart into paragraph form on chart paper. Ask group members to copy the paragraphs in their notebooks. Require groups to also prepare and use visuals for making their point, such as skits, pictures, and props. Assign ELLs roles that are appropriate to their level of English proficiency. While circulating among the groups, work one-on-one with beginning ELLs, checking comprehension with questions and tasks appropriate for their level of proficiency.**

http://kidshealth.org/parent/system/medical/pre-natal_tests.html [**available in Spanish**]
http://www.genome.gov/10002401 [**completely text based—no visuals or translations available**]
http://www.geocities.com/geneinfo/facts/disabilities.html [**completely text based—no visuals or translations available**]
http://www.hejweca.org/benoc/papers/ethicalhgp.doc [**completely text-based—no visuals or translations available**]

Although Wikipedia can be a questionable source, it can be helpful to ELLs because its articles are often available in multiple languages. The entry on "genetic engineering" http://en.wikipedia.org/wiki/Genetic_engineering **is available in 35 languages other than English although some languages' entries are brief and do not include the details of the English version.**

4. Before the debate, remind students that each group will get a chance to voice its opinion and that they should not interrupt each other's argument. Allow teams to defend their positions for 30 to 45 minutes. **Make sure each group includes visuals in the presentations.** At the end of the debate discuss the results of the debate: Did one group make a better case than the other? Which argument was the strongest? **Write the team names on the board and list their strengths.** Did any of the students change their views on the issue after the debate?
5. Post-assessment: Ask students to review their answers to the question they were given at the beginning of the lesson. Tell them to write a short paragraph about whether or not their suggestion would be different, based on what they have learned. Why or why not?

ELL prompt—My position before our lesson was: Now it is:

Use the following three-point rubric to evaluate students' work during this lesson.

Note: This lesson can be made more culturally responsive by discussing other countries' laws and policies on genetic manipulation. The class can explore how deep cultural aspects impact opinions on these types of controversial topics.

The following section focuses on teaching physical science.

TABLE 3.7b. Modified evaluation rubric

	3	2	1
Quality of student work	Students described in-depth new technologies that have made genetic manipulation possible; identified a variety of situations in which genetic manipulation could solve a problem; and developed clear and persuasive arguments of the ethical issues surrounding the use of genetic manipulation.	Students satisfactorily described new technologies that have made genetic manipulation possible; identified some situations in which genetic manipulation could solve a problem; and developed adequate arguments of the ethical issues surrounding the use of genetic manipulation.	Students had difficulty describing the new technologies that have made genetic manipulation possible; could not identify situations in which genetic manipulation could solve a problem; and did not develop complete arguments of the ethical issues surrounding the use of genetic manipulation.

3.7
Physical Science

Physical science standards cover physics and chemistry disciplines of science. At the elementary grade levels, students focus on basic knowledge and skills, such as ability to identify the properties of objects and materials, describe relative position and motion of an object, and understand light, heat, electricity, and magnetism. At the secondary level, physical science concepts relate to understanding the interactions of matter, the influence of forces and motion on objects, conservation and transfer of energy, atoms and chemical reactions. Physical science concepts can be challenging even for English-speaking students as they are considered more abstract compared with other areas of science. Therefore, the material needs to be presented on a conceptual and concrete level to make the content comprehensible for ELLs. There are a number of strategies that can be used to facilitate acquisition of physical science knowledge for ELLs, namely demonstrations, laboratory activities, concept maps, videos, etc.

Physical science concepts, physics in particular, can be intimidating for ELLs and non-ELLs alike. Concepts such as forces and motion, and conservation of energy are abstract and difficult for students to comprehend. Watts and Zylberstain (1981), for instance, found that students in their study believed that forces caused motion and a constant force must be required to maintain motion. This study further revealed that students had difficulty identifying the forces acting on the object in motion, such as a thrown ball, and understanding the gravitational force acting on an object at rest. Researchers studying students' misconceptions in physical science concepts have reported that the aspects of the physical science concepts that are least understood by students were those most in dissonance with their sensory perceptions of the concepts (Novick & Nussbaum, 1978). Students often carry their alternative conceptions, or misconceptions, resulting from lack of appropriate understanding of these concepts in secondary grades, into college. In fact, Halloun and Hestenes (1985) found that although students had a basic understanding of the concept of mechanics, their understanding was often at odds with scientific ones. For instance,

47% of their students believed that an object slows down even though the net force acting on it is zero and 66% of the participants stated that objects under the effect of a constant force move at a constant speed.

The "formula-based" aspect of physics is a major factor—although not the only one—contributing the problem of lack of conceptual understanding. In many schools, physical science concepts have been taught principally as applied mathematics, geared toward students who possess the required mathematics skills. As each formula explains a concept and/or a principle, in order for students to understand how and when to use them in a given problem they first need to understand the concept or the principle behind the mathematical formula. Teaching physical science concepts *conceptually* can provide ELLs and beginning science students with a meaningful way to understand the core concepts in physical science. With this approach, students are better equipped to understand the formulas of physics, and are motivated to explore thought-provoking exercises. Conceptual teaching of physical science concepts does not mean that teachers dumb down the concepts and sacrifice high-level thinking. On the contrary, through challenging problem solving or inquiry-based activities, students can achieve a high level of conceptual understanding.

While teaching potential[1] energy, for instance, instead of lecturing about the concepts and providing the definitions of the terms and the formulas right at the beginning, a teacher can engage students in a "Marbles and Sliders" activity in which students construct their understanding of potential energy. In this activity, student groups are provided with a ruler, a marble, a small "V"-shaped cardboard (slider), and a block of wood or a book, and are asked to answer five major challenges by simply creating a ramp and releasing the marble along the ruler. In the first one, students create their ramps as shown in Figure 3.2 and try to work out what to do to get the greatest sliding distance without pushing the marble down the ramp or changing the slider. Students will record the greatest sliding distance they acquired, describe how they measured the sliding distance, and describe or draw what they did to get the greatest sliding distance.

In the second challenge, they try to answer if doubling the starting distance (the distance between the releasing point on the ruler and the table-end of the ruler) measured along the ramp, doubles the sliding distance. They are encouraged to use different pairs of starting positions such as 5 cm and 10 cm, and 6 cm and 12 cm, to come up with the best conclusion. In the third challenge, students investigate how doubling the mass of the marble (e.g., rolling two identical marbles instead of one) changes the sliding distance. The fourth challenge requires them to design investigations to determine which of the two variables, the "distance along the ruler" or "vertical distance/height," has the greatest effect on sliding distance. Once again, students gather data, describe what they do, and come up with their best conclusions. In the final challenge, students use what they have learned in the previous challenge to create two different ramps that produce the same sliding distance.

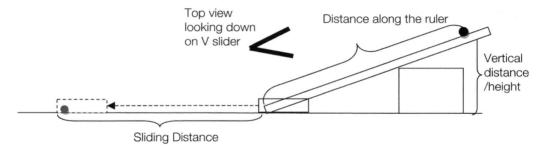

FIGURE 3.2. Marble and slider activity.

Once students recognize that the mass of the marble and the vertical distance affect how far the slider will go, the teacher can introduce potential energy and its formula: potential energy = weight × height. To make sense of the formula and its relationship to the concept that they have just learned, students practice several new problems, such as determining how the potential energy of an object changes after increasing its mass three times or decreasing it to half of its original mass. In order to evaluate student learning and to review the concept learned, science teachers can provide the figures and questions below.

Assume that you are given two different marbles, one being twice as heavy as the other (M = 2m). By using a block and a ruler, four different slopes are created as shown in Figure 3.3. In all four situations, the marbles are initially at rest. In A, the small marble (m) is released from the top of the wall (h). In B, the slope is decreased in a way that the small marble travels the same distance along the ruler as in A, but the height is half of the height travelled in A. The large marble in C (M = 2m) and small marble in D (m) are released from the middle of the ruler and they only travel half of the height.

Which two should be used to investigate if height affects the amount of energy a marble has? Explain your answer.

Which two should be used to investigate if distance along the ruler affects the amount of energy a marble has? Explain your answer.

Which two should be used to investigate if mass affects the amount of energy a marble has? Explain your answer.

Find the potential energy of the marbles at the time they were released and arrange the potential energies from the greatest one to the smallest one.

The benefit of this activity for ELLs is that, no matter what values they use for the vertical height and distance along the ruler, they will still be able to discover the same relationships between the variables (e.g., height and sliding distance). Although students at upper middle and high school are expected to create their own data table, for ELLs to see the relationships easily and focus only on the experiment, it might be helpful for the teacher to have a data table ready before the investigation. The discovered relationships can later be noted as:

The _____ (higher/shorter) the vertical height is, the _____ (longer/shorter) the sliding distance is.

The _____ (heavier/lighter) the marble is, the _____ (longer/shorter) the sliding distance is.

Another example of support for ELLs' learning of physical science is the study of the periodic table in chemistry. As there is a significant body of complicated terminology involved in chemical reactions, we can focus on the Latin and Greek roots of the elements on the table, which is especially helpful for the ELLs whose native languages have Latin and Greek roots, such as Spanish. While ELLs are learning English and the language of science, they must now be able to understand some Latin to be successful at truly understanding the periodic table of elements. How can secondary science teachers help? Web-based resources with hyperlinks are great resources to help

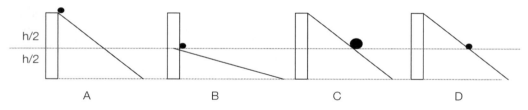

FIGURE 3.3. Review activity.

explain the elements. A good site is http://www.webelements.com/ where each element has its own explanatory page with photos and other graphics as well as its name in a variety of languages.

Understanding how objects behave has been the life work of many famous scientists—Aristotle, Galileo, Kepler, and numerous others. However, Sir Isaac Newton's work best represents and summarizes how we explain the motion of objects and the forces that act upon them. The publishing of *Principia mathematica philosophiae naturalis* in 1686 (over 300 years ago!) remains the foundation upon which all study of the motion of objects is based. Newton's three laws of motion are summarized below:

Newton's First Law (or the Law of Inertia): An object at rest or in motion will stay at rest or in motion unless acted upon by an external force. In other words, an object will maintain its current state of motion unless and until some external push or pull causes it to behave differently.

Newton's Second Law of Motion (F = ma): The net force on an object (of mass m) is equal to the mass of the object times the object's acceleration.

Newton's Third Law of Motion: For every action there is an equal and opposite reaction.

One can immediately see that these three laws can be quite abstract and difficult to understand, yet there are strategies that science teachers can use to make Newton's laws come to life for all students, including ELLs. For each law, we present some ideas that have proven successful in the physical science classroom with ELLs.

For the first law, it is critical that ELLs experience what it means to stay in one position and not be moved by outside forces. One way to do this is to have a student stand still in front of the room. The ELL can describe, sketch or draw a diagram of the student's movements. Next, have someone push the student gently (enough to make the student move). The ELL must then describe, sketch or draw a diagram of what she or he observed. Newton's first law of motion just occurred!

Newton's Second Law of Motion involves a formula that can be easily understood (relatively speaking) from a mathematical perspective. However, it is much more difficult to grasp the idea at a conceptual level. Yet the conceptual framework for this law is most critical, as it is arguably the most powerful of the three laws, based on its formulaic nature. For an explanation of this law, we can go back to our example for Newton's First Law. Once the student begins to move, we can describe the student's increase in speed (acceleration) and discuss the force that was applied to the student to cause this acceleration. If we calculate the student's mass and acceleration (with technological equipment such as motion detectors), we can determine the amount of force that was applied to the student.

For Newton's Third Law, ELLs can be engaged in something as common as sitting in a chair and identifying the force that is keeping them from falling to the floor. Their weight is pushing down on the chair, and the chair is pushing back up with an equal and opposite force. Otherwise, they would fall to the floor!

There are numerous websites that explain Newton's Laws of Motion, with several providing videos and podcasts that can be used in your work with ELLs. See Part 4 of this book for more information on these fantastic technological resources.

Physics offers many opportunities for hands-on, inquiry-based instruction, which increases comprehension for ELLs. The following lesson plan (adapted from lesson plans at http://school.discoveryeducation.com/lessonplans/) shows a lesson before and after modification for ELLs, using the SIOP principles offered in Part 2.

Activity: Understanding the Laws of Gravity (Before Modification)
Grades: 6–8; 9–12
Duration: 60 minutes
Physical sciences

Objectives

Students will be able to:

1. Define gravity as the pull force applied by earth on all objects.
2. Explain that all objects, regardless of their mass, would fall with the same acceleration where air resistance is negligible.
3. Describe air resistance as a type of friction working against gravity to decrease the acceleration of a falling object.

Materials

The following materials should be provided for each group: balls of different sizes and weights, rock, a small stone, marble, a pencil, a feather, a sheet of paper, a cotton ball, internet.

Procedures

1. Pre-assessment: Show students a heavy object, such as a rock, and a lighter object, such as a tennis ball, and ask which one will fall faster when both are released at the same time. Have students write their predictions in their journal along with their reasoning for their answer.
2. Tell students that they will test their predictions. Divide them into small groups and provide each group with a variety of objects to explore with.
3. Group members meet and go over their predictions and collectively determine how to test them. They design their experiment by identifying the control, dependent and independent variables. Remind students to create a table to record their data and results.
4. The students who will drop the object should stand on a chair or desk. While they drop the object pairs, other students in the group make careful observations to see which one reached the floor first or if both objects reached the floor at the same time.
5. After the groups have finished exploring with the given objects, have them write their conclusion, which they will share with the rest of the class. Students should state that all objects fell at the same time regardless of how heavy they were. This means that objects with different masses fall at the same rate of speed or with the same acceleration.
6. Tell students that they did an experiment that is believed to have been performed by Galileo Galilei (1564–1642), an Italian scientist. Have students use the internet or an encyclopedia to find out about Galileo's experiment in which he dropped objects from the Leaning Tower of Pisa in Italy.
7. Give each group a feather and a paper sheet, and ask students to repeat their exploration by including these items. Here they will discover that the feather and paper fall slower. Ask them to bunch a sheet of paper up into a ball and drop it from the same height. They will find out that the ball of paper reaches the floor faster than the sheet of paper. The purpose here is to help students understand the role of air resistance in free fall. Thus, have students discuss possible reasons for what they observed. They should conclude that air resistance, a type of friction, is slowing down the feather and the sheet of paper.
8. Ask students what they think would happen if they performed the same experiment in a vacuum tube, which has no air in it. Have students discuss it in their groups and then share their answers. They should predict that the feather would reach the floor at the same time as a ball or a brick.
9. Post-assessment: Have students write a report explaining the results of their experiments and draw conclusions regarding the effects of both gravity and air resistance on the acceleration of falling objects. Encourage them to accompany their paragraphs with labeled drawings and diagrams. Use a three-point rubric to evaluate students' reports (see Table 3.8).

TABLE 3.8. Unmodified lesson final report evaluation rubric

	3 points	2 points	1 point
Student Final Report	Results accurately reported; illustrations or diagrams clearly labeled; conclusions explained logically in well-written, well-organized paragraphs.	Results adequately reported; illustrations or diagrams included; paragraphs lacking in organization	Reporting of results sketchy or inaccurate; no illustrations or diagrams; conclusions lacking in logic; paragraphs poorly organized

Extension: Use the discussion questions below to help students apply their knowledge of gravity and its effect on the freely falling objects to other real-life incidents.

Discussion Questions
1. What characteristics of a human body provide evidence that it has adapted to the earth's gravitational pull? How might a human body be different if there was no gravity?
2. Do other planets have a gravitational pull? If they do, are their forces of gravity the same? Which planets have the strongest and the weakest gravitational pulls? How would a human body evolve if we were on a planet with a stronger gravitational pull?
3. How does gravity affect the formation of some physical features on the earth's surface? How would having stronger or weaker gravity affect their appearance?
4. Have students research about the gravity experiments conducted by Galileo, Newton, and Cavendish. How are these experiments similar? What evidence is there that these scientists built on each other's research observations to make their discoveries?
5. How does a roller coaster "defy" the laws of gravity? (Sometimes the back car is moving slightly faster than the others, thanks to the acceleration due to gravity, and at other times the first car is going slightly faster.) With that in mind, which seat in a roller coaster is the scariest? How might a roller coaster designer make a roller coaster that gives the greatest sensation to the passengers?

Activity: Understanding the Laws of Gravity **(*After Modification following SIOP principles in Bold*)**
Grades: 6–8; 9–12
Duration: 60 minutes
Physical sciences

Content *Objectives*
Students will be able to:
1. Define gravity as the pull force applied by earth on all objects.
2. Explain that all objects, regardless of their mass, would fall with the same acceleration where air resistance is negligible.
3. Describe air resistance as a type of friction working against gravity to decrease the acceleration of a falling object.

Language Objectives
Students will analyze and produce the structure of the conditional mood: What would happen if_____? The_____would_____.

Materials

The following materials should be provided for each group: balls with different sizes and weight, rock, a small stone, a pencil, a feather, a sheet of paper, a cotton ball, internet.

Supplementary Materials

Website on Galileo's experiment: http://www.visionlearning.com/library/module_viewer. php?mid=45

This site includes a Flash animation of the Pisa experiment with various objects. In addition, the explanation of the scientific method is provided in English and Spanish.

Procedures

1. Pre-assessment: [**Comment: Starting with a visual helps ELLs at beginning levels to understand the topic from the start of the lesson. Hold up a baseball and a marble. Point to each object while stating, "A baseball and a marble." Hold up both palms and let them fall parallel to the floor, asking, "Which will fall to the floor faster?" Point to the baseball: "Will the baseball fall faster?" then the marble, "Or the marble? What do you think? Which weighs more?" Pantomime heavy weights in palms. "Which is heavier?"**] Show students a heavy object, such as rock, and a lighter object, such as a tennis ball, and ask which one will fall faster when both are released at the same time. Have students write their predictions on their journal along with their reasoning for their answer.

2. Tell students that they will test their predictions. Divide them into small groups and provide each group with a variety of objects to explore with. **Pair the ELLs within the groups with a more proficient speaker of English.**

3. Group members meet and go over their predictions and collectively determine how to test them. **Write terms regarding the qualities of a good experiment on the board: a) Control/ experimental treatment; b) One variable at a time.** They design their experiment by identifying the control, dependent and independent variables. Remind students to create a table to record their data and results. **Make a chart handout for beginning ELLs:**
   a) **Object (name)___same ___faster ___slower; object (name)___same ___faster ____slower.**
   b) **Object (name)___same ___faster ___slower; object (name)___same ___faster ___slower.**

4. The students who will drop the object should stand on a chair or desk. While they drop the object pairs, other students in the group make careful observations to see which one reached the floor first or if both objects reached the floor at the same time.

5. After the groups have finished exploring with the given objects, have them write their conclusion, which they will share with the rest of the class. Students should state that all objects fell at the same time regardless of how heavy they were. This means that objects with different masses fall at the same rate of speed, or with the same acceleration.

6. Tell students that they did an experiment that is believed to have been performed by Galileo Galilei (1564–1642), an Italian scientist. **Hold up a picture of Galileo Galilei and the Tower of Pisa.** Have students use the internet or an encyclopedia to find out about Galileo's experiment in which he dropped objects from the Leaning Tower of Pisa in Italy. **Beginning level ELLs can search for and read information in their native languages.**

7. Give each group a feather and a paper sheet, and ask them to repeat their exploration by including these items. Here students will discover that the feather and paper fall slower. Ask them to bunch a sheet of paper up into a ball and drop it from the same height. They will find out that the ball of paper reaches the floor faster than the sheet of paper. The purpose here is

to help students understand the role of air resistance in free fall. Thus, have students discuss possible reasons for what they observed. They should conclude that air resistance, a type of friction, is slowing down the feather and the sheet of paper. **While circulating among the groups, work one-on-one with beginning ELLs, checking comprehension with questions and tasks appropriate for their level of proficiency.**

8. **Show a vacuum tube or a picture of a vacuum tube.** Ask students what they think would happen if they performed the same experiment in a vacuum tube, which has no air in it. Have students discuss it in their groups and then share their answers. They should predict that the feather would reach the floor at the same time as a ball or a brick. **Make a supplemental sentence completion form for ELLs to respond to the question: The _____ would fall at the same (=) speed as _____. The _____ would fall faster than _____. The _____ would fall slower than _____. Include a word bank with graphics (marble, baseball, etc.).**

9. Post-assessment: Have students write a report explaining the results of their experiments and draw conclusions regarding the effects of both gravity and air resistance on the acceleration of falling objects. Encourage them to accompany their paragraphs with labeled drawings and diagrams. **ELLs can use the modified Science Writing Heuristic template to guide their report. Beginning ELLs may create a labeled drawing or diagram in place of a written report.** Use a three-point rubric to evaluate students' reports (see Table 3.9).

Paragraph evaluation (italicized in Table 3.9) can be omitted for beginning level ELLs.

Extension: Use the discussion questions below to help students apply their knowledge of gravity and its effect on the freely falling objects to other real-life incidents.

Discussion Questions

Prepare blank graphic organizers to support discussion questions. Question 2 can use a Venn diagram. Question 3 can use a cause and effect diagram. Question 6 can use an attribute chart. Due to the sentence structure complexity of the question responses, the teacher can assign one or more of these three graphic organizer supported questions to groups that include beginning ELLs and check for comprehension one-on-one as needed.

1. What characteristics of a human body provide evidence that it has adapted to the earth's gravitational pull? How might a human body be different if there was no gravity?
2. Do other planets have a gravitational pull? If they do, are their forces of gravity the same? Which planets have the strongest and the weakest gravitational pulls? How would a human body evolve if we were on a planet with a stronger gravitational pull?
3. How does gravity affect the formation of some physical features on the earth's surface? How would having stronger or weaker gravity affect their appearance?

TABLE 3.9. Modified lesson final report evaluation rubric

	3 points	2 points	1 point
Student Final Report	Results accurately reported; illustrations or diagrams clearly labeled; *conclusions explained logically in well-written, well-organized paragraphs.*	Results adequately reported; illustrations or diagrams included; paragraphs lacking in organization	Reporting of results sketchy or inaccurate; no illustrations or diagrams; conclusions lacking in logic; paragraphs poorly organized

4. Have students research about the gravity experiments conducted by Galileo, Newton, and Cavendish. How are these experiments similar? What evidence is there that these scientists built on each other's research observations to make their discoveries?

5. How does a roller coaster "defy" the laws of gravity? (Sometimes the back car is moving slightly faster than the others, thanks to the acceleration due to gravity, and at other times the first car is going slightly faster.) With that in mind, which seat in a roller coaster is the scariest? How might a roller coaster designer make a roller coaster that gives the greatest sensation to the passengers?

3.8
Earth and Space Science

The earth and space sciences are typically studied together to develop an understanding of the earth and the solar system as a set of closely related systems. Students at elementary grade levels develop an understanding of the properties of earth materials, such as hardness and texture of rocks and minerals, and similarities and differences among these materials. They investigate daily and seasonal weather changes and movements of the sun, moon and stars across the sky. As students begin to develop abstract thinking, they start studying the solar system in general, and the sun, the earth, asteroids, and planets in particular. They investigate the earth's place in the solar system along its movements that causes day/night and seasons and its history. High-school students are expected to understand the role of energy in the evolution and operation of the earth system. Through studying renewable and non-renewable energy resources and various cycles that have continuously shaped the earth, students develop a knowledge base of the issues that are currently affecting society, such as global warming. They further study the origin and evolution of the earth systems and universe.

Both ELLs and non-ELLs experience the majority of the processes and concepts learned in this science content area on a daily basis (e.g., days, seasons, moon phases). However, they are not able to observe what causes these processes first hand. For instance, students can observe the moon going through phases, but without directly observing the location of the sun, moon and earth it is difficult for students to make sense of what causes the moon phases. Thus, not having direct contact with most of these phenomena, and the long-term nature of the processes, make it difficult for students to understand these concepts. Consequently, many leave K–12 education with either incomplete understanding of these concepts or with misconceptions.

A private universe (1987), a video documentary prepared by Harvard-Smithsonian Center for Astrophysics, provides examples to address this problem and makes a strong point regarding the lack of an accurate understanding of the relationship among the earth, moon, and sun. In the video, some new graduates and faculty members of Harvard University explain what causes seasons. Their answers reveal that they all believe seasons are caused by the distance between the sun and the earth during different times of the year. In other words, they believe that it is winter when we are further away from the sun, and it is summer when we are closer to the sun. In reality, however, the distance between the earth and the sun doesn't create such significant temperature changes. Additionally, on the Northern Hemisphere winter takes place when we are closer to the sun and summer is when we are further away from it. The tilt of the earth's axis (23.5°) is the real cause of the seasons. When the tilt is toward the sun, the northern hemisphere receives more direct sunlight and thus it is summer time. However, the southern hemisphere receives less direct sunlight and thus it is winter.

Appropriate understandings of these concepts can be reinforced by the use of powerful simulation and modeling activities as well as by conducting long-term observations and using software such as *Starry night*® can be helpful to both ELLs and non-ELLs in making sense of these abstract concepts. In the example of the moon phase lesson from the previous section, teacher Sally London revised her teaching to make the instruction more comprehensible for ELLs. Looking more closely at that lesson, we can see that a number of principles were followed to improve it. Her initial lesson depended on explanation and discussion, but her revised lesson took a more experiential approach. Table 3.10 provides a summary of the lesson before and after revision.

In part one of the lessons, an oral discussion was changed to a hands-on experience. In part two, a brief explanation of a diagram in the textbook was replaced with a step-by-step reference to the diagram and the associated parts of the hands-on experience, connecting the terms with the experience and illustrations. Phase three originally required students to read the textbook explanation independently, but the revised version pairs students to increase interaction and to support writing about the experience. Comprehension is checked through individual notebook entries in phase four rather than a quiz that may be worded in a way that ELLs don't understand. Lastly, the SQ3R strategy is employed to support reading the text whose content the students have already experienced (background knowledge), and ELLs are paired with students who are more proficient in English in order to discuss the meaning of the text to improve comprehensibility and increase interaction. Ms. London made simple changes to her instruction that benefitted all students and improved comprehensibility for her ELLs.

TABLE 3.10. Comparison of Ms. London's lessons

	Initial Lesson	Revised Lesson
1	Ask students to tell what they know about the phases of the moon and why they think they happen	Assemble students holding ping pong balls in a circle around a light source and demonstrate moon phases
2	Explain diagram	Show diagram & point to each phase on the diagram as students experience the moon phase—emphasize the terms & point to them
3	Independent student reading	Pair work to add to notebook—word bank, phrase bank, Science Writing Heuristic
4	Quiz	Evaluation of notebook entries
5		Pair reading of the textbook explanation of moon phases using the survey, question, read, recite, and review (SQ3R) technique (http://www.studygs.net/texred2.htm)

Moon Phases: Language Intensive Instruction Compared to Hands-On, Minds-On Instruction

Staying with the theme of moon phases, the following lesson plans and video clips present the stark contrast between a typical language intensive lesson, using teacher explanation, student discussion, and objective assessment and a hands-on, minds-on lesson, using demonstration, experiential learning, and paired activities and reflection. Research shows that students who engage in science inquiry activities that do not require them to think about what is going on tend not to gain the conceptual understanding that was expected of them. However, when attention is explicitly and specifically paid to making sure students are thinking before, during, and after an activity (probing questions, checking for understanding, embedded assessments, etc.), student retention of new knowledge tends to improve (Driver, Asoko, Leach, Mortimer, and Scott, 1994; Flick, 1993). As can be seen in the following video clips and lesson plans, the teacher in the hands-on, minds-on lesson has deliberately paired students who can support each other's completion of their tasks and circulates to check comprehension as displayed on leveled worksheets that the pairs complete. By deliberate pairing, the teacher can also encourage the use of the native language to support critical thinking throughout the activity.

Before watching the video clip, read the following lesson plan and consider what aspects of the lesson may make it inaccessible to ELLs.

Moon Phase Lesson Plan—Language Intensive Instruction

Objectives: 1) Describe and explain the motion of celestial bodies. 2) Describe the composition and characteristics of the components of the solar system. 3) Describe the effects of solar phenomena on the earth.

Materials: moon phase diagram; multiple-choice quiz.

Preliminary Discussion (Introduction)
1. Teacher begins by asking the class in a very friendly tone what they know about moon phases.
2. Teacher praises and confirms answers. Teacher asks others who did not respond if they can add anything.

Presentation
1. Teacher holds up diagram of moon phases and explains how the moon phases change:

   New moon—When the moon is roughly in the same direction as the sun, its illuminated half is facing away from the earth, and therefore the part that faces us is all dark: we have the new moon. When in this phase, the moon and the sun rise and set at about the same time.

   Waxing crescent moon—As the moon moves around the earth, we get to see more and more of the illuminated half, and we say the moon is waxing. At first we get a sliver of it, which grows as days go by. This phase is called the crescent moon.

   Quarter moon—A week after the new moon, when the moon has completed about a quarter of its turn around the earth, we can see half of the illuminated part; that is, a quarter of the moon. This is the first quarter phase.

Waxing Gibbous moon—During the next week, we keep seeing more and more of the illuminated part of the moon, and it is now called waxing gibbous (gibbous means "humped").

Full moon—Two weeks after the new moon, the moon is now halfway through its revolution, and now the illuminated half coincides with the one facing the earth, so that we can see a full disk: we have a full moon. As mentioned above, at this time the moon rises at the time the sun sets, and it sets when the sun rises. If the moon happens to align exactly with the earth and sun, then we get a lunar eclipse.

Waning Gibbous moon—From now on, until it becomes new again, the illuminated part of the moon that we can see decreases, and we say it's waning. The first week after full, it is called waning gibbous.

Last quarter moon—Three weeks after new, we again can see half of the illuminated part. This is usually called last quarter.

Waning crescent moon—Finally, during the fourth week, the moon is reduced to a thin sliver from us, sometimes called waning crescent.

A while after four weeks (29.5 days, more precisely) the illuminated half of the moon again faces away from us, and we come back to the beginning of the cycle: a new moon. Sometimes, when the moon is almost new, it is possible to dimly see its darkened disk. The light from the sun cannot reach this part of the moon directly; but at this time the earth (as viewed from the moon) is at its full and very bright, and what we see is light reflected from the earth, that then bounces back at us from the moon. It's a long trip for this light: from the sun to the earth, to the moon, and back to the earth.

1. Teacher questions class—What phase follows the first quarter? Answer: "waxing gibbous." What do we call the moon when we see it as completely dark? Answer: "new moon." What do we call the moon when we see it as completely lit? Answer: "full moon."

Practice
2. Teacher asks students to work in pairs, taking turns stating the phases of the moon to each other.

Performance (Individual Assessment)
3. Teacher passes out a multiple-choice quiz to individuals.

Adapted from http://home.hiwaay.net/~krcool/Astro/moon/moonphase/.

Moon Phases Quiz

Name:_____   Date:_____

Circle the best answer for each question.

1. When the illuminated part of the moon decreases, we call that:
    a. New
    b. Waxing
    c. Waning
    d. Subtraction

2. What occurs two weeks after the new moon?
    a. First quarter
    b. Full moon
    c. Eclipse
    d. Waxing crescent

3. When the moon and sun rise and set at approximately the same time:
    a. Full moon
    b. Last quarter
    c. New moon
    d. Waning gibbous

4. What causes the moon to appear different throughout the month?
    a. The earth
    b. The sun
    c. Both a and b
    d. None of the above

To experience this language-intensive lesson as a student who is not proficient in the language of instruction, please view the following video to see this lesson in action in Hebrew: http://engage.ucf.edu/v/p/h65d4ak After watching the video clip, read the following lesson plan and consider what aspects of the revised lesson may make it accessible to ELLs.

Moon Phase Lesson Plan—Hands-On, Minds-On Instruction

Objectives: 1) Describe the phases of the moon. 2) Explain the process of the moon's changing appearance from the earth's perspective.

Materials: Ping-pong ball on a stick for each student; a larger sphere (15 cm or so) on a stick for teacher; a lamp with a bright bulb (400 W) and the shade removed. A dark room is also required. Diagram handout for three levels of English proficiency.

Procedure
Assemble students in a circle around the lamp. Pair ELLs with native speakers for assistance, asking native speakers to help the ELLs complete the activity and the handout. At each step, model each placement of the "moon" while clearly stating the directions. With the lamp in the center of

the room have each student place the ball at arm's length between the bulb and their eyes. They should hold the pencil in their left hand. State while pointing to each object: "The bulb is the sun, the ball is the moon and you are earth." Show the labeled pictures of each as well as the labeled diagram.

Usually the moon passes above or below the sun as viewed from earth. Have the students move their moon up or down a bit so that they are looking into the sun. As they look up (or down) at their moon they will see that all of the sunlight is shining on the far side, opposite the side that they are viewing. This phase is called "new moon" (like "no moon"). Gesture to them to pick up their handouts and pencils to complete their task for new moon. Model the task of shading in the drawing.

They should now move their hand towards the left, about 45 degrees (1/8) of the way around counterclockwise. Have them observe the sunlight on their moon now. They should see the right-hand edge illuminated as a crescent. The crescent will start out very thin and fatten up as the moon moves farther away from the sun. Gesture to them to pick up their handouts and pencils to complete their task for this phase of the moon.

When their moon is at 90 degrees to the left students will see the right half of the moon illuminated. This phase is called "first quarter." Remember that fully one half of the sphere is illuminated at all times (except during lunar eclipses) but the illuminated portion that we observe changes as the moon changes position. Gesture to them to pick up their handouts and pencils to complete their task for this phase of the moon.

As they continue to move counter-clockwise past first quarter, the moon goes into its "gibbous" phase (more than half but less than fully illuminated), which grows as the moon moves towards 180 degrees. Gesture to them to pick up their handouts and pencils to complete their task for this phase of the moon.

When the moon reaches the position directly opposite the sun, as viewed from earth, the half viewed from earth is fully illuminated (unless the student's head is causing a lunar eclipse). Of course only half of the moon is illuminated. It has taken the moon about two weeks to move from new to full. This growth in illumination is known as "waxing." Gesture to them to pick up their handouts and pencils to complete their task for this phase of the moon.

Students should now switch the pencil to their right hand and face in the general direction of the sun. Starting with the moon at full, students should continue the moon's counterclockwise motion. They will observe the reverse of the moon's phases seen so far with the left portion of the moon illuminated. As with the previous phases of the moon, gesture to them to pick up their handouts and pencils to complete their task after experiencing each phase of the moon.

After the gibbous phase diminishes, the moon will reach the 270 degrees position, straight out to the right. This is "third" or "last quarter." It is followed by a thinning crescent and a return to new moon. From full to new, the moon has been "waning" and leading the sun. The phase cycle takes 29.53 days.

Ask students to check their papers with their partners.

Have native speakers complete a science writing heuristic in their science journals while teacher meets with ELLs to review their diagrams, clearly stating each word while pointing to the appropriate term. The teacher can provide language clues, such as pointing out the word "quarter" in both "first quarter" and "last quarter" and writing "¼" next to it, etc.

(*Adapted from Educator's Guide to moon Phases: http://education.jpl.nasa.gov/educators/moon-phase.html.*)

For English-proficient students—shade each moon picture in Figure 3.4 and write the correct

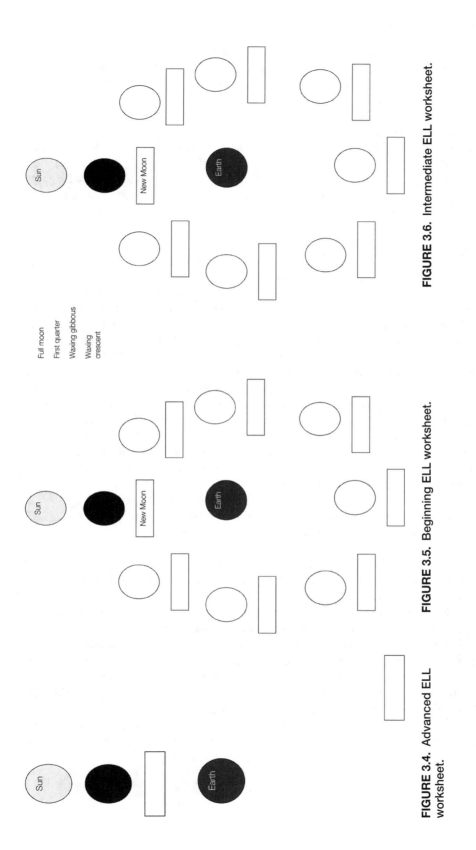

Full moon
First quarter
Waxing gibbous
Waxing crescent

Sun
New Moon
Earth

Sun
New Moon
Earth

Sun
Earth

FIGURE 3.6. Intermediate ELL worksheet.

FIGURE 3.5. Beginning ELL worksheet.

FIGURE 3.4. Advanced ELL worksheet.

term. For beginning English language learners—shade each moon picture in Figure 3.5 and draw a line from the correct term to the drawing of the phase of the moon. For intermediate English language learners—shade each moon picture in Figure 3.6 and copy the correct term next to the drawing of the phase of the moon.

To experience this hands-on, minds-on lesson as a student who is not proficient in the language of instruction, please view the following video to see this lesson in action in Hebrew: http://engage. ucf.edu/v/p/rra6jCM
Now that you have analyzed both lesson plans and have seen the lessons in action in a language other than English, consider how the principles for science instruction to ELLs were demonstrated in the hands-on, minds-on lesson.

Understanding the Seasons

In order to address potential misconceptions about the causes of seasons, students can model the elliptical orbit of earth around the sun by drawing an ellipse on a big poster paper. They place a light bulb simulating the sun inside the ellipse in a way that when students model the earth's revolution about the sun the light bulb is closer to the earth at one side versus further away from it on the opposite side (see Figure 3.7). Small desk globes with an axis will be used to model the earth's motion around the sun. The teacher asks students to find their State (e.g., Ohio) on the globe and a country on the southern hemisphere such as Argentina. As students place the globe on the labeled locations of their model, they describe the position of their state and Argentina compared to the sun using terms such as "tilted away," "tilted toward," and "no tilt" (or, tilted but not toward or away from the sun). While they investigate, the light hits the surface of the globe when it is tilted toward or away from the sun, and students are challenged to infer about the seasons that take place at both locations and support their inferences by providing observational evidence (e.g. the light hits more directly). In order to address the misconception about the distance causing seasons, students should answer questions such as:

According to your model, during what season is [State] farthest from the sun? _____
According to your model, during what season is [State] closest to the sun? _____

It is important to note that before this modeling activity, students should investigate and understand the earth's rotation on its axis and that the axis always points toward the same direction, the northern star, but it changes relative to the sun.

Fouzder and Markwick (1999) used a similar modeling activity, accompanied by observation of the comet Hale-Bopp and lunar eclipse, to teach about the solar system to 18 14-to-15 year olds, 13 of whom were ELL students. Students' native languages included Arabic, Bengali, Bulgarian, Somali, Filipino, Portuguese, and Patois (Caribbean) and all students fell below the level of *intermediate fluency*. The authors reported that students' test scores increased significantly from 28.1 out of 56 points (54%) to 34.6 (66.5%) as a result of the model-making activity. They further emphasized the importance of small-group work and oral class presentations of the models in helping ELLs practice and improve their verbal English language skills. The box below presents the concepts and the vocabulary they aimed to teach with this modeling activity, which other science teachers of ELLs may adapt to teach the same or similar concepts.

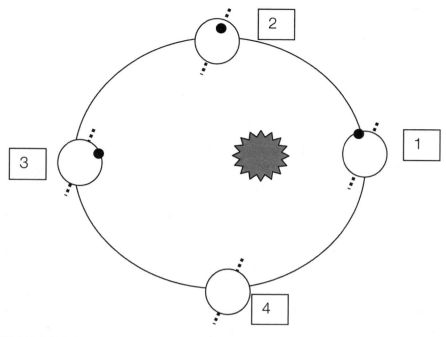

FIGURE 3.7. Model of the Earth's motion around the Sun.

The Solar System

Concepts

Size, shape and order of planets from the sun
Composition and structure of planets
Orbiting of planets around the sun defining one year on earth
Rotation of planets causing day and night
Radiation of heat and light
Moons
Artificial satellites
Solar and lunar eclipses
Comets
Creation of the universe/big bang theory
Outer space
Galaxy
The atmosphere and its layers
Seasonal changes

Vocabulary

Asteroid	Meteor
Axis	Milky Way
Center	Motion

Circumference	Orbit
Constellation	Pollution
Density	Rings
Diameter	Rocket
Distance (light year)	Rotation
Elliptical	Speed
Eruption	Telescope
Light year (distance)	Volcano
Mass	Weight

Adapted from Fouzder and Markwick (1999).

Another way to address the misconceptions about seasons is to have students investigate the weather, temperature changes in particular, in cities that are located on the equator line throughout the year. The assumption behind this investigation is that if the distance between the earth and the sun is the cause of the seasons, these cities should experience significant temperature changes, regardless of the tilt of the earth's axis. Students gather the relevant weather information by using the internet and visiting websites such as World Weather Information Center (http://www.worldweather.org/) or Weather Underground (http://www.wunderground.com/). If students pick Brunei, for instance, they will find out that the average annual temperature is 80 °F (27 °C), the minimum average daily temperature has been reported as 75 °F (~24 °C) and the maximum as 90 °F (~32 °C). Students can discuss and debate whether these values are significant enough to claim that the distance between the earth and the sun is the real cause of the seasons.

Earth science offers many opportunities for links to language development for ELLs. In their activity, "Crusty (Rock) Writing", Hassard and Dias (2009: 469–470) offer a unique strategy for teaching about rocks and the scientific skill of observation. This lesson includes the opportunity for students to write poems about the rocks they have observed. This activity can be an excellent motivational tool, especially for students who enjoy and/or are interested in poetry. For ELLs, this approach can be extended to allow them to write their poem in their first language (L1), with the opportunity to translate their poem to English. As the ELLs continue along the second language acquisition continuum, they can benefit from seeing how two languages compare in a unique way such as poetry. Another option for beginning level ELLs to use poetry to write about earth science topics is to use what Christison (1982a, b) calls concrete poetry, which includes pictures and words. Students can be given a handout with a drawing of a rock. They can write descriptors of the rock in different parts of the drawing, such as, "sharp, rough, speckled, shiny" and they can embellish the drawing as well. Richard-Amato (1988) suggests using structured poetry prompts for more advanced ELLs, such as a cinquain. Given such a template as well as a sample poem, ELLs can insert nouns, adjectives, and verbs into the template to craft their own cinquain. A cinquain follows the following pattern: 1st line: one or two words that name the topic; 2nd line: two or three descriptive words; 3rd line: three or four action words; 4th line: four or five words regarding attitude toward topic; 5th line: one or two words to rename topic. For a rock, the poem could be: Crusty Rock; Sharp, rough, shiny; Fell down the mountain; I like you in my pocket; Crusty Rock. To expand students' vocabulary and improve the poem, they could be encouraged to use a thesaurus for some of the descriptors or verbs.

There are also benefits for ELLs in reading native speakers' more complex poetry, because language learners can comprehend more than they can express. Posting and reading out loud the Crusty Rock poems of students who are more proficient in English can be a good model for ELLs because, according to Richard-Amato (1988), they enable beginners to internalize language chunks (e.g., "You have tumbled …" "You have survived …") and they allow intermediate and advanced students to internalize pronunciation and intonation patterns.

Crusty (Rock) Writing

Content Objectives

1. Collect data on rocks using observational skills.
2. Record notes about a natural object, a rock.
3. Reconstruct notes in poetry form.

Description

As part of a science unit on a local geology, students select a rock that they observe carefully, using all five senses. They then write words and phrases based on their observations. After reading and thinking about their notes, they write an ode to their individual rock, beginning, "O, rock …"

Procedures

Have students gather rocks as part of a field trip or bring enough rocks from a local scene so that each student will have one to observe.

Stimulus: All students have a rock on their desk. Discuss what the students can observe about a rock based on each of the senses. Have student recorder write key words on the board or on chart paper, such as:

- Sight: size, shape, and color.
- Hearing: rattle, scraping.
- Taste: mineral content, dirt.
- Touch: shape, roughness, smoothness, unevenness, bumps.
- Smell: sweet fragrance, earthiness.

Have students fold a sheet of composition paper in thirds, labeling one section for each sense, and the sixth one entitled "Other ideas." Ask students to observe their rocks and to jot down notes about what they observe.

Activity: After students have had time to observe and write notes, tell them that they can use their observation to write an ode to their rocks. Tell them that an ode is a song that begins, "O …" and usually praises a person. Students can begin their poem with "O rock …" and speak to their rock as a person, using personification.

Follow-up: After students have written for a while, have them read their poems to a partner. Partners can assist each other in adding ideas or revising the poem, as needed. Their poems might be something like this:

[O], wonderful gray rock,
Bumpety, lumpety, and tough.
You have tumbled down from the high mountain,
You have survived the trampling of many rough feet,
The crush of an automobile's wheels.
I will give you an easier life now
Perched on my bedroom windowsill.

Evaluation: Circulate around the room to observe student participation as the class observes, writes, and shares. Have students determine criteria (scientific and poetic) for an especially good poem after they have shared and have them answer the question: "What made some poems stand out / especially effective?" Students can revise their poems based on the established criteria. Have students display the rock writing with rocks laid on a table or shelf.

The original activity was published in *The art of teaching science*, by Hassard and Dias (2009).

3.9
Science as
Inquiry

Scientific inquiry involves an understanding of the many ways scientists study nature and develop their ideas. Thus, teaching inquiry-based science means that students are engaged in inquiry-based activities and understand that scientific knowledge is produced as a result of scientific inquiries. The NSES defines inquiry-based science as follows:

> Inquiry is a multifaceted activity that involves making observations; posing questions; examining books and other sources of information to see what is already known; planning investigations; reviewing what is already known in light of experimental evidence; using tools to gather, analyze, and interpret data; proposing answers, explanations, and predictions; and communicating the results. Inquiry requires identification of assumptions, use of critical and logical thinking, and consideration of alternative explanations. (p. 23)

Therefore, in an inquiry-based classroom, learners should:

- be engaged with scientifically-oriented questions;
- develop and evaluate explanations based on evidence;
- evaluate their explanations in light of alternative scientific explanations; and
- communicate and justify their proposed explanations.

As a teaching technique, Colburn (2000) describes several forms of inquiry: *structured, guided,* and *open-ended inquiry*. Structured inquiry refers to activities in which students follow specific steps and/or guidelines the teacher provides while investigating a hands-on problem. The difference between structured inquiry and traditional expository activities is that in structured inquiry students are not informed about the outcomes of their investigation. Rather, they come to understand these relationships between variables as a result of the inquiry. In expository activities, on the other hand, students already know what the outcomes of their investigation are. Below you will find examples of structured inquiry and expository activities:

Examples of Structured Inquiry and Expository Activities

Traditional Activity: Floating and Sinking

Kate starts her unit on floating and sinking by asking students to describe what they know about floating and sinking. She then gives groups of students four vials: two vials (A and B) have different bottom areas, but the same weight; and two vials (C and D) have different weights, but the same bottom areas. Kate writes the following propositions on the board:

1. When two objects have the same bottom area, the heavier object will float lower in the liquid.
2. When two objects have the same weight, the object with the smaller bottom area will float lower in the liquid.

Kate passes out tanks of water and the students are challenged to find the two vials that show proposition 1. and the two vials that show proposition 2. The students float the objects and for the most part perform the activity correctly. Kate then reviews the two propositions and selects students to show how the correct vials demonstrate the propositions. Kate then shows the students two lumps of clay that weigh the same. She asks the students how they would form one lump of clay so it floated high in the liquid.

Structured Inquiry Activity: Floating and Sinking

Jackie starts her unit on floating and sinking by asking students to describe what they know about floating and sinking. She then gives group of students four vials: two vials (A and B) have different bottom areas, but the same weight, and two vials (C and D) have different weights, but the same bottom areas. She asks students how these vials might float differently in water. Students give their ideas. Jackie then passes out tanks of water and challenges students to discover how weight and bottom area determine how high or low the vials float. After the students have floated their vials in the water, Jackie asks students a series of questions (What did you find out? How is bottom area related to how high or low and object sinks? How is weight related to how high or low and object sinks?). Students not only answer the questions but float the vials to show evidence that supports their answers. Jackie summarizes by writing the following statements on the board:

1. When two objects have the same bottom area, the heavier object will float lower in the liquid.
2. When two objects have the same weight, the object with the smaller bottom area will float lower in the liquid.

Jackie then has the students apply the new concepts to new events or situations. As students apply the new concepts, provide them with praise and corrective feedback.

The major responsibility of a teacher in a guided inquiry activity is to provide the materials and the scientific problem to investigate. Students are responsible for designing their investigation, collecting, analyzing, and interpreting the data. They later communicate their results and outcomes to others in the classroom.

In open-ended inquiry, students pose and investigate scientific questions. Although it is the ideal way to conduct and learn about scientific inquiry, open-ended inquiry is very difficult to implement for most students, especially for those whose background is not congruent with science and those who are from different cultures, like ELLs. Unless the teacher provides some guidelines, many students will not understand what it means to do scientific inquiry, or the outcomes of their investigation.

We suggest that science teachers of ELLs start with more structured inquiry activities that are based on concrete and observable concepts, centered on questions that students can answer directly via investigation, and can be investigated using materials and situations that are familiar to students. Once the students become comfortable with this technique, teachers should give more responsibility to students, such as deciding what type of investigation to conduct and the type of data to collect. The more familiar students become with the context of inquiry and materials, the easier it becomes for them to learn through inquiry.

Science teaching techniques, called the "Learning Cycle" (Atkin & Karplus, 1962) and 5Es (Bybee, 1997), are the most popular strategies to use for guided inquiry. Although the framing of these techniques is different, they both provide students with opportunities to explore scientific concepts and apply what they learned in new situations. Developed by the Science Curriculum Improvement Study (SCIS), the Learning Cycle has three stages. In the first stage, called *exploration*, students work individually or in small groups to investigate scientific phenomena. In the second stage, *concept introduction*, students share the results of their investigations with their peers and the teacher who then guides students to the appropriate understanding. In the last

TABLE 3.11. Comparison of traditional expository activities and various modes of inquiry-based investigations

	Expository	Structured inquiry	Guided inquiry	Open-ended inquiry
Problem	Teacher	Teacher	Teacher	Student
Hypothesis	Teacher	Teacher	Teacher	Student
Research design	Teacher	Teacher	Student	Student
Data collection	Teacher/Student	Student	Student	Student
Data analysis	Teacher	Student	Student	Student
Data Interpretation	Teacher	Student	Student	Student

stage, students are given a new situation to apply what they learned in the previous two stages. Hence, it is called *concept application*.

5E was developed by Biological Sciences Curriculum Study (BSCS) and stands for *Engage, Explore, Explain, Elaborate,* and *Evaluate.* In the *engagement* stage, teachers uncover what students already know. Students then perform hands on investigations designed to help them understand a scientific phenomenon in the *exploration* stage. Like concept introduction, in the *explanation* stage, students share the results of their investigations with one another and the teacher draws on these results to explain the new concept. In *elaboration*, students apply the newly acquired knowledge as they investigate a new situation. The *evaluation* stage is a chance for the teacher to assess students' progress and for students to reflect on what they learned.

Regardless of the teaching technique used, a teacher can guide ELL students through inquiry by asking questions that are at an appropriate level of difficulty and then scaffolding to more challenging ones. This scaffolding of questions is necessary to avoid intimidating ELL students. The questioning strategy, called HRASE: Questioning Hierarchy, created by Penick, Crow, and Bonnstetter (1996), is an appropriate one to use with ELL students because it is particularly suited to science teaching in that it emphasizes students' prior experiences and uses these experiences to build relationships, apply knowledge and create explanations.

HRASE: Questioning Hierarchy Suggested by Penick, Crow, and Bonnstetter (1996)

*H*istory—questions that relate to students' experience:
- What did you do …?
- What happened when you …?
- What happened next …?

*R*elationships—questions that engage students in comparing ideas, activities, data, etc:
- How does this compare to …?
- What else does this relate to …?
- What do all these procedures have in common?

*A*pplication—questions that require students to use knowledge in new contexts:
- How could this idea be used to design …?
- What recognized safety issues could this solution solve?
- What evidence do we have that supports …?

*S*peculation—questions that require thinking beyond given information:
- What would happen if you changed …?
- What might the next appropriate step be?
- What potential problems may result from …?

*E*xplanation—questions that get at underlying reasons, processes, and mechanisms:
- How does that work?
- How can we account for …?
- What justification could be provided for …?

These questioning categories correspond closely to the types of tasks that ELLs at different stages of second language acquisition can reply to in English (see Table 3.1 for more information). For example, history questions require ELLs to use the past tense, the structure for which tends to emerge in the early production or speech emergence stage. Relationship questions require comparing and contrasting. If they are answered verbally rather than with a diagram or drawing they require the use of comparative adjectives (bigger than, more voluminous than, etc.), and depend on using structures learned in the early production or speech emergence stages. Application, speculation, and explanation questions require far more complex command of the language to respond to verbally, the language for which typically does not emerge until the speech emergence or intermediate fluency stages. This is not to say that ELLs at low levels of English proficiency cannot engage in higher order thinking activities. Quite the contrary. It simply means that the questions and the means for responding to them need to be scaffolded according to the ELL's level of English proficiency. For example, expecting an ELL at early production to respond verbally to the question, "What would happen if you changed …?" could be scaffolded as follows: The teacher shows a piece of clay that is shaped as a bullet and places it in a bin full of liquid. The clay sinks toward the bottom of the bin. She then flattens the clay into a square and states, "I changed the shape of the object. Before it was like a bullet, and now it is like a square. The surface is larger. What will happen now?" Even beginning ELLs can either gesture or say that it will float higher than the other object (even in simple English or with grammatical errors). While using this questioning strategy with ELL students of any level of proficiency, teachers should wait long enough for them to think and formulate their answers, repeat and paraphrase their answers to check if the student's thinking was communicated correctly, and avoid praising or criticizing their answers to encourage them to think for themselves and stop looking for the teacher's validation.

While engaged in an inquiry-based activity, ELL students can document their experiences by using the Science Writing Heuristic (SWH) (Keys, Hand, Prain, & Collins, 1999). Consistent with the heuristic idea discussed in Part I of this book, the SWH is a method of scaffolding the learning that takes place in scientific inquiry. The SWH has been used with elementary through college students, and has been found to be quite effective in helping students negotiate meaning from their work (Cavagnetto, Hand, & Norton-Meier, 2009). The main focus of the SWH is how the science or laboratory report is written. For the ELL, this report will be important, as it is often the most informative artifact for the secondary science teacher in determining students' progress. The SWH has seven key questions that serve as the template for the student report:

1. What are my questions?
2. What do I do?
3. What can I see?
4. What can I claim?
5. How do I know? Why am I making these claims? (This is considered evidence.)
6. How do my ideas compare with other ideas?
7. How have my ideas changed?

(Burke, Hand, Poock, & Greenbowe, 2005)

With the SWH, the key departure from the typical lab report is the expectation that students will work with others throughout the inquiry activity, as ideas, strategies, claims and evidence are gathered. The ELL will have ample opportunities to consult with her/his peers in making meaning of the experiment and will have a consistent set of questions that reduce the language demands. Social constructivism permeates the use of SWH when it is implemented effectively. ELLs should benefit from this instructional strategy, especially in their writing to learn science.

English language learners at beginning and intermediate levels of English proficiency, however, may need additional scaffolding for the SWH. Because the seven key questions are the basis of repeated written reports, the time needed to have them translated into students' native languages

TABLE 3.12. Word banks

Scientific Inquiry Word Bank	Today's Topic (Gravity) Word Bank
Hypothesis Test Experiment Theory Observation Data Inference Evidence Investigate Understand Explain Conclusion Collect Record Analyze	Predict Air Resistance Objects Acceleration Mass Gravity Increase Decrease Heavier Lighter Control Variable Ball Feather Sheet of Paper Drop Land

is well invested. In cases where this is not practical, companion graphics or diagrams can help provide the meaning, such as a photo of someone looking at something for the "what do I see?" question. Beyond comprehension of the questions used to frame the inquiry process, ELLs' written responses require even greater English proficiency. Generally speaking, ELLs' receptive language skills (comprehension) are typically greater than their productive language skills (expression), so the scaffolding required for beginning students' writing is more extensive. In order to promote language growth, sample sentence completions can be provided so that ELLs can supply main nouns and verbs. For example, the question "How do I know?" can be supported with a sentence completion such as, "I know _____ because _____," which requires more complex sentence structure than beginning ELLs have acquired. Completing the sentence gives ELLs a model to incorporate into their growing grammatical competence in English. Another possibility is to include a bank of words (see Table 3.12) used in the inquiry process on a handout with the sentence completions. The following is an adaptation of the SWH for beginning ELLs:

1. What are my questions?
   What is _____? What does _____? Which _____? Is _____? Does _____? How does _____? How _____ does _____? How _____ is _____?

2. What do I do?
   I _____.

3. What can I see?
   I can see _____.

4. What can I claim?
   I can claim _____.

5. How do I know? Why am I making these claims? (This is considered evidence.)
   I know _____ because _____.

6. How do my ideas compare with other ideas? [ELLs can also complete a Venn diagram.]
   My idea is different from _____ idea because _____.
   My idea is like _____ idea because _____.

7. How have my ideas changed?
   My first idea (before the experiment) was _____. My idea now is _____.

The following section focuses on the history and nature of science.

3.10
History and Nature of Science

Although it is not a new phenomenon, teaching the history and nature of science in schools has gained emphasis in the last two decades with the publication of *Science for all Americans: a Project 2061 report on literacy goals in science, mathematics, and technology* (Rutherford & Ahlgren, 1989), *Benchmarks for scientific literacy* (American Association for the Advancement of Science, 1993), and the NSES (National Research Council, 1996). These three documents state a common goal for science education in the United States: creating scientifically literate citizens who can compete in an increasingly technological world (Bybee, 1997, 2000; DeBoer, 1991). They all advocate that all people involved in teaching and learning science understand scientific inquiry and the nature of science. In today's society in particular, when there is public questioning about scientific claims (e.g., global warming; evolution), it is imperative for students to be able to effectively understand what science is (and what it is not) to fairly evaluate scientific knowledge (Moore, 1993).

Scientific literacy is generally thought of as having three components: scientific content knowledge, process skills (observing, inferring, collecting and interpreting data), and the nature of science (American Association for the Advancement of Science, 1993; National Research Council, 1996). The nature of science (NOS), also known as "science as a way of knowing," consists of the values and beliefs that underlie scientific ideas and activities. Lederman (1998) outlined the following aspects of nature of science: a) scientific knowledge is tentative; b) science relies on empirical evidence to support its claims; c) science is based on current theories and understandings and as such is subjective; d) scientific theories and laws are different types of knowledge; e) science is partly the product of inference, imagination and creativity; and f) science is socially and culturally embedded. In order to be scientifically literate, students must have the informed understanding of these aspects in addition to the science content and process skills.

Studies conducted in K–12 schools as well as college settings have reported that most science courses are focused on teaching of science content knowledge and process skills to do scientific investigations. This means that students learn the scientific concepts and technical skills necessary to do science, but not the underlying principles of how scientific knowledge develops. Unfortunately, science educators have assumed that students implicitly learn about NOS if students are engaged in inquiry-based investigations and developed inquiry-based science curricula that mimic scientific processes to be implemented in schools. However, there has been no evidence to show that inquiry-based instruction alone inherently develops students' understanding of the nature of science (Lederman, 1998; Lederman & Abd-El-Khalick, 1998; Ryder, Leach, & Driver, 1999).

Research indicates that an explicit and reflective teaching approach is needed for students to understand the nature of science properly (Gess-Newsome, 2002; Khishfe & Abd-El-Khalick, 2002; Schwartz, Lederman, & Crawford, 2004). The phrase "explicit and reflective" means that objectives for NOS understandings are explicitly included in the learning objectives and students are provided with structured in- and out-of-class opportunities to reflect on their understanding of NOS in relation to the course activities. This approach has been successfully integrated in elementary and secondary science classrooms (Akerson & Volrich, 2006; Khishfe, 2008; Khishfe & Abd-El-Khalick, 2002) and can be a useful strategy to help ELL students develop an appropriate understanding of the nature of science.

An explicit and reflective approach to teaching the nature of science goes hand in hand with Lee and Fradd's (2001) "instructional congruence" framework that we mentioned while reviewing ESOL-focused science education research in Part 2. This framework suggests that teachers should consider ELL students' language and cultural experiences while planning their science instruction and provide "explicit" guidance for ELL students to link their language and cultural experiences with the science content, especially if their culture's educational practices do not support inquiry-based classroom practices.

In order to help ELLs develop appropriate views of NOS, teachers must state specific NOS objectives along with the content and language objectives and share them with the students. Teachers should prepare discussion questions that enable students to reflect on their understanding of the nature of science and link their cultural experiences with the content they are learning in class. Classroom discussions will make all students aware of the possibility of different viewpoints on the same issue. Thus, students should be given additional opportunities to reflect individually on what they learned outside of the classroom. Teachers should encourage ELL students to provide examples, when necessary, from their own cultures to be able to assess whether they mastered the targeted understanding.

The Draw-a-Scientist activity (Finson, Beaver & Cramond, 1995) is a way to help ELLs better understand who does science. For this activity, the science teacher provides the students with a blank sheet of paper and a variety of different instruments (e.g., pens, pencils, and colored markers). The students are then directed to draw a picture of what they think a scientist looks like (Finson, Beaver, & Cramond, 1995; Jones & Bangert, 2006). After students have drawn their pictures, the teacher evaluates the pictures by looking for those visuals that are typically associated with scientists. Among these are:

- male scientist;
- White;
- unkempt hair;
- pocket protector;
- eye glasses;
- symbols of science;

- the lab is inside;
- the person is nerdy looking.

(Jones & Bangert, 2006)

Once the science teacher has made note of these visuals, a discussion with the students can then be conducted, where students' ideas about scientists are revealed. Many stereotypes about scientists can be discussed and hopefully abandoned, leading ELLs to the conclusion that they can be scientists, too.

The Draw-a-Scientist activity is particularly helpful in dispelling ELLs' misperceptions about who does and does not do science, and it can be adapted for ELLs at beginning levels of proficiency. The teacher can write "scientist" on the board at the beginning of the lesson, which gives beginning-level ELLs the opportunity to look up the word in a bilingual dictionary while their classmates are beginning their drawings. In cases where students do not yet possess dictionary skills, the teacher can supply the word in the native language (researched in advance, provided either orally or in print). In order to improve comprehensibility and develop vocabulary, the teacher should ask students to name each characteristic while pointing to it on their drawings, and the teacher should write each descriptor on the board. For example:

Male   White   Messy Hair   Nerd   Indoors

The teacher can then ask students to identify classmates' drawings that possess most of the listed features, showing the picture to the class and identifying each descriptor again by pointing. When discussing the stereotypes, the teacher can show resources profiling scientists that do not possess these characteristics, such as the book Hispanic Scientists (St. John, Amram, & Henderson, 1996), asking for a yes/no or thumbs-up/thumbs-down response to each of the descriptors on the board when showed a picture of the featured scientists.

TABLE 3.13. History of the atomic model

Scientist/ philosopher	Proposed model	Description of the model	Notes
Democritus 400 B.C.	Model did not have a specific name	All matter is composed of indivisible particles called atoms.	The word "atom" is from a Greek word "atomos"- meaning "uncuttable." Hypothesized that atoms were different in shape and size, small and hard, always moving, and capable of joining.
John Dalton 1803	Billiard Ball Model	Atom is a small solid sphere. Atom is indivisible and indestructible.	His ideas built on those of Democritus. 1. All matter is made of atoms. 2. Atoms of an element are identical in mass and properties. 3. Each element has different atoms. 4. Compounds are composed of atoms of different specific ratios. 5. Chemical reactions are rearrangements of atoms.

TABLE 3.13. *(continued)* **History of the atomic model**

Scientist/ philosopher	Proposed model	Description of the model	Notes
Joseph John Thomson 1897	Plum Pudding Model	Atom is a sphere filled with a positively charged fluid, called "pudding." Scattered in this fluid are electrons and "positively charged particles," together called "plums." Atom is NOT an "indivisible" particle as Dalton suggested.	Thomson discovered that electrons were smaller parts of an atom and were negatively charged. For his discovery, Thomson was awarded the Nobel Prize in physics in 1906. Thomson knew atoms were neutral, but could not find the protons. E. Goldstein discovered the protons in 1900.
Ernest Rutherford 1911	Rutherford Model or Solar System Model	Atom is mostly empty space with a dense positively charged center, called "nucleus," surrounded by negative electrons.	Discovered nucleus. Knew that atoms had positive and negative particles, but could not decide how they were arranged. Received the Nobel Prize in chemistry in 1908 for his contributions to better understanding the structure of the atom.
Neils Bohr 1915	Bohr Model or Planetary Model (Particle model of atom)	Atom has a dense core, called "nucleus," that contains neutrons and protons, and the electrons orbit the nucleus much like planets orbiting the Sun. The key differences are: 1) the orbits are not confined to a plane as is approximately true in the Solar System, and 2) electrons orbit because of electrical interaction, not because of gravitational interaction.	Proposed that electrons travelled in fixed paths around the nucleus. This model of the atom helped explain the emission spectrum of the hydrogen atom. Received the Nobel Prize in physics in 1922 for his theory. (James Chadwick discovered neutrons in 1932)
Erwin Schrodinger and Werner Heisenburg 1926	Electron Cloud Model (Wave model of atom)	Atom consists of a dense nucleus composed of protons and neutrons surrounded by electrons that exist in different clouds at various energy levels.	Electrons do not travel in distinct orbits. Rather, this model showed the most common probable location of an electron. The probability of location was represented by the density of the cloud. Electrons move so fast that they appear to form a cloud around the nucleus.

Table 3.13 presents a summary of the history of the atomic model. Looking at science from a historical perspective helps students to appreciate the challenges associated with gaining knowledge. Appreciating that scientific ideas may have a different origin, depending on the cultures that produced them, helps students appreciate the diversity of knowledge and experiences in science.

3.11
Personal and Social Perspectives in Science

The study of science-related personal and societal issues is an important endeavor for ELLs at the secondary grade level. The NSES are clear about the importance of students understanding the role science plays in their daily lives. Students should understand that science does not occur in a vacuum. Rather, science is around them all the time, and the better they understand the people, places, and things that have scientific components, the better and more productive citizens they can become.

At primary grade levels, students learn about personal health through learning about the human body and how it functions. They further learn that human beings are part of the environment and that some external factors, such as disease, can cause the population of human beings to decrease or increase. The issue of human consumption of non-renewable and renewable resources and the role of science and technology in their local community is also emphasized at these grade levels.

Secondary science students can undertake sophisticated studies of personal and societal challenges. They can expand their study of health and establish linkages among populations, resources, and environments; they can develop an understanding of natural hazards, and unforeseen effects of science and technology in their society. Issues such as smoking and drug use, and causes of global warming and acid rains and their effects on the environment are among the concepts that can help both ELLs and non-ELLs make connections between the science concepts they are learning and the world beyond the school walls.

Most of these issues are global, so it may not be too difficult to engage ELLs in studies that are related to personal and social perspectives. Projects that enable ELLs to work on health or environmental problems (e.g., water pollution and its effect on human lifestyles) that actually take place in their native/home country can help them better understand the role of science in society.

Even more important is the need to start in the local context as the precursor to moving to native land and then global issues.

One way to engage ELLs in local context issues is through the use of 10-minute field trips (Russell, 1998). Critical to ELLs for this instructional strategy is the pre-teaching and follow-up that is necessary to prepare and reinforce the concepts learned on the field trip. For example, the ecology of the school grounds can be studied through the observation and data collection on several trips outside the classroom. The science teacher must prepare the ELLs for what they can expect to find, identify key words related to plant and animals that may be seen, and re-visit these points while outside, but no later than upon returning to the classroom.

An example of preparing for and debriefing for a 10-minute field trip is the "four seasons of a tree" activity from www.geoec.org/lessons/5min-fieldtrips.pdf. This activity requires students to spend 30 minutes each month observing and noting changes in one tree or plant of their choice in the schoolyard. For ELLs, a word bank with graphics and translations where appropriate/feasible would be helpful. Terms such as date, estimate, leaves, needles, and branches can be pre-taught. Providing a form for them to record data also helps reduce the language demands rather than expecting them to write about it in a narrative science journal. Having them use digital cameras to document the changes they recorded links visuals to new vocabulary. Help with the future tense can be provided so that students can make predictions about changes in the plant. For example, I think my plant will_____by the next time I visit (word bank: grow, millimeter, centimeter, change color, etc.).

A popular science assignment, namely "science-in-the-news," can be used to help ELLs identify and be aware of the scientific and technological issues in their community while helping them to improve their reading and oral communication skills. English language learner students can bring a newspaper article that addresses an issue, such as the construction of a new super mall by their city's main tourist attraction site, the county park including a lake. By using colored markers, ELLs can identify and highlight the problem on the text, the scientific facts mentioned, if there are any proposed solutions, and political, economic, and environmental implications of the problem (e.g., creating more jobs while destroying the habitats of local animals). English language learners can then be paired up with English-speaking students to present the information they highlighted orally. Once ELL students become familiar with this activity, at the end, science teachers should encourage them to state their own personal opinion regarding the problem they identified and what decision they would make as active members of their community. This will enable ELLs to make connections between what they have learned and the life outside of their classroom, recognize that they are the decision makers and they can contribute to the solution of the societal problems.

The ability to put current science-related issues into local and global perspectives is important for ELLs. One way to help them do this is through the use of debates. There are several issues that have become topics of widespread discussion over the last few years that lend themselves to debates (e.g., stem-cell research, cloning, deforestation, oceanic dead zones, particle accelerators, space exploration). Each of these topics has economic, environmental, health and/or societal implications. Let's take a closer look at such a topic—that of global warming.

English language learners can be partnered with their peers to explore the causes and remedies of global warming. Needed in this research is an historical and chronological review of the issue of how the earth is becoming warmer. Indeed, it will be necessary for the students to consider that some people do not believe that global warming is actually occurring or that it is a crisis. It is important for students to consider multiple viewpoints in preparation for the debate. There are numerous websites that can assist ELLs in understanding various sides of the global warming issue.

English language learners can be quite helpful in looking at global warming from the perspective of other countries and how they are addressing this issue. For example, some ELLs may have personal experiences or stories that highlight how some countries may not be able to do as much as other countries in addressing greenhouse gas emissions because of the financial costs associated with the implementation of some of the global warming interventions.

After a week of research and preparation, the teams are ready to attend a "global summit" to debate the merits of the variety of ways to address global warming's deleterious effects, knowing that the entire world is affected. Countries must realize that they are interdependent on this issue and they must work together to find common ground. However, common ground cannot be found until each party knows where the others stand on this world-impacting issue.

Charts and prompts, such as those in Tables 3.14 and 3.15, can be provided to ELLs to assist them in their work with their team during the research part of the class debate.

TABLE 3.14. Global warming causes research preparation table

Causes	Effects

Ideas to Research for Your Country

How is _____ (name of my assigned country) contributing to global warming?

What is my country doing to reduce the release of greenhouse gases through fossil fuel combustion and deforestation?

As a follow-up activity, ELLs can write a brief essay on how they might be contributing to the problem of global warming in their personal lives and what type of changes they need to bring to their personal lives to prevent global warming.

Activities that enable ELL students to become part of a decision-making process, such as debates, can reduce the cultural barriers. Through sharing and discussing different viewpoints, ELLs can realize that their ideas count and they can contribute to the solution of global problems, such as global warming. From the instructional standpoint, this will help science teachers to monitor the improvement in ELLs' understanding of the science concepts and the process of problem solving and their English-language development.

TABLE 3.15. Global warming solutions research preparation table

Solution	Financial costs

The following section focuses on understanding the relationship between science and technology, differentiating their respective roles and relationships.

3.12
Science and Technology

The NSES identifies two important outcomes for all students, regardless of grade level, to accomplish under the *Science and Technology* content standard. The first is to understand the relationship between science and technology. More specifically, students should differentiate between science and technology, yet recognize that science and technology work together to help us better understand the world. The second is to acquire abilities to design solutions to problems through the use of technology, which is what the NSES calls *technological design*. The idea here is for students to learn about technology by participating in design. To point out the importance of technological design, the NSES states that what inquiry is in science is similar to what design is in technology (National Research Council, 1996).

A technological design framework is described as having a sequence of five stages:

- identify a problem;
- propose a solution;
- implement proposed solutions;
- evaluate the solution or design; and
- communicate the problem, design, and solution (National Research Council, 1996: 137–138).

With this framework, technological design looks very similar to processes of scientific inquiry. However, it is important to note that scientific inquiry is conducted to produce evidence-based explanations, whereas technological design focuses on creating a solution. Another important point is that the NSES suggest that the number of stages or which stages to be included in a design must be determined based on the identified problem. For instance, some classroom activities may involve only evaluating an existing solution or product, rather than designing one.

At elementary grade levels, students start carrying out simple design activities in which they learn about science and technology, their goals, processes, benefits and risks, and tools. The problems can be defined by students and/or teachers. In either case, it should be simple, clearly stated, and relevant to students' everyday lives. Additionally, students should be informed about the criteria for success. For instance, students can participate in a challenge in which they design a strong and cost-effective house that can survive strong winds, heavy rains, and earthquakes by using a pool of materials that are given to them, such as blocks, aluminum foil, straw, and paper. Such design challenges also help students understand the role and importance of technology for their community and local economy, and how to evaluate benefits and risks of technology.

At middle school, students should start clearly stating the difference between science and technology as well as recognizing that scientific investigations drive technological innovations and technological advancements support investigations in science. Similar to elementary grade levels, teacher guidance remains important but allows for more variation in students' approach to the problems. Technological design activities should be related to the science concepts they have learned and followed by classroom discussions during which the relationship between science and technology and its impact on their community are specifically addressed. For instance, after learning about thermal energy, how to measure it, and thermal conductors, students can be given a challenge to build a solar cooker and test its effectiveness by actually cooking with it. Such activity is an extension that includes the concept of energy transfer and utilization through reflection, conduction, and the greenhouse effect. While developing abilities to perform a technological design, students will elaborate on their understanding of thermal energy. After testing each design, students should be given opportunities to revise their design to make it better.

Performance objectives established for high-school students are the same as for middle-school students. However, the complexity of the problems addressed and extended ways the principles are applied change. High-school students develop greater independence in their designs for possible solutions. They can also relate scientific concepts and principles they have learned with the knowledge they gained in technological design. For instance, after learning the concepts of energy and transfer of energy, they should be able to identify and work on problems associated with energy conservation. Possible problems can be identified within students' community and wider regional, national, or global contexts. It should be open ended so that different students can come up with different designs to tackle the same problem and meet the established criteria for success. For instance, given the current global emphasis on energy efficiency, students can be challenged to design an energy efficient home for their families that is also aesthetically pleasing, functional, and marketable. Other than a few limitations, such as the maximum area the house occupies and a specific budget to build the house, which the teachers provides, students are free to come up with their own designs. In order to accomplish this, students will need to do research on materials and techniques to build such a house, and may even need to interview local architects to come up with the best design.

English language learners' performances in design challenges depend on their level of familiarity with the process. For those who never participated in technological design activities, the problem should be stated by the teacher and relevant to the concept that ELLs have been learning. For instance, after exploring with thermal conductors, they can engage in a design to answer the question of "How can you design a thermos that keeps the liquid hot for a long time?" To help students understand the design stages, teachers can write down the technological framework on poster papers and ask ELLs to write down the problem, their solution, how they plan to implement it, and so on before they actually start implementing their solutions. Teachers can also limit the type and number of materials they can use, but give them enough time to design and implement their solution. Communication is an important aspect of technological design activities, so pairing ELL students with English-speaking students can help them practice their oral language skills. As students develop familiarity with the design process and its purpose, they can be asked to identify their own problems to be solved which can be relevant to their own culture and community as well as to the science concepts they have learned.

Another key point to help ELLs understand is that technology is a tool in science, and is not the science. Using probes in physics classes can help make this point lucid. Two companies provide the most widely used probes and computer software for secondary physics and physical science teachers—Pasco® (www.pasco.com) and Vernier® (www.vernier.com). While both companies obviously boast of the utility of their probes and software compared to the other, emphasis for the secondary science teacher should be on how ELLs will come to understand how to use the probes to collect and analyze their data more efficiently and effectively. For example, both companies have a motion-detector probe. English language learners can use this probe to calculate the acceleration of a lab partner as she moves toward or away from him/her. The challenge for the science teacher is to ensure that the ELLs understand Newton's laws of motion in enough detail that they are able to use the data that are collected via the probe. Unless this understanding is in place, the information provided by the probe will be useless to the ELL. Some of the strategies mentioned in this book can be used to address Newton's laws of motion. Garrett and Shade (2004) also provide some humorous approaches to helping students understand Newton's laws.

It is tempting to assume that if the ELL successfully used the technology then comprehension has taken place, but the technology is simply a tool in collecting, measuring and analyzing data and does not supplant the conceptual understanding required to make sense of the results. The statement of Newton's laws—"anything in motion stays in motion unless acted upon by an outside force; force = mass × acceleration; any action has an equal and opposite reaction"—uses complex language and must be clearly connected to each step of the demonstration of the laws. For example, when showing a pendulum that the teacher lifts to one side and releases, the teacher can state and write on the board, "anything in motion" and indicate that the *pendulum is in motion*. When the pendulum stops moving, the teacher can point to it, stating and writing on the board, "the pendulum is not in motion." Then the teacher can state and write "outside force" on the board and state "An outside force stopped the pendulum. What outside force(s) stopped it?" In the case of the probe, the ELL would need to understand all three of Newton's laws of motion to know how to use the acceleration data. It is possible that an ELL may have learned the formulas while in school in their native countries but they don't fully understand the concepts. While it may appear that they can calculate correctly from the data collected from the probes, they may in fact not fully understand the concepts behind the theories.

WebQuests are other beneficial technological tools that ELLs can use to learn about various science concepts. A WebQuest is designed to connect students with a sampling of internet resources containing audios, videos, animations, and other materials. A quality WebQuest is more than a workbook that students follow the links to fill in the blanks. It should be aligned with the national goals of science education and promote inquiry with purposefully chosen internet resources within well-defined tasks. One concern about WebQuests is that they lack the hands-on manipulation aspect of scientific inquiry. However, engaging students in critical thinking activities promotes the minds-on aspect of inquiry.

In contrast to the concerns about substituting the use of technology for conceptual understanding, various types of technology can be especially helpful to ELLs for increasing comprehension. A wonderful resource that gives excellent suggestions on this topic is *Teaching English language learners through technology* (Erben, Ban, & Castañeda, 2008).

The following section focuses on the most recent NSES area, unifying concepts and processes.

3.13
Unifying Concepts and Processes

The NSES state that students need to be actively engaged in scientific inquiry, develop a rationale and objective framework for solving problems, and understand the concepts and processes that unify the various fields of science. Unifying concepts and processes create connections within and among various fields of science, such as biology and geology. As a result, a focus on unifying concepts helps K–12 students to construct a holistic understanding of science and its role in society. The application of these concepts provides students with insightful ways of considering and integrating a range of basic ideas that help them to explain their surroundings.

The unifying concepts and processes provide students with a framework to organize their thinking about science. As students implement these concepts and processes in scientific investigations, they will recognize the broad patterns that cut across all fields of science. Unifying concepts and processes should be the focus of science instruction across the K–12 continuum and be linked to the objectives of other content standards.

The unifying concepts and processes standard is not clustered as K–4, 5–8, and 9–12 like other content standards. Instead, it is presented for K–12 grades, because these concepts and processes should be developed and mastered by students throughout their K–12 education. However the complexity of each will be different for elementary, middle- and high-school grades. Elementary students study the functions of different parts of plants, while high-school students study the functions of different organelles in a plant cell. The NSES have grouped the unifying concepts in the following manner:

- systems, order, and organization;
- evidence, models, and explanation;
- constancy, change, and measurement;

- evolution and equilibrium;
- form and function.

Systems, order, and *organization* refer to abilities to think about the whole in terms of its parts, and about the parts as they relate to one another as well as to the whole. *Systems* refer to organized groups of items that are regularly interacting or independent and that form a whole. The solar system, nervous system, and weather systems are all examples of this group. *Order* refers to the behavior of a group of or individual objects, organisms, or events, such as seasons, life cycles, subatomic particles, and planets of the solar system. *Organization* is a systematic way to think about the world. The periodic table of elements and classifications of animals and plants are examples of this group.

Scientists use *evidence* and *models* to understand, and *explain* scientific phenomenon. This group can be addressed in activities focusing on history and nature of science concepts. Observations and data to back up a scientific explanation are considered evidence. Models are constructs that help us explain a scientific phenomenon, not simply copies of reality, such as the atomic model and biodiversity models. Scientific explanations refer to the interpretations and meanings made from evidences gathered. Hypotheses, laws, theories, and principles represent various forms of scientific explanations.

Through observations, students learn that some characteristics of living things, materials, and systems remain *constant* over time, whereas others *change*. By engaging in scientific explorations, students develop an understanding of the processes and conditions in which *change, constancy,* and *equilibrium* take place. Physical science concepts such as physical and chemical changes, properties of materials, and motion can help students understand the change. Characteristic properties of matter, such as boiling and freezing points and density, can be used to explain constancy. Measurement is a science process skill that can be integrated in all scientific concepts, such as in exploring thermal energy by measuring temperature, and in investigating uniform motion by measuring distance over time.

Evolution is a process of change over a long period of time in a certain direction, usually from a lower simpler form to a more complex one. Technological advancement as well as evolution of organisms is an example of this group. *Equilibrium*, on the other hand, refers to balance in systems. Equilibrium can be emphasized during studying concepts such as air pressure and transfer of thermal energy.

Form refers to the shape of an object while *function* refers to what this object or item is for. In other words, functions are used to explain the forms. Interdependence of living things and behavioral patterns of living organisms provide students with opportunities to investigate the relationship between form and function. For instance, through studying various birds, their beak and feet shapes and structures (forms), students can understand what type of food each type of birds can eat (function), and whether they can swim or not (function).

Science teachers of ELLs should explicitly address these unifying concepts and processes while teaching various science concepts. Re-emphasizing the concepts and processes can help ELL students understand their meaning and purpose, and can help them recognize how these processes and concepts unify various fields of science. Depending on the ELLs' levels of language proficiency, while focusing on ecosystems at middle-school grades, the teacher can have students identify animal behavior as a response and the variety and effect of population of organisms within an ecosystem with visual aids, or, have them identify the interconnectedness of populations of organisms within an ecosystem.

Exploring the eight topics discussed in this section with your ELLs will certainly improve their understanding of science and English. Hopefully, the activities, lesson plans, and instructional strategies mentioned will serve as a springboard for generating more ways and opportunities for ELLs to become engaged and learn scientific knowledge and skills needed to be successful in school, beyond the school campus and after their formal schooling is complete.

In Part 3 we looked at specific learning activities for ELLs in eight categories of science education. In Part 4 we provide a wealth of resources for teaching science to ELLs.

Part 4
Resources

The following are ELL teaching and learning resources from which secondary grade level science and ELL teachers, curriculum specialists, middle- and high-school students, parents, and anybody who is interested and involved in ELL teaching can benefit. Annotations are provided to assist them to access science or science-relevant ELL information easily without sifting through hundreds of websites. We gave priority to sites that are accurate, credible, and durable. Nevertheless, we remind readers that these sites are continuously being updated and information presented is subject to change. Hence, readers should carefully review the content of the resources suggested.

4.1
Internet Resources for Teachers

This section presents a series of annotated websites that will be of most use to science teachers as well as teachers of ELL students. Lesson plans and activities being presented include ELL-infused science lessons, general secondary grade level science lessons, and general ELL activities. We also included a list of websites that focus on current scientific issues, such as global warming and stem cell research. Science museum websites are other valuable sources of information when it comes to science teaching and learning. Thus, the websites of science museums that provide science teaching materials (e.g., lesson plans), professional development programs, and student resources (e.g., games and puzzles) are also presented in this section. Finally, websites of professional ESL organizations listed here provide teaching materials as well as a wide range of texts and articles that can foster science-relevant ELL teaching.

Lesson Plans and Activities

ELL-Infused Science Activities

EverythingESL
http://www.everythingesl.net/lessons/
EverythingESL.com is created by Judy Haynes, an ESL teacher from New Jersey with thirty years of teaching experience, the co-author of four books on ESL and a chapter for TESOL's *Integrating standards into classroom practice*, and the current editor of the NJTESOL/NJBE *Voices*. The website presents content-based lesson plans, which are regularly updated, for beginning through intermediate students.

Lanternfish: ESL Science
http://bogglesworldesl.com/esl_science.htm
Lanternfish offers content-based ESL lesson plans and worksheets that aim to teach English using content such as science. The ESL Science Center is part of this website and a monthly web magazine with science articles geared towards ESL learners.

Canadian Association of Second Language Teachers
http://www.caslt.org/resources/english-sl/classroom-resources_activities_Science_en.php
The Canadian Association of Second Language Teachers (CASLT) website provides ESL science lesson plans and activities for middle-school grades (4–8). One of the strengths of this website is that all lesson plans (regardless of the content area emphasized) are differentiated for beginners, intermediate and advanced level students.

E. L. Easton: English Online
http://eleaston.com/science.html
Created by Eva L. Easton, an ESL teacher of speech and pronunciation at Bergen Community College in Paramus, NJ, this site presents many ESL teaching and learning materials for content-area teachers. The site consists of two types of items. First, there are materials created by other people, such as links to language sites from around the world. The second group includes the materials she has created, such as pages devoted to "pronunciation." There are no explanations as to how to use the site, so it is geared more towards teachers than learners.

Lesson Plans and Resources for ESL, Bilingual, and Foreign Language Teachers
http://www.csun.edu/~hcedu013/eslindex.html
Developed by Marty Levine, Professor Emeritus in the Department of Secondary Education at California State University, Northridge. The website offers many content-relevant lesson plans and resources for ESL, bilingual, and foreign language teachers.

National Aeronautics and Space Administration
http://spaceplace.nasa.gov/sp/kids/index.shtml
The National Aeronautics and Space Administration (NASA) website is available in both English and Spanish. The site includes games, quizzes, and activities that can be used to teach middle grade level science.

Science Lesson Plans and Activities that can be Differentiated for ELL Students

The Educators' Reference Desk
http://ericir.syr.edu/cgi-bin/lessons.cgi/Science
The Educators' Reference Desk (ERIC) offers many science activities and lesson plans that can be easily modified for ELL students. The major strengths of this resource are that: 1) the activities focus on variety of science topics in areas, such as agriculture, geology, paleontology, meteorology, physics, and many more; 2) they target all grade levels.

Ohio Resource Center
www.Ohiorc.org
Ohio Resource Center website includes hundreds of science activities that are aligned with both

Ohio Academic Content and the NSES, peer reviewed and of high quality that teachers across the United States can easily access.

Hands-On Universe
http://www.handsonuniverse.org/for_teachers/index.html
Hands-On Universe™ (HOU) is an educational program that enables students to investigate the Universe while applying tools and concepts from science, math, and technology. Besides science instructional materials, teachers and their students can download images from a large archive of images and analyze them with the aid of user-friendly image processing software available on the website. The website is hosted by the Lawrence Hall of Science at University of California.

Galápagos Education
http://www.nsta.org/publications/interactive/galapagos/index.html
This activity presented by NSTA can be used to teach history of science. More specifically, students learn important facts about Darwin's voyage on the *Beagle* and his visit to the Galápagos Islands, including the names and locations of the various islands of the archipelago with an online map. Then, by clicking on selected islands, they read journal entries, both real and fictional, from a modern-day exploration of the islands that were visited by Darwin.

Do-It-Yourself Science
www.csiro.au/csiro/channel/pchar.html
Australia's national science organization, The Commonwealth Scientific and Industrial Research Organization (CSIRO), provides a collection of science experiments and games in the areas of physics, biology, environment, geology, technology, and math for grades 3–8.

Rainforest Alliance
http://www.rainforest-alliance.org/education.cfm?id=teachersmain
The Rainforest Alliance Learning Site offers multidisciplinary curricula (science, math, and social studies) that promote understanding of how rainforests contribute to our collective well-being. It provides a global perspective on the importance of protecting the world's natural resources and gives students opportunities for direct action. Illustrated stories (available in English, Spanish and Portuguese) and lesson plans aligned with National Science Education targets elementary and middle grade levels.

Audubon: Educators' Lounge
http://www.audubon.org/educate/educators/
Audubon Educators' Lounge presents tips, strategies, projects, activities, games, and resources for science teachers. Teachers can also find information on variety of scientific issues, such as global warming, endangered species, and energy, which is helpful in developing instruction.

New Horizons for Learning
www.newhorizons.org/strategies/multicultural/freed.htm
New Horizons for Learning provides an example of a culturally responsive lesson plan in science, developed by Andrea B. Freed—an Assistant Professor in the Department of Early Childhood / Elementary Education at the University of Maine at Farmington, which centers on myths, legends, and moon phases.

Education Place

http://www.eduplace.com/activity/

Education Place is an activity search engine. It is a curriculum database for K–8 teachers who want to find science lesson plans and activities on a variety of topics, such as plants, animals, and physical systems by grade level.

Open Educational Resources: Commons

http://www.oercommons.org/

Open Educational Resources' website provides teaching and learning materials that can be used by K–12 teachers and teacher educators. Some examples of these materials include, but are not limited to: full university courses, complete with readings, videos of lectures, and homework assignments; interactive mini lessons and simulations; electronic textbooks that are peer-reviewed and frequently updated; and K–12 lesson plans, worksheets, and activities that are aligned with the national standards.

Smithsonian Education: Science and Technology

http://smithsonianeducation.org/educators/lesson_plans/science_technology.html

The Smithsonian Center for Education and Museum Studies provides leadership in education at the Smithsonian and produces a variety of programs, services, and resources for the education and museum communities. The Science and Technology site offers many secondary level science activities that teachers can adapt for ELL students.

Science-Teachers.com

www.science-teachers.com

Science-Teachers.com is a teaching resource providing lesson plans, worksheets, and activities for upper elementary and middle-school science teachers. Aligned with national science standards, lesson plans and activities focus on physical, life, earth, and space sciences. All resources on this site are free to distribute to students in classrooms.

Science NetLinks

http://www.sciencenetlinks.com/

Science NetLinks is part of Thinkfinity, a partnership of the Verizon Foundation, the AAAS, the National Endowment for the Humanities, the National Council on Economic Education, the National Geographic Society, the National Council of Teachers of Mathematics, the International Reading Association, the National Council of Teachers of English, the J. F. K. Center for the Performing Arts, the Smithsonian National Museum of American History, and the Literacy Network. The website provides numerous science lesson plans aligned with the national standards and resources for K–12 science educators.

Learningscience.org

http://www.learningscience.org/index.htm

Learningscience.org presents newer and emerging learning tools, such as real-time data collection, simulations, inquiry-based lessons, interactive web lessons, and imaging that can be used by teachers, learners, and parents. All lesson plans are aligned with the NSES.

Science-Teachers.com

http://www.science-teachers.com/

Science-Teachers.com provides science lesson plans, worksheets, and activities in the areas of physical, life, earth, and space sciences, for upper elementary- and middle-school science teachers.

AT&T Education: Blue Web'n

www.kn.pacbell.com/wired/bluewebn/

Blue Web'n is a database for more than 2000 educational websites categorized by subject, grade level, and format (e.g., tools, references, lessons, and activities). The website is updated monthly.

RubiStar

http://rubistar.4teachers.org/index.php

The purpose of this website is to help teachers create rubrics for their assignments in many content areas, including science.

Websites that are Specifically for ELL Teaching and Learning

The Internet TESL Journal

http://iteslj.org/links/

"TESL/TEFL/TESOL/ESL/EFL/ESOL Links" is a website maintained by the Internet TESL Journal and provides two select lists of links for students and teachers of ELLs. Some of the links for students include games, bilingual articles, podcasts, and self tutoring tools (e.g., vocabulary and pronunciation). Teacher links include articles, book reviews, teaching tips, lesson plans, weblogs and podcasts.

Colorín Colorado

http://www.colorincolorado.org/educators/content

This bilingual site for educators and families of ELL students presents articles focusing on teaching content areas with ELL students and provides teachers with ideas and strategies to help them develop lesson plans that are inclusive of ELL students.

Songs for Teaching: Using Music to Promote Learning

http://www.songsforteaching.com/esleflesol.htm

EFL/ESOL/ESL Songs and Activities present lyrics and sound clips for a variety of songs that teachers can use to help students learn vocabulary for things such as colors, shapes, and food, among many other topics.

ESL-lounge.com

http://www.esl-lounge.com

ESL-Lounge focuses on verbal communication and provides hundreds of ESL lesson plans and materials that can be used for communicative English lessons in the classroom. The website also offers grammar worksheets, surveys, flashcards, reading comprehension and communication activities, board games and song lyrics. Additionally, this website recommends the most interesting books to read on every possible aspect of teaching and ESL.

Dave's ESL Café

http://www.eslcafe.com

Dave's ESL Café serves as an "internet meeting place" for teachers and students. It offers resources for both teachers and students. Student resources include, but are not limited to, grammar lessons, idioms, phrasal verbs, quizzes, and student forums. For teachers, the website offers an idea cookbook, teacher forums, job forums, and teacher training forum.

National Postal Museum

http://www.postalmuseum.si.edu/educators/letters.pdf

This website offers enrichment materials for the advanced ESL classrooms at 8th grade level and above. These materials help build language and communication skills. The dynamic power of personal letters is highlighted in this collection while students develop English proficiency.

ESL Monkeys

www.eslmonkeys.com/teacher/lessonplans.html

The purpose of the website is to share ESL materials and online ESL resources with teachers and students. Teachers can benefit from the lesson plans and free ESL books as well as post their resumes to find ESL teaching related jobs. Students can use the free online English lessons and English books, find a mentor to work with, and participate in a student forum.

Scientific Issues

Sierra Club

http://www.sierraclub.org/

Sierra Club is an environmental organization whose mission is to protect the environment and preserve wildlife. The website provides information on current environmental issues and initiatives that teachers can use to engage higher grade level ESL students in class discussions.

National Wildlife Federation

http://www.nwf.org/

National Wildlife Federation's website educates public about current environmental issues, such as global warming. Teachers of 7–12 grade students can benefit from this site to engage students in class discussions, and debates.

Science Friday

www.sciencefriday.com and www.kidsnet.org/sfkc/

Science Friday is a weekly radio show on technical topics by National Public Radio. Besides presenting information on scientific innovations and legislations, the website offers activities and other resources that are aligned with the NSES.

National Science Digital Library

http://nsdl.org/resources_for/k12_teachers/

The National Science Digital Library website is created by the National Science Foundation (NSF) to provide organized access to high-quality resources and tools that support innovations in teaching and learning at all levels of science, technology, engineering, and mathematics (STEM) education. This site offers hundreds of science lesson plans and professional development opportunities for middle- and high-school science teachers.

Science Learning Network
http://www.sln.org/index.html
Science Learning Network is an online community of educators, students, schools, science museums and other institutions demonstrating a new model for inquiry science education.

National Geographic
http://www.nationalgeographic.com/xpeditions/
National Geographic website provides up-to-date and in-depth information on current scientific issues that can easily be adopted by higher grade level science teachers for classroom use. The Xpeditions page of the website provides science and social studies integrated lesson plans, aligned with national content standards, for K–12 classrooms.

Public Broadcasting Station (PBS)
http://www.pbs.org/teachers/sciencetech/
Teachers presents hundreds of science activities for K–12 science educators. Teachers can easily access the lesson plans by browsing based on the grade level and the topic of interest.

The New York Times
http://www.nytimes.com/learning/teachers/lessons/science.html
The New York Times' website contains hundreds of free lesson plans for grades 6–12. Teachers may perform a keyword search to retrieve a lesson, browse the lesson plan archive by subject, or scroll down the page to view the most recently published lessons.

Project Learning Tree
http://www.plt.org/cms/pages/21_44_19.html
Project Learning Tree's Energy and Society program kit provides formal and informal educators with tools and activities to help students in grades Pre-K–8 learn about their relationship with energy and investigate the environmental issues related to energy's role in society.

Texas State Energy Conservation Office
http://www.infinitepower.org/lessonplans.htm
Created and hosted by Texas State Energy Conservation Office, this site presents lesson plans on renewable energy for K–12 classrooms. The lesson plans were developed by a team of educators and renewable energy experts and include teacher resource guides, reading texts, and worksheets. All the materials are available for the teachers free of charge.

Museum Resources

Exploratorium
http://www.exploratorium.edu/explore/index.html
The Exploratorium is a museum of science, art, and human perception located in San Francisco, California. This site contains hundreds of science activities and over 18 000 web pages exploring hundreds of different topics.

The Franklin Institute Online
http://www.fi.edu/msp/index.html
Philadelphia MSP Curriculum resources collected in this website are intended to help upper elementary and middle-school science teachers. The lesson plans and activities presented are inquiry-based and aligned with the NSES.

Ingenious

http://www.ingenious.org.uk/

Ingenious is developed by the National Museum of Science and Industry (NCMI) in the UK. It brings together images and viewpoints to create insights into science and culture. It weaves unusual and thought-provoking connections between people, innovations, and ideas. It invites the audience on a voyage of discovery through the content, exploring new perspectives on human ingenuity.

Science Museum

http://www.sciencemuseum.org.uk/educators/classroom_and_homework_resources.aspx

The Science Museum of London's website provides a collection of science activities, classroom and homework resources for elementary, middle and high school teachers and students. Although the lesson plans are aligned with British National Curriculum Standards, they can be easily adapted to the United States NSES because of the similarities amongst concepts and indicators.

Science Museum of Minnesota

http://www.smm.org/explore/

The Science Museum of Minnesota website contains a variety of interactive science activities, such as "Disease Detectives," "Tissues of Life," "Low Life Lab," and "Simply Science," for middle-school teachers. Each activity includes a teacher resource, exploration activities, quizzes, informational texts and stories about the topic, and many more supplementary materials (e.g., videos) that are available to teachers free of charge.

Science Center Singapore

http://www.science.edu.sg/ssc/virtual_ssc.jsp?type=4&root=0&parent=0&cat=140

The Science Center of Singapore website contains science content information that is explained in relation to real-life cases (e.g., endangered species of Singapore). Although the website does not provide specific lesson plans, teachers can benefit from the science concepts explained on this website while developing their lesson plans.

Museum of Science and Industry

http://www.msichicago.org/online-science/activities/

The website of the Museum of Science and Industry in Chicago provides science lesson plans and activities for middle- and high-school science teachers. Even though the activities are not specifically differentiated for ESL students, pictorial explanations of the materials and procedures make the procedure and the content understandable for ESL students.

The Children's Museum of Indianapolis

http://www.childrensmuseum.org/teachers/online_resources_activities.htm

The Children's Museum of Indianapolis presents teacher resources and interactive activities in the areas of life sciences and earth sciences for elementary and middle-school teachers. All activities are differentiated based on the students' reading levels (non-reader, early-reader and reader) Therefore, they can be easily adapted to teach ESL students with varying English language skills.

Professional ESL Organizations

There are quite a few organizations that are dedicated to fostering ESL infusion into content areas. Besides providing many online resources for teaching, they also publish a host of research-based and practitioner-oriented journals.

- American Council on the Teaching Foreign Languages http://www.actfl.org/i4a/pages/index.cfm?pageid=1
- International Association of Teachers of English as a Foreign Language (IATEFL) www.iatefl.org/
- Illinois Association for Multilingual Multicultural Education (IAMME) www.iamme.org
- California Association for Bilingual Education (CABE) www.bilingualeducation.org
- California Teachers of English to Speakers of Other Languages (CATESOL) www.catesol.org
- National Network for Early Language Learning (NNELL) www.nnell.org
- Texas Association for Bilingual Education (TABE) www.tabe.org
- International Association for Languages and Intercultural Communication (IALIC) http://www.ialic.arts.gla.ac.uk/

4.2
Literature for Teachers

This section will provide an annotated list of articles and texts that focus on teaching science for ELL students. You will find links to online articles, texts, and PowerPoint presentations, a list of reader-friendly research articles, classroom-based articles that provide specific examples and ideas for teaching science for ELLs at middle and high schools, content-based articles, books and book chapters, and a list of science education journals.

Online Articles and Texts that Focus on Teaching Science for ELLs

Haynes, J. (2008). Content-based science instruction for ELLs.
http://www.everythingesl.net/lessons/content_based_science_instruct_64209.php
This short article explains how to increase interest and add excitement to ELL instruction through science-based thematic units. It briefly defines "thematic unit," discusses reasons for content-based ESL instruction, and provides tips as to how to teach content-based ESL instruction.

NSTA position: Multicultural Science Education.
http://www.nsta.org/about/positions/multicultural.aspx
This position statement by the NSTA emphasizes that ALL children can learn and be successful in science regardless of their background. It provides a list of principles that schools and teachers should follow to ensure quality science teaching for ALL learners.

Northwest Regional Educational Laboratory (1999). *The Inclusive Classroom: Teaching Mathematics and Science to English-Language-Learners.*
http://www.nwrel.org/msec/just_good/8/introduction.html

This online book focuses on teaching science and mathematics to ELLs and offers ideas about how to link standards-based teaching strategies with techniques from the field of second-language acquisition. It also emphasizes the importance of communication among content area teachers of ELLs as well as of involving families in ELLs science and mathematics learning.

Salt Lake City School District.
http://www.slc.k12.ut.us/staff/larmad/science/Pages/ELLScience.htm
This short text is hosted by Salt Lake City School District and explains the important instructional approaches (e.g., including language objectives, adaptation of text, activating prior knowledge, and using hands-on activities and co-operative groups) to meet the instructional needs of ELL students.

Bassoff, Tobey. How to: Adjust your teaching styles for ELLs in ESL/bilingual classrooms: Teaching science to your ELL/ESL learners: Breaking the language barriers.
http://www.teachersnetwork.org/ntol/howto/eslclass/science.htm
This short article suggests using visually dynamic literature, simple tactile projects, and internet sites with ELL students, and explains that these techniques can be effective in building science vocabulary with the ELL students.

English Language Learners in Science: Find effective ways to support your ELLs in science.
http://teachingtoday.glencoe.com/howtoarticles/english-language-learners-in-science.
This how-to article explains how to differentiate science instruction for ELL students, and the importance of creating positive science classroom environment, increasing opportunities for communication, and managing safe and productive laboratory exercises.

Differentiating Science Instruction: Learn how science is an ideal content area for differentiating instruction.
http://teachingtoday.glencoe.com/howtoarticles/differentiating-science-instruction
This how-to article points out four factors (reading ability, competency in mathematics, prior knowledge, and English-language proficiency) influencing students' comprehension of the science concepts. It explains that differentiation can be based on concepts and skills, and describes various instructional strategies for implementing differentiated science instruction.

Finding Science in Real World: Making connections to real-world applications motivates students and improves learning.
http://teachingtoday.glencoe.com/howtoarticles/finding-science-in-the-real-world.
This article points out that when material is relevant to students' lives and when they see the connection between the knowledge acquired in school and what is happening in the world beyond school walls, students learn and retain information better, and become more interested in the subject. The article suggests seven ways to making real-life connections in science, such as using the news.

Improving Reading Skills in Science.
http://teachingtoday.glencoe.com/howtoarticles/improving-reading-skills-in-science.
This article points out the challenges with scientific texts with technical vocabulary, detailed concepts and relationships, and multi-step processes and cycles. It describes a variety of teaching strategies to improve students' comprehension of simple and detailed science texts and science vocabulary.

Integrating the Inquiry Approach in Science.
http://teachingtoday.glencoe.com/howtoarticles/integrating-the-inquiry-approach-in-science
This short article describes important aspects of inquiry-based science teaching practices, such as picking a topic that can easily be investigated, and modeling appropriate safety procedures.

Managing a Science Lab.
http://teachingtoday.glencoe.com/howtoarticles/managing-a-science-lab
The article provides guidelines for teachers (e.g., creating an organized and focused atmosphere, and teaching students the lab safety) to implement safe laboratory practices at schools.

Identifying and Dispelling Misconceptions in Science.
http://teachingtoday.glencoe.com/howtoarticles/identifying-and-dispelling-misconceptions-in-science
This how-to article emphasizes the importance of eliciting students' prior knowledge to identify possible misconception they may have about the topic to be studied. It describes common sources of misconceptions, ways to identify them, strategies to help students overcome their misconceptions.

Anstrom, K. (1998). Preparing Secondary Education Teachers to Work with English Language Learners: Science. *National Clearinghouse for Bilingual Education.* 11.
http://citeseerx.ist.psu.edu/viewdoc/download?doi=10.1.1.120.3798&rep=rep1&type=pdf.
The focus of this first report is on the education of secondary-level ELL students within mainstream language arts classes. The intent of this document is to give teachers and teacher educators a better understanding of how mainstream language arts instruction can be designed and implemented to enhance academic achievement for these students.

Crandall, J., Spanos, G., Christian, D., Simich-Dudgeon, C., and Willetts, K. (1987). Integrating Language and Content Instruction for Language Minority Students. *National Clearinghouse for Bilingual Education.* 4.
http://nelson.k12.va.us/HighSchool/users/ktucker/Integrating%20Language%20and%20Content%20Instruction.doc
The purpose of this teacher resource guide is to introduce teachers and administrators to approaches for combining language and content instruction (in ESL, bilingual, foreign language, mainstream, and content classes), and to provide suggestions and resources for implementing these approaches.

Incorporating Reading and Writing In Teaching Science to English Language Learners (ELL) by Benjamin C. Ngwudike, Jackson State University.
www.shellsconference.org/presentations/SHELLS-08-Ngwudike.ppt
This PowerPoint presentation explains the commonalities between science and language instruction and describes ways to integrate reading and writing into teaching science to ELL students. It also lists the effective strategies for teaching ELL science and assessing ELL students' science knowledge.

WIDA Standards and Assessments for English Language Learners in Science Education HIGH SCHOOL Developed and Adapted for AEEP by Miguel Mantero (2008).
http://edonline.ua.edu/aeep/WIDA%20web.pdf
World-class Instructional Design and Assessments (WIDA) is a consortium of sixteen states

dedicated to the design and implementation of standards-based education for ELL students. This PowerPoint presentation describes Title III requirements of the NCLB Act (related to the ELL issues), reviews literature about second language acquisition, presents WIDA ELP (English Language Proficiency) standards, and explains how to use them in instruction and assessment. The examples of these implementations are in the area of science.

Research Articles

Amaral, O. M., Garrison, L., and Klentschy, M. (2002). Helping English learners increase achievement through inquiry-based science instruction. *Bilingual Research Journal, 26*(2). http://brj.asu.edu/content/vol26_no2/pdf/ART2.PDF.
This article presents the results from a four-year project conducted in rural setting with ELL students in grades K–6 in the El Centro Elementary School District in southern California. Results of this research indicated that the impact of the project on student achievement depended on the number of years students participated in the project. The longer they were in the program, the higher their scores were in science, writing, reading and mathematics.

Brown, C. L. and Bentley, M. (2004). ELLs: Children left behind in science class. *Academic Exchange Quarterly*, 8(3): 152–157.
This article presents results of a year-long study conducted in two rural elementary science classes for ELL students in a southeastern state. The researchers found that mainstream teachers did not accommodate ELL students and that hands-on, inquiry-based learning was not provided in science classes. It was also noted that science education has been pushed aside in the classrooms due to NCLB state-mandated testing.

Buck, G., Mast, C., Ehlers, N., and Franklin, E. (2005). Preparing teachers to create a mainstream science classroom conducive to the needs of English language learners. *Journal of Research in Science Teaching, 42*(9): 1013–1031.
This article presents an action-research study conducted by a science educator, an ELL educator, a first-year science teacher, and a graduate assistant to explore the process a beginning teacher goes through to establish a classroom conducive to the needs of middle-level ELL students. The results of this research revealed that successful strategies a beginning teacher must utilize for teaching middle-level ELL students in a mainstream classroom involve complex structural considerations that are not part of the teacher's preparation; that learning increases for all children, but there are differences in learning achievement between ELL and non-ELL children; and that student and peer feedback proved to be an effective means of enhancing the growth of a beginning teacher seeking to increase her skills in teaching ELL learners.

Buxton, C., Lee, O., and Santau, A. (2008). Promoting science among English language learners: Professional development for today's culturally and linguistically diverse classrooms. *Journal of Science Teacher Education, 19*(5): 495–511.
This article describes a model professional development intervention that was implemented to support 3rd through 5th grade teachers' science instruction in nine urban elementary schools with high numbers of ELL students. It provides in-depth information about the curriculum materials and workshops that were designed to complement and reinforce each other in improving teachers' knowledge, beliefs, and practices in science instruction and English language development for ELL students.

Buxton, C. (1999). Designing a model-based methodology for science instruction: Lessons from a bilingual classroom. *Bilingual Research Journal, 23*(2–3): 147–178.
This article reports findings from the "Science Theater/Teatro de Ciencias" project in a second/third grade two-way class in a small Western town, where science was taught in both English and Spanish on alternating days. This instructional approach not only provided opportunities for students to think, analyze, and talk about science concepts, but also allowed them to relate science to their personal lives and to society as a whole. The activities were related to students' experiences and previous knowledge, and also to issues that had social implications.

California Council on the Education of Teachers, the California Association of Colleges of Teacher Education, the State of California Association of Teacher Educators, and the Independent California Colleges and Universities Council on the Education of Teachers (2001). Success for English language learners: Teacher preparation policies and practices, *Teacher Education Quarterly, 28*(1): 199–208.
This is a position paper of the California Council on the Education of Teachers, the California Association of Colleges of Teacher Education, the State of California Association of Teacher Educators, and the Independent California Colleges and Universities Council on the Education of Teachers. It establishes the position of the three organizations on educational policy and regulations affecting ELL students, recommending action relative to teaching ELL students. The paper presents a background on the California Standards for the Teaching Profession, makes recommendations related to each standard, and offers a rationale for the recommendations in relation to their potential impact on ELL students.

Colombo, M. W. and Colombo, P. D. (2007). Blogging to improve instruction in differentiated science classrooms. *Phi Delta Kappan, 89*(1): 60–63.
In this article, the authors show how the wise use of classroom blogs, coupled with podcasts and vodcasts, can help teachers extend and differentiate their instruction to meet the needs of diverse learners.

Courtney, M. (2005). Teaching Roberto. *Bilingual Research Journal, 29*(2): 475–484.
This article presents a case study in the form of a teacher's personal diary of experiences during a semester teaching a class of academically at-risk high-school students. It focuses on the interactions among the teacher, the class, and Roberto, a student with negligible English skills. It investigates Roberto's movement from a withdrawn and unengaged state to becoming an engaged member of the classroom.

Fathman, A. K., Quinn, M. E., and Kessler, C. (1992). *Teaching science to English learners, Grades 4–8.* NCBE Program Information Guide Series, *11.*
http://www.eric.ed.gov/ERICDocs/data/ericdocs2sql/content_storage_01/0000019b/80/12/d5/1e.pdf
This guide is intended to help teachers plan, design, and implement science activities for ELL students in grades 4–8, in mainstream science classes, ESL classes, and bilingual education programs. It presents steps for designing science experiments that integrate language and science content, explains the principles of learning and teaching proposed by the AAAS, and outlines the specific strategies for integrating language and science. It also offers a model procedure in which science concepts are examined through three activity types: teacher demonstration, then group investigation, and finally, individual investigation. Sample activities on heat, animals, and plants using this procedure are outlined in detail.

Firestone, W., Martinez, M. C., and Polovsky, T. (2006). Teaching mathematics and science to English language learners: The experience of four New Jersey elementary schools. *New Jersey Math Science Partnership Bilingual Report.*
http://nj.mspnet.org/index.cfm/13069
This paper explores the challenges of teaching math and science to ELL students and some approaches to addressing those challenges identified in four schools serving ELL students working with the New Jersey Math Science Partnership.

Fradd, S. H., Lee, O., Sutman, F. X., and Saxton, M. K. (2001). Promoting science literacy with English language learners through instructional materials development: A case study. *Bilingual Research Journal,* 25(4): 479–501.
Authors point out that a science curriculum focusing on science inquiry with ELL students has not been developed, and current science programs do not meet the needs of this group of students. In this paper, they discuss the learning needs of specific groups of ELL students and their teachers by describing their research with groups of fourth-grade ELL students and their teachers, including perspectives of inquiry with teachers who shared their students' languages and cultures and features of materials developed to integrate science and literacy instruction. They present the student achievement resulting from the use of these materials.

Fradd, S. H. and Lee, O. (1999). Teachers' roles in promoting science inquiry with students from diverse language backgrounds. *Educational Researcher, 28*(6): 14–20.
The purpose of this paper is to point out possible differences in ways teachers use inquiry with diverse groups of students, particularly those who are bilingual or developing English language proficiency and literacy. Authors suggest that a single approach is not appropriate for many students whose language and cultural backgrounds differ from the mainstream. They discuss teachers' roles in identifying effective approaches to science inquiry with students from diverse language backgrounds, explain differences in ways teachers perceive and engage in science inquiry, and discuss the importance of a research agenda to effectively implement science inquiry in ways that enable all students to succeed.

Fradd, S. H. (1997). School–university partnerships to promote science with students learning English. *TESOL Journal, 7*(1): 35–40.
This paper describes the teaching–learning process occurring as two university professors and eight fourth-grade teachers collaborated to promote science instruction by building on the teachers' insights about their students' languages and cultures.

Fradd, S. H. and Lee, O. (1995). Science for all: A promise or a pipe dream for bilingual students? *Bilingual Research Journal, 19*(2): 261–278.
The paper focuses on two ethnically and linguistically diverse elementary schools that considerably differed with regard to students' prior knowledge and background, teacher and administrator attitudes toward science education and toward the capabilities of students with cultural and linguistic differences, and instructional environment. The authors describe their efforts to promote science learning.

Hansen-Thomas, H. (2008). Sheltered instruction: Best practices for ELLS in the mainstream *Kappa Delta Pi Record, 44*(4): 165–169.
The author provides an overview of sheltered instruction, shows how it can be implemented in mainstream classes, and encourages its implementation in Pre-K–12 classrooms.

Laplante, B. (1997). Teaching science to language minority students in elementary classrooms. *New York State Association for Bilingual Education Journal*, 12.
http://www.ncela.gwu.edu/pubs/nysabe/vol12/nysabe124.pdf
This article proposes nine language- and science-related teaching strategies that are appropriate for elementary science teachers working with language minority students. The author describes each of the proposed strategies, discusses their theoretical underpinnings, and gives examples of the classroom implementations.

Lee, O. (2004). Teacher change in beliefs and practices in science and literacy instruction with English language learners. *Journal of Research in Science Teaching, 41*(1), 65–93.
This paper focuses on six 4th-grade bilingual Hispanic teachers and investigates the patterns of change in their beliefs in practices as they learned to establish "instructional congruence," a process of mediating academic disciplines with linguistic and cultural experiences of diverse student groups. The authors conclude that establishing instructional congruence is a gradual and demanding process requiring teacher reflection and insight, formal training, and extensive support and sharing.

Lee, O. and Avalos, M. A. (2002). Promoting science instruction and assessment for English language learners. *Electronic Journal of Science Education, 7*(2).
http://wolfweb.unr.edu/homepage/crowther/ejse/ejsev7n2.html
This paper addresses issues of science instruction and assessment with ELL students. The authors emphasize the importance of science learning for all students, particularly ELL students, review the current status of science instruction and assessment for ELL students, and describe effective policies and practices for science instruction and assessment that enables ELL students to become effective learners.

Lee, O. and Fradd, S. H. (1998). Science for all, including students from non-English-language backgrounds. *Educational Researcher, 27*(4): 12–21.
The authors stress the lack of attention given to the attainment of educational equity for all students. In this article, they propose the notion of "instructional congruence" as a way of making academic content accessible, meaningful, and relevant for diverse learners, more specifically ELL students. The authors also discuss an agenda for research, practice, and policy in promoting high standards for all students across subject areas.

Lee, O. and Fradd, S. H. (1996). Literacy skills in science learning among linguistically diverse students. *Science Education, 80*(6): 651–671.
Focuses on two aspects of literacy related to science performance: interpretations of science task cards depicting a series of activities and written language samples summarizing science tasks. They highlight difficulties that students experience in developing and expressing their understandings of science activities and point out the need to consider the multiple roles of literacy in science learning.

Moore, F. M. (2007). Language in science education as a gatekeeper to learning, teaching, and professional development. *Journal of Science Teacher Education, 18*(2): 319–343.
In this study, the author used a feminist post-structural perspective to explain how language is a gatekeeper in learning science, in achieving professional honors in teaching science, and in teaching science to ELL students. The results of the study revealed that the various uses of language

revealed dynamics related to the culture of power of language and the culture of power of science along ethnicity, gender, and class dimensions for teachers.

Richardson Bruna, K., Vann, R., and Perales Escudero, M. (2007) What's language got to do with it? A case study of academic language instruction in a high school "English learner science" class. *Journal of English for Academic Purposes*, 6(1): 36–54.
This article presents a case study of academic language instruction in a high school "English learner science" course. It illustrates how a teacher's understanding of academic language affects her instruction and students' opportunities for learning. The authors assert that the teacher's emphasis on vocabulary serves to obscure important semantic relationships among the phenomena she is teaching about in her lesson, as well as ignoring the linguistic resources needed to express those relationships. They propose that the social action accomplished by this didactic tension may be to produce an economy of discourse for ELL students, which serves to withhold from them opportunities to not only talk, but also think, like scientists.

Sandefur, S. J., Watson, S. W., and Johnston, L. B. (2007). Literacy development, science curriculum, and the adolescent English language learner: Modifying instruction for the English-only classroom. *Multicultural Education*, 14(3): 41–50.
This article stresses the need for resources to support teachers as they accommodate their science instruction to meet the needs of culturally and linguistically diverse students—more specifically ELL students. The authors call for teacher collaboration and recommend use of good curriculum, challenging assignments, and assessment and grading that reflects growth. They also share literacy strategies to help teachers scaffold ELL students to empower and enrich the experience of mainstream students.

Settlage, J., Madsen, A., and Rustad, K. (2005). Inquiry science, sheltered instruction, and English language learners: Conflicting pedagogies in highly diverse classrooms. *Issues in Teacher Education*, 14(1): 39–57.
The authors state that the research about teaching diverse learners focuses on pre-service teacher education settings and point out the need to follow graduates into the classrooms. They examine the inquiry-based science teaching practices of several new elementary teachers with ELL students.

Shaver, A., Cuevas, P., Lee, O., and Avalos, M. (2007). Teachers' perceptions of policy influences on science instruction with culturally and linguistically diverse elementary students. *Journal of Research in Science Teaching*, 44(5): 725–746.
This study investigated elementary school teachers' perception of how educational policies affected their science instruction with a majority of ELL students. The results suggest that it is important to understand how teachers perceive the influence of policies, particularly those relating to ELL students, as science accountability becomes more imminent across the United States.

Siegel, M. A. (2007). Striving for equitable classroom assessments for linguistic minorities: Strategies for an effect of revising life science items. *Journal of Research in Science Teaching*, 44(6): 864–881.
The authors investigated classroom assessments for English learners in middle-school life science courses in two California schools. They used a framework for equitable classroom assessments, "McCes—Sounds like Success," to refine and evaluate assessments in the study. They provide detailed information on the ways they modified the instruments and their results revealed that

both English only students and advanced English learners scored significantly better on the modified classroom assessments. The authors further discussed a new perspective on validating equitable classroom assessments as opposed to standardized assessments for English learners.

Shaw, J. M. (1997). Threats to the validity of science performance assessments for English language learners. *Journal of Research in Science Teaching, 34*(7): 721–743.
This case study investigates the use of performance assessment with 96 ELL students in five high-school science classes. The results showed that both teachers and students had an overall favorable response to the assessment, although students' English comprehension and expression skills were determining factors for certain items. The authors recommend increasing the clarity of an assessment's design, allowing ELL students more time to complete assessments, and scoring by raters who are knowledgeable about typical patterns in written English for this student population.

Spurlin, Q. (1995). Making science comprehensible for language minority students. *Journal of Science Teacher Education. 6*(2): 71–78.
The purpose of this article is to present to science teacher educators with information from the second language acquisition literature that is useful in understanding the linguistic needs of second language learners in today's classrooms. The authors also include examples of how this material can be incorporated into science methods courses.

Theoretical

Stoddart, T., Pinal, A., Latzke, M., and Canaday, D. (2002). Integrating inquiry science and language development for English language learners. *Journal of Research in Science Teaching, 39*(8): 664–687.
The authors state that the integration of inquiry science and language acquisition enhances learning in both English language and science content. They describe a conceptual framework for science–language integration and the development of a five-level rubric to assess teachers' understanding of curricular integration. They use examples from teacher interviews to illustrate teacher thinking at each level.

Westby, C., Dezale, J., Fradd, S. H., and Lee, O. (1999). Learning to do science: Influences of culture and language. *Communication Disorders Quarterly, 21*(1): 50–64.
This article discusses components of scientific literacy on discourse and describes the academic and social participation structures of science lessons in four classrooms of elementary school students learning English as a second language.

Zúñiga, K., Olson, J. K., and Winter, M. (2005). Science education for rural Latino/a students: Course placement and success in science. *Journal of Research in Science Teaching, 42*(4): 376–402.
This study investigated the effects of one rural high school's science course placement practices on Latino/a student success in science, as measured by performance in a required science course and enrollment in subsequent science courses. The results indicate that track placement was inappropriate, as Latino/a students with demonstrated success on standardized tests written in English, and with high grade point averages, were placed in the lower-level science course. Thus, despite this rural school's attempt to provide for the needs of all the students, the result in this case was decreased success in science for Latino/a students, regardless of their English fluency.

Classroom-Based Articles: Middle School Science

Armon, J. and Morris, L. J. (2008). Integrated assessments for ELL. *Science and Children, 45*(8): 49–53.

This paper explains the importance and benefits of integrating writing and drawing with science investigation, and illustrates how teachers can use this integration to meet the needs of students learning English. It concludes by noting some of the difficulties posed by integration and offers some recommendations.

Bittel, K. (2006). Differentiated assessment. *Science Scope, 29*(3): 49–51.

The author describes a unique form of assessment that not only encourages students to work at the highest critical-thinking level possible, but also allows them creative liberty to express their understandings of the big ideas. This enables *all* students, including English language learners and special education students, to achieve their potential through the use of peer support and a menu of final projects.

Bittel, K. and Hernandez, D. (2006). Kinesthetic writing, of sorts. *Science Scope, 29*(7): 37–39.

In this article, the authors focused on the 8th grade students' ability to write quality conclusions at the end of every laboratory investigation. They found out that the activity involving the use of flipbooks was very successful not only with their mainstream students, but also with their ELL and special education students.

Corder, G. (2007). Supporting English language learners: Reading in the science classroom. *Science Scope, 31*(1): 38–41.

This article reports that students with limited reading skills, such as ELL students, also have limited educational opportunities. The author briefly reviews the body of research providing specific techniques for supporting and developing this group of students' reading ability and provides examples of the ways to apply these techniques in science classrooms.

Hansen, L. (2006). Strategies for ELL success. *Science and Children, 43*(4): 22–25.

The author describes how to use a version of the learning cycle (engage, explore, develop, and apply) to address language issues with ELL students in a science classroom.

Hansen, L. (2003). Science in any language. *Science and Children, 41*(3): 35–39.

This article describes how Guided Language Acquisition Design (GLAD) teaching strategies can help ELL students with science. GLAD is a model for planning science, social studies, and literature-based units. It includes a collection of innovative strategies designed to help all levels of ELL students access core curriculum while acquiring English skills and vocabulary.

Johnson, C. C. (2005). Making instruction relevant to language minority students at the middle level. *Middle School Journal, 37*(2): 10–14.

The author describes an instructional strategy, called instructional congruence, which has been widely used with success in middle level science, and stresses its potential to help ELL students succeed in science.

Lincoln, F. and Beller, C. (2004). English language learners in the science classroom. *Science Scope, 28*(1): 28–31.

The authors indicate that teachers can meet the needs of language learners without compromising the content by writing goals and objectives for the entire class. They present strategies that have been successfully used by both pre- and in-service teachers in teaching language and cultural minorities.

Verma, G., Martin-Hansen, L., and Pepper, J. B. (2008). Using sheltered instruction to teach English language learners, *Science Scope, 32*(3): 56–59.
The author describes the four elements of sheltered instruction (group work, wait time, group-response technique, supplemental materials), and explains how it should be implemented in science classes.

Classroom-Based Articles: High School Science

Creech, J. and Hale, G. (2006). Literacy in science: A natural fit. *The Science Teacher, 73*(2): 22–27.
In this article, the authors share how they used reading in their science classrooms through implementing four quarterly reading projects with yearlong literacy routines that they used successfully with their 9th-grade students, including ELL students. These projects were based on Reading Apprenticeship, an instructional framework offered by the Strategic Literacy Initiative to support middle- and high-school student literacy in content areas. The authors state that this framework encourages reading as an active problem-solving process and creates a classroom climate that supports inquiry. They conclude that this connection to inquiry made this framework a natural fit in science classrooms.

Greathouse, D. and Lincoln, F. (2008). Using all available tools: effective strategies to teach English language learners in the science classroom. *The Science Teacher, 75*(5): 48–52.
The authors present a survey of tools and methods to enhance science learning for culturally diverse students who are non-English speakers.

Hanes, C. (2004). Chemistry as a second language. *The Science Teacher, 71*(2): 42–45.
In this article, the author shares an approach to a basic curriculum that makes chemistry accessible to all students, especially ELL students. This approach incorporates multiple intelligences, the learning cycle, and specially designed academic instruction in English (SDAIE) strategies.

Johnson, C. C. (2006). Enabling all students to learn science. *The Science Teacher, 73*(2): 32–37.
The author cites the benefits of using portfolios for instruction, provides ideas on how to use portfolios in instruction, and shares her own experience with regards to how using portfolios has helped her overcome the challenge of preparing pre-service teachers of secondary science who are expected to teach at schools with increasing ELL populations.

Medina-Jerez, W., Clark, D. B., Medina, A., and Ramirez-Marin, F. (2007). Science for ELLs: Rethinking our approach. *The Science Teacher, 74*(3): 52–56.
The authors look at possible issues in diverse classrooms and offer some ideas to provoke curiosity and confidence in ELL students. These ideas include: 1) Encourage group work; 2) Incorporate collaboration; 3) Explicitly teach new vocabulary; 4) Use alternative assessment; 5) Promote democratic classrooms; 6) Include the contributions of non-Western scientists; 7) Make sure pre-service educators have diverse field experiences; 8) Use technology in the classroom; and 9) Encourage parent involvement.

Richardson Bruna, K., Chamberlin, D., Lewis, H., and Ceballos, E. M. L. (2007). Teaching science to students from rural Mexico: learning more about ELL students' communities of origin. *The Science Teacher,* 74(8): 36–40.
This article reports on the science teaching practices of a 9th grade teacher who has only Mexican ELL students in his classroom and examines aspects of the students' former lives that stand to impact their experience in this classroom.

Watson, S. (2004). Opening the science doorway: Strategies and suggestions for incorporating English language learners in the science classroom. *The Science Teacher,* 71(2): 32–35.
In this article, the author, who has conducted two workshops for teachers interested in learning new methods to teach science to ELL students, shares successful instructional strategies compiled by teachers at the seminars; strategies the author has used as a science teacher in the high-school setting, and references to other suggestions found in the literature.

Westervelt, M. (2007). Schoolyard inquiry for English language learners. *The Science Teacher,* 74(3): 47–51.
This article presents scaffolded outdoor inquiry activities to help ELL students learn life-science concepts. Through inductive outings, nature journaling, and multicultural gardening, her beginner and intermediate level ELL students gain science-inquiry skills and improve the language skills they need to succeed in an English-immersion public high school. These students also develop a sense of ownership and belonging as contributing members of the school community.

Content-Based ESL Articles

Brown, C. L. (2004). Content-based ESL curriculum and academic language proficiency. *The Internet TESL Journal, 10*(2).
http://iteslk.org/Techniques/Brown-CBEC.htm
This article provides a critical needs rationale for implementing a content-based ESL curriculum and discusses ways to implement it.

Brown, C. L. (2007). Content-based ESL instruction and curriculum. *Academic Exchange Quarterly, 11*(1): 114–119.
This article presents theoretical, pedagogical, and empirical reasons why content-based instruction is more beneficial for ELL students. The author discusses necessary paradigm changes in ESL education from an oral English proficiency orientation to an academic English proficiency orientation. She further claims that content-based ESL instruction, which integrates language instruction with content areas, can meet both the linguistic and academic needs of ELL students, and thus offers a more meaningful path to academic language acquisition.

Pawan, F. (2008). Content-area teachers and scaffolded instruction for English language learners. *Teaching and Teacher Education, 24*(6): 1450–1462.
This study reports that scaffolding provides content-area teachers with an effective means to integrate language instruction into content-area instruction for ELL students.

Books and Book Chapters

Calderón, M. E. (2007). *Teaching reading to English language learners, grades 6–12: A framework for improving achievement in content areas.* Thousand Oaks, CA: Corwin Press.

This book provides a field-tested, research-based approach to expediting reading comprehension that results in higher test scores not just for ELL students, but for all students.

Cary, S. (2000). *Working with second language learners: Answers to teachers' top ten questions.* Portsmouth, NH: Heinemann.
The author responds to teachers' ten most frequent and most problematic questions with examples drawn from actual classes that demonstrate outstanding ELL practices, coaching commentary that highlights key teaching strategies and ties together theory and practice, and professional reflection questions and action items.

Carrasquillo, A., Kucer, S. B., and Abrams, R. (2004). *Beyond the beginnings: Literacy intervention for upper elementary English language learners.* Clevedon, UK: Multilingual Matters.
In this book, the authors address the curricular, instructional, and assessment needs of upper grade elementary teachers who are struggling to promote literacy development in their ELL students.

Echevarria J., Vogt, M. E., and Short D. J. (2000). *Making content comprehensible for English language learners: The SIOP model.* Boston, MA: Allyn & Bacon.
This is a resource book for both in-service and pre-service teachers to learn how to use sheltered instruction for ELL students. It presents the first field-tested model of sheltered instruction, the Sheltered Instruction Observation Protocol (SIOP), which provides teachers with an easy-to-use tool for planning effective sheltered lessons and reflecting on their own teaching experience.

Fathman, A. K. and Crowther, D. T. (2006). *Science for English language learners: K–12 classroom strategies.* Arlington, VA: NSTA Press.
The collection of classroom-based articles in this book focuses on teaching science content and processes, on language development and literacy, and on inquiry-based teaching.

Forte, I. (2001). *ESL active learning lessons: 15 complete content-based units to reinforce language skills and concepts.* Nashvile, TN: Incentive Publications.
This book provides practice and reinforcement in the use of listening, speaking, reading, and writing. The human body, following directions, fruits, insects, animals, money, measurement, signs, plants, cafeteria, safety, weather, and transportation are among the topics covered in the book.

Forte, I., Pangle, M. A., and Drayton, M. (2001). *ESL content-based language games, puzzles, and inventive exercises.* Nashville, TN: Incentive Publications.
The book consists of many literacy activities designed to help students learn, practice, and master a wide variety of essential language-based skills connected to specific curriculum areas, including science. The activities are appropriate to use in peer tutoring, centers, or whole group directed teaching situations.

Law, B. and Eckes, M. (2000). *The more-than-just-surviving handbook: ESL for every classroom teacher.* Winnipeg: Peguis Publishers.
The book reviews the latest research on first- and second-language learning, literacy theory, and integrating the skills of reading, writing, speaking, and listening how to apply the latest research to the regular classroom that contains both native-English-speaking and non-English-speaking students.

Lee, O., and Fradd, S. H. (2001). Instructional congruence to promote science learning and literacy development for linguistically diverse students. In D. R. Lavoie and W. M. Roth (Eds.), *Models of science teacher preparation* (pp. 109–126). Dordrecht, The Netherlands: Kluwer Academic Publishers.

In this chapter, the authors explain a model that they created, called "instructional congruence." They first explain the theoretical framework for the model and illustrate its key aspects. They then describe professional development activities for elementary teachers to help them establish instructional congruence in their classrooms. Finally, they provide examples of how the teachers can establish instructional congruence to promote students' science learning and literacy development.

Reiss, J. (2005). *Teaching content to English language learners.* White Plains, NY: Longman.

This book shows content-area teachers how to transform second-language learning theories into useful tools for ensuring the success of their ELL students. The book's three parts present easy-to-incorporate techniques to make content more accessible, strengthen vocabulary, and increase student participation.

Roseberry, A. S. and Warren, B. (2008). *Teaching science to English language learners: Building on students' strengths.* Arlington, VA: NSTA Press.

This book addresses the questions of whether a student's cultural background supports learning in science and whether concentrating on the specialized vocabulary of science is the best way to help ELL students. It combines research findings with classroom vignettes and the perspectives of teachers and encourages teachers to see diversity as a resource rather than as an obstacle in the science classroom.

Short, D. J. (1991). *How to integrate language and content instruction: A training manual.* Washington, DC: Center for Applied Linguistics.

The purpose of this manual is to help educators effectively integrate language and content instruction in teaching ELL students. The manual is targeted at elementary and secondary school level teachers, administrators, and teacher educators involved in ESL or bilingual instruction and content-area instruction for limited-English-proficient students. The manual provides specific strategies for integrating language and content instruction and information on specific techniques for adapting materials and for developing lesson plans.

Journals

The list below is a selection of journals that publish research-based or classroom-based articles in the area of science education. Readers are more likely to find articles that focus on teaching science to ELLs in these journals.

Science Education publication of NARST
Journal of Research in Science Teaching publication of NARST
Journal of Science Teacher Education, publication of ASTE
Journal of Elementary Teacher Education, publication of ASTE
Journal of College Science Teaching, publication of NSTA
The Science Teacher, publication of NSTA
Science Scope, publication of NSTA
Science and Children, publication of NSTA
Science Educator, publication of NSELA

4.3
Materials for Teachers

This section provides a list of instructional materials that teachers can use in classrooms to help accommodate ELLs. In what follows you will find training modules for science teachers to work with ELL students, and lists of instructional videos, DVDs, podcasts, videocasts, webcasts, and software.

Teacher Professional Development

A Descriptive Study of Content-ESL Practices
Burkart, G. S. and Sheppard, K. (1995). *Content-ESL across the USA. Volume III: A training packet. A descriptive study of content-ESL practices.* Washington, DC: Center for Applied Linguistics. http://eric.ed.gov/ERICDocs/data/ericdocs2sql/content_storage_01/0000019b/80/14/29/cd.pdf
This training packet presents the practices and results from a 3-year study of content-ESL programs across the United States. The 15 guides explained in the document include information on curriculum development, material selection and adaptation, and lesson planning. Guidance is also offered on choosing techniques, learning co-operatively, and teaching thematically. Sample surveys, checklists, assessment protocols, and student profiles are included along with program profiles and additional resources.

Project MORE
http://education.uncc.edu/MORE/StartResources/OnlineRes.htm
Project MORE (Making, Organizing, Revising and Evaluating) is an initiative funded through the Training All Teachers Program for the Office of English Language Acquisition (US DoE Grant T 195B010018). Developed by University of North Carolina-Charlotte, the website provides

resources for content-area teachers, including science teachers. All materials are aligned with North Carolina Standards.

Annenberg Media
http://www.learner.org/teacherslab/aboutlab.html
The goal of the Teachers' Lab is to provide teachers and educators with a deeper understanding of commonly taught math and science concepts. Many of the Labs are based upon professional development workshops broadcast on the Annenberg Channel (http://www.learner.org/channel/channel.html).

Exploratorium Teacher Institutes
http://www.exploratorium.edu/ti/
The Teacher Institute offers a variety of hands-on science activities based on Exploratorium exhibits, content-based discussions, classroom materials, and online teaching resources. The Institute offers summer workshops and district-wide in-services for both new and experienced teachers. All participants receive a stipend for attending the institutes and workshops.

Museum of Science and Industry
http://www.msichicago.org/education/educator-resources/teacher-workshops/
The Institute for Quality Science Teaching offers year-long and full- and half-day teacher development workshops for new and experienced teachers. All workshops are provided at no cost to teachers.

Panhandle Area Educational Consortium (PAEC)
http://www.paec.org/teacher2teacher/math_science.html
PAEC offers e-learning workshops for teachers of science, mathematics, English, and language arts. Teachers can review the courses offered and earn graduate credits upon completion of each course.

Videos and DVDs

PCI Education
http://www.pcieducation.com/store/default.aspx?CategoryId=20&DepartmentId=49
PCI Education is an online store that contains a variety of curriculum materials (e.g., videos, software, books, and manipulatives) that are developed with the intention for teaching science to ELLs at secondary grade levels.

Learningscience.org
http://www.learningscience.org/index.htm
Learningscience.org is an organization that shares the newer and emerging learning tools (e.g., real-time data collection, simulations, inquiry-based lessons, interactive web lessons, microworlds, and imaging) of science education. Learning tools are aligned with the NSES and are reviewed by an editorial panel of science educators and scientists for content and design. Although the main emphasis is on students, teachers, and parents, anyone interested in science education will find the site useful and informative.

EduMedia

http://www.edumedia-sciences.com/en/

EduMedia fosters improvement of learning techniques through internet-based educational methods. The website features more than five hundred interactive simulations and videos to facilitate science learning.

Discover Primary Science

http://www.primaryscience.ie/site/index.php

Discover Primary Science is a flagship project run by the Discover Science and Engineering (DSE) awareness program in Ireland. The program aims to develop creativity in children, show them how important science is in everyday lives and more importantly how much fun it can be. The website provides hundreds of short videos (some animated) on a variety of science topics.

The Futures Channel

http://www.thefutureschannel.com/index.php

The Futures Channel's goal is to use new media technologies to create a channel between the scientists, engineers, explorers and visionaries who are shaping the future, and today's learners who will one day succeed them. The website offers a variety of real-world and teaching and learning videos for teachers.

The SIOP model: Sheltered instruction for academic achievement.
Video (VHS) (2002).

This seventy-seven minute video illustrates eight components of the SIOP Model for sheltered instruction in detail. The video presents extended footage from middle- and high-school classrooms, and features interviews with six outstanding teachers and the SIOP researchers. It is designed for use in sustained programs of staff development and teacher education.

Helping English learners succeed: An overview of the SIOP model.
Video (VHS) (2002).

This 26 minute video provides an introduction to a research-based model of sheltered instruction. The video uses classroom footage and researcher narration to concisely present components of the SIOP Model. The video will be useful to administrators, policy makers, and teachers. It also serves as a fitting supplement in teacher methodology courses.

Teachers' Domain

http://www.teachersdomain.org/

Teachers' Domain is an online library of more than a thousand free media resources from the best in public television. These classroom resources, featuring media from NOVA, Frontline, Design Squad, American Experience, and other public broadcasting and content partners, are easy to use and correlate to state and national science standards.

Annenberg Media

www.Learner.org

Annenberg Media provides educational video programs with co-ordinated web and print materials for the professional development of K–12 teachers. Annenberg Media's multimedia resources help teachers increase their expertise in their fields and assist them in improving their teaching methods. Many programs are also intended for students in the classroom and viewers at home. All Annenberg Media videos exemplify excellent teaching.

ABC Science

http://www.abc.net.au/science/labnotes/

ABC Science is created by the ABC broadcasting station of Australia. The website contains a variety of science teaching resources for teachers, including videos, audios, and field-based activities.

NASA

http://search.nasa.gov/search/edFilterSearch.jsp?empty=true

NASA Education Resource Center's search engine for middle-school and high-school science teaching materials, including videos and activities.

Podcasts, Videocasts, and Webcasts (Science and Science Teaching)

Science journal, AAAS

http://www.sciencemag.org/about/podcast.dtl

Science's weekly podcast takes listeners on a tour of some interesting stories in the journal and on the affiliate websites. The topics may vary from scientific issues (e.g., "genetic influences on cognition") to educational issues (e.g., "Improving minority student performance").

Scientific American

http://www.sciam.com/podcast/

The website offers four podcast programs. *Sixty-Second Science* provides quick reports and commentaries on the world of science. Hosted by Steve Mirsky, Science Talk explores the latest developments in science and technology through interviews. Sixty-Second Psych is a quick commentary on the latest news in behavior and brain research. Finally, *Sixty-Second Earth* is for quick reports on the science of the environment and the future of energy.

Science@NASA

http://science.nasa.gov/podcast.htm

NASA posts the podcast of the last twenty scientific stories they have published on their website Science@NASA. Listeners can go to the story page and read along and look at any images while listening to the podcasts.

Science Friday, NPR

http://www.sciencefriday.com/feeds/radio/

Science Friday is a radio program on National Public Radio (NPR). The latest show segments can be heard on this website.

National Geographic Society

http://www.nationalgeographic.com/podcasts/

The website offers podcasts of the latest nature and science news, eye-opening photography, audio travel guides, classic video clips, world music coverage, and wild animal adventures.

Science and the City

http://www.nyas.org/snc/podcasts.asp?PartnerCD=odeo&TrackCD=pcast

Hosted by the New York Academy of Sciences, Science & the City posts a new podcast every Friday featuring interviews, conversations, and lectures by scientists and authors.

National Science Foundation (NSF)
http://www.nsf.gov/news/mmg/index.cfm?s=1
NSF offers the podcast series called *The Discovery Files,* which focuses on a variety of scientific issues.

Museum of Science of Boston
http://www.mos.org/events_activities/podcasts
The museum's podcasts offer an in-depth look at the latest issues in science and technology through weekly interviews with guest researchers and the museum's staff.
http://www.mos.org/events_activities/videocasts
The museum's series of videocasts covers the latest issues and breakthroughs in the areas of health, technology, and science.

Museum of Science and Industry—Chicago
http://www.msichicago.org/online-science/podcast/
The website posts the interviews conducted with the people in and behind the exhibits.
http://www.msichicago.org/online-science/videos/
The museum also offers a variety of informative videos in the areas of agriculture, environment, space, biology, chemistry, energy, geology, physics, technology, geography, health, industry, and social studies.

Microbe World
http://www.microbeworld.org/
Meet the scientists and *This week in virology* (TWIV) are two podcast series the website offers. Each episode of *Meet the Scientist* provides information on a scientist and his or her current research. *This week in virology*, on the other hand, focuses on the latest issues in microbiology.

Science Teaching Tips
http://scienceteachingtips.podomatic.com/
Science Teaching Tips is produced by the Exploratorium's Teacher Institute. The short, five-minute episodes are created by science teachers to share with others. Episodes can be on hands-on activities, science facts, science history, pedagogy tips for new teachers, or other ideas for the science classrooms.

NSTA
http://www.nsta.org/publications/laboutloud.aspx
Two science teachers, Brian Bartel and Dale Basler, host the podcast. They discuss science news and science education with leading scientists, researchers, science writers, and other important figures in the field.

Heartland
http://www.aea11.k12.ia.us/prodev/science/podcast.html
The website is a collection of science podcasts created by students and teachers from schools in the Heartland Area Education Agency 11.

WonderHowTo
www.wonderhowto.com
WonderHowTo is a collection of "how to" instructional videos purposefully selected from about 2000 websites.

Colorín Colorado

www.colorincolorado.org/webcasts/

Colorín Colorado offers 45-minute instructional video programs for the teachers of ELL students. Each program includes recommended readings, suggested discussion questions, and a PowerPoint presentation accompanying the video.

4.4
Resources for Students

This section provides an annotated list of resources for ELL students. The list includes web resources that are helpful in learning science and English, print and online science dictionaries, and other helpful links for science learning. It is important to note that, in addition to the resources presented here, students can also utilize resources that are listed in each of the chapters.

Web Resources

Science Learning

The Franklin Institute
http://www.fi.edu/learn/learners.php
The Franklin Institute offers variety of resources for science learning. Targeting secondary grade level students, the website provides information on emerging scientific issues.

Natural History Museum
http://www.nhm.ac.uk/kids-only/
Students can play games and download images and pictures while gaining content knowledge on life sciences at the Natural History Museum's website.

Science Friday
http://www.kidsnet.org/sfkc/
Kids' Connection is an educational resource based on Science Friday, a radio program by NPR. Learners can browse through a variety of science subjects or topics. Each content page has a sum-

mary of the radio program, discussion ideas, activities, links to the audio, selected resources, and related science standards.

NASA Education Resource Center
http://www.nasa.gov/audience/forstudents/index.html
Student pages offer a variety of resources for elementary, middle, high school, and college students. They can use the website to interact with scientists, get help with their homework, ask questions, watch videoclips, and search many science and technology topics.

NASA Kids' Club
http://www.nasa.gov/audience/forkids/kidsclub/flash/index.html
NASA Kids' Club features interactive science games for students. The website also provides information for teachers and parents with regards to how to teach kids safe surfing habits and what they can do to protect their children's and students' identity.

KIDIPEDE
http://www.historyforkids.org/
Kidipede – History and Science for Middle School Kids is a search engine for students organized and run by Dr. Karen Carr, an associate professor of History at Portland State University. Although the site targets children and teenagers, the level of the information presented is appropriate for college students, parents, and teachers.

National Geographic Kids
http://kids.nationalgeographic.com/
National Geographic Kids features informative videos, activities, games and stories that make learning science fun for elementary and secondary level students. The website won the Parents' Choice Recommended award in 2008.

Teachers First
www.teachersfirst.com/getsource.cfm?id=9615
This interactive water cycle video (Grades 3 to 7) follows the steps of the water cycle and interactivity with living things, the earth, and the processes that occur in the water cycle. Students click on the individual steps to learn the vocabulary and interrelatedness of the water cycle on the earth.

Children's Museum of Indianapolis
http://www.childrensmuseum.org/games/grades_6-8.htm
The website features science activities for middle-school (6th through 8th grades) students. Each activity has a task, procedures for students to follow, online resource links on the focus topic, and rubrics to evaluate student performance. It also provides teacher resources for each activity.

Kidport
www.kidport.com/
Kidport is an online educational service designed to help K–8 students excel in school. The website focuses on the standard-based content, how kids learn, and what kids like. "Think-and-Learn" modules featured are to make students aware of the thinking skills they need to use while learning. Projects are integrated into the learning modules to provide compelling real-world experiences and applications for students.

The Biology Place

http://www.phschool.com/science/biology_place/index.html

The purpose of this resource is to inform students about various biological concepts and help them apply their understanding. Activities featured on this website includes manipulating graphs, biological puzzles, and answering questions.

Discover Primary Science

http://www.primaryscience.ie/site/kids_introduction.php

Discover Primary Science is a project run by the Discover Science and Engineering (DSE) awareness program in Ireland. The program aims to develop creativity in children, show them how important science is in everyday lives and more importantly how much fun it can be. The website provides hundreds of short videos (some animated) on a variety of science topics. Students can also play games and ask science content related questions to experts on this website.

How Stuff Works

http://www.howstuffworks.com/

HowStuffWorks provides easy-to-understand explanations of how the world actually works. Founded by North Carolina State University Professor Marshall Brain in 1998, the site is now an online resource for people of all ages and covers a range of topics from car engines to stem cells.

ABC Science

http://www.abc.net.au/spark/?site=science

ABC Science is created by ABC broadcasting station of Australia. The website contains a variety of fun science videos, audios, and activities for middle-school students.

Ciencia Loca

http://cientec.or.cr/ciencias/experimentos/index.html

This Spanish online resource provides many biology, physics, and chemistry activities for students. ELL students whose native tongue is Spanish, or students who are fluent in Spanish, can benefit from the activities and experiments featured on this website.

Learn Out Loud

http://www.learnoutloud.com/Podcast-Directory/Science

Learn Out Loud is a collection of hundreds of podcasts providing information on current scientific issues as well as on a variety of science concepts in language that is easy to understand. Programs include *Slacker astronomy, Planetary radio, The naked scientist, The science show, This week in science, Living on Earth, Arthritis central,* and *All in the mind.* The kids' pages on the site also provide educational audio and videos for young children and teenagers.

LabWrite

http://www.ncsu.edu/labwrite/

This NSF funded (DUE-9950405 and DUE-0231086) and sponsored resource is developed by North Carolina State University to help students, laboratory instructors, and professors understand how to use "writing" in science labs. Students learn how to reflect on the critical components of laboratory activities while writing pre-lab and post-lab assignments as well as during the lab.

ELL Learning

ESL Kid Stuff
http://www.eslkidstuff.com/
Specifically designed for ELL students and their teachers, this online resource provides thousands of flashcards, worksheets, songs, word lists, and ESL games, and features articles, and teaching tips for teachers and parents.

ESL-Kids.com
http://www.esl-kids.com/
ESL-Kids.com offers instructional tools for young learners including flashcards, worksheets, classroom games and children's song lyrics. It's also available in Japanese and Korean.

English 4 Kids
http://www.english-4kids.com/teachers.html
English 4 Kids features lesson plans, videos, games, and flashcards for ELL students and their teachers. Student pages of the website provide learning resources for kids in the form of videos and interactive quizzes based on the level of the ELL students (easy, medium, and high levels).

Les JEUNES
http://www.ac-nancy-metz.fr/enseign/anglais/Henry/youth.htm
Les JEUNES offers hundreds of supporting materials for young adults to learn English. The website is available in English and French.

The Purdue Online Writing Lab
http://owl.english.purdue.edu/owl/resource/678/01/
The ESL pages of the Purdue Online Writing Lab offer hundreds of "writing" resources for ELL students and their teachers. The topics include writing and teaching writing, grammar and mechanics, style guides, and professional writing. The site features practice guides and writing exercises.

Childrensoftware.com
www.childrensoftware.com
Childrensoftware is a search engine for educational software for children. The website also provides comprehensible reviews, tips, ratings, and articles on software programs so that teachers and parents can make informed decisions.

Dictionaries

Print

Allaby, M. (2008). *Oxford dictionary of earth sciences*. New York, NY: Oxford University Press.
American Heritage student science dictionary (2002). Boston, MA: Houghton Mifflin.
American Heritage children's science dictionary (2003). Boston, MA: Houghton Mifflin.
Berger, M. (2000). *Scholastic science dictionary*. New York, NY: Scholastic.
Daintith, J. (2008). *Oxford dictionary of chemistry*. New York, NY: Oxford University Press.
Daintith, J. (2005). *Oxford dictionary of science*. New York, NY: Oxford University Press.
Daintith, J. (2005). *Oxford dictionary of physics*. New York, NY: Oxford University Press.

Hine, R. (2008). *Oxford dictionary of biology*. New York, NY: Oxford University Press.

Kingfisher science encyclopedia. (2006) London: Kingfisher.

Morris, C. (1991). *Academic Press dictionary of science and technology*. San Diego, CA: Academic.

Ridpath, I. (2007). *Oxford dictionary of astronomy*. New York, NY: Oxford University Press.

Scientific American: science desk reference. (1999). New York, NY: John Wiley & Sons, Inc.

Stockley, C., Oxlade, C., and Wertheim, J. (2007). *The Usborne illustrated dictionary of science*. London: Usborne Books.

Trefil, J. (2003). *The nature of science: An A–Z guide to the laws and principles governing our universe*. Boston, MA: Houghton Mifflin.

Online

The following is a list of free-access dictionaries on the World Wide Web:

- Encyclopedia of Life (http://www.eol.org/).
- McGraw-Hills' AccessScience Encyclopedia of Science and Technology Online (http://www.accessscience.com/).
- Enchanted Learning (www.enchantedlearning.com/science/dictionary/).
- English Science Manager Editing (http://www.sciencemanager.com/science_dicts.htm).
- Jefferson Lab (http://education.jlab.org/glossary/).
- EnvironmentalChemistry.com (http://environmentalchemistry.com/yogi/chemistry/dictionary/).
- One Look Dictionary Search (www.onelook.com).
- Edventures Term Browser (http://discover.edventures.com/functions/termlib.php).
- Biology-Online Dictionary (http://www.biology-online.org/dictionary/?Term=A).
- ChemicCool (http://www.chemicool.com/dictionary.html).
- Feimer's Physics Page (http://www.physicsphenomena.com/Physicsdictionary.htm).
- Alpha Dictionary-Physics. (http://www.alphadictionary.com/directory/Specialty_Dictionaries/Physics/).
- International Society for Complexity, Information, and Design—Encyclopedia of Science and Philosophy (http://www.iscid.org/encyclopedia/).
- Cambridge Dictionaries Online (http://dictionary.cambridge.org).
- Dictionary.com (http://dictionary.reference.org).
- Encarta World English Dictionary (http://encarta.msn.com/encnet/features/dictionary/dictionaryhome.aspx).
- Lexicool (www.lexicool.com).
- Merriam-Webster Dictionary (www.m-w.com/dictionary.htm).
- Oxford Dictionaries (www.askoxford.com/dictionaries/?view=uk).
- Omniglot (www.omniglot.com/links/dictionaries.htm).

Glossary

5Es: An instructional model developed in order to allow students to discover relationships among their experiences. The 5 Es stand for Engagement, Exploration, Explanation, Elaboration, and Evaluation.

AAAS: American Association for the Advancement of Science.

Accommodation: The process of re-framing one's mental representations as a result of new information or new experiences.

Active learning: A process in which learners are actively engaged in the learning process, rather than passively absorbing lectures.

AIMS: Activities Integrating Math and Science.

Alternative assessment: Any type of assessment in which students create a response to a question. This is different from assessments in which students choose a response from a list given, such as multiple choice, true/false, or matching. Alternative assessments can include short answer questions, essays, performance assessments, oral presentations, demonstrations, exhibitions, and portfolios.

Analogy: Drawing a comparison in order to show a similarity in some respect.

Assimilation: The process of incorporating new experiences into existing mental schemes without changing them.

Authentic assessment: Evaluating student learning and ability in real-life tasks and situations. Portfolios, performance-based assessments and/or observations in place or in conjunction with more traditional measures of performance such as tests and written assignments can all be used during authentic assessment.

Basic Interpersonal Communication Skills (BICS): Speech that is informal, everyday, and colloquial.

Benchmarks for Science Literacy: A set of science literacy goals developed through Project 2061, AAAS's long-term initiative to reform K–12 science.

Biological Sciences Curriculum Study (BSCS): An organization that aims to improve all students' understanding of science and technology by developing curricular materials, supporting their widespread and effective use, providing professional development, and conducting research and evaluation studies.

Classifying: A basic science process skill. Grouping or ordering objects or events into categories based on similarities or differences in properties. Lists, tables, or charts are generated.

Cognitive Academic Language Proficiency (CALP): Level of language required to understand academically demanding subject matter in a classroom.

Cognitive demand: Mental complexity of a task.

Collaborative learning: An instructional technique in which learners at various performance levels work together in small groups toward a common goal. Learners in the same group are responsible for one another's learning as well as their own. Thus, the success of one learner helps other students to be successful.

Comprehensible input: Language delivered at a level understood by a learner.

Concept maps: A visual representation of relationships between ideas, images or words.

Conceptual change (framework): Process of learning during which learners' prior knowledge has to be fundamentally restructured in order to allow understanding of the intended knowledge, that is, the acquisition of science concepts.

Content-Based Instruction: A second-language learning approach where teachers use instructional materials, learning tasks, and classroom techniques from academic content areas as the vehicle for developing second language, content, and cognitive skills.

Context-embedded: Language where there are plenty of clues, shared language understanding, and where meaning is relatively obvious due to help from the physical and social nature of the conversation.

Context-reduced: Language where there are few clues as to the meaning of language of the communication apart from the words themselves.

Communicating: A basic science process skill. Using words, graphic symbols, diagrams, tables, or demonstrations to describe an action, object, or event.

Cookbook labs: Experiments based on detailed instructions that prompt students to follow step-by-step directions, requiring little intellectual involvement.

Cooperative learning: An instructional technique that allows students to work in small groups within the classroom, often with a division of assignment of several specific tasks or roles. This group strategy allows students to practice working in a group and taking leadership roles.

Deductive approach/reasoning: Using an accepted premise or generalization to predict observations and facts.

Discovery teaching/approach: An approach to engage students in inquiry through which, guided by the teacher and materials, they "discover" the intended content.

Discrepant event: An observed event that is unexpected. It may surprise or puzzle the observer.

Disequilibrium: Dissonance between learners' prior knowledge about a phenomenon and newly presented information.

Educational Resources Information Center (ERIC): Online digital library of education research and information. ERIC is sponsored by the Institute of Education Sciences (IES) of the United States' Department of Education.

English for speakers of other languages (ESOL): Teaching English to non-native speakers.

English language learner (ELL): The term used in the United States to describe many individuals who are in the process of learning English.

Experiment: The method of investigating causal relationships among variables.

Exploration: A careful systematic search.

Expository laboratory: Refers to cookbook or verification labs in which students follow a step-by-step procedure to arrive at an end result.

Formal assessment: An assessment procedure for obtaining information that can be used to make judgments about characteristics of a learner using standardized instruments (e.g., tests, and quizzes). Learner receives a numerical score or a grade based on his or her performance.

Formative assessment: A self-reflective process that intends to promote student attainment. It is the bidirectional process between teacher and student to enhance, recognize and respond to the learning.

FOSS: Full Option Science System. An organization that has been designed to combine the content of science with the process of science to meet two main goals: scientific literacy for students and instructional efficiency for teachers.

Guided inquiry: Teachers guide students through projects by giving them starting questions, prompting new discussions with ideas and methods, or acting as supervisors in other ways; it can be at the beginning of a course with naive students and followed by open-ended inquiry. In contrast, open-ended inquiry is less structured.

Hands-on science: Hands-on quite literally means having students "manipulate" the things they are studying—plants, rocks, insects, water, magnetic fields—and "handle" scientific instruments—rulers, balances, test tubes, thermometers, microscopes, telescopes, cameras, meters, calculators. In a more general sense, it seems to mean learning by experience.

Hypothesis: A proposal intended to explain certain facts or observations.

Inductive approach/reasoning: Making empirical generalizations based on a large number of observations and facts.

Inferring: A basic process skill. Interpreting or explaining observations; making predictions about an object or event based on previously gathered data or information.

Informal assessment: An assessment procedure for obtaining information that can be used to make judgments about characteristics of a learner using means other than standardized instruments (e.g., observation, rubrics, portfolios, peer and self-evaluations, and discussions).

Informal science education: Science education programs developed by institutions and organizations, such as museums, planetariums, zoos, and parks that provide science learning opportunities outside of classrooms.

Inquiry-based science: An instructional technique in which students are engaged in open-ended, student-centered, and hands-on activities.

Integrated science process skills: Higher level process skills, such as formulating hypotheses, manipulating variables, defining operationally, interpreting data, formulating models, and experimenting, which are used by older learners.

Interaction: A theory in second language acquisition (SLA) that maintains that a second language learner needs comprehensible input, opportunity for output, interaction, and opportunity to negotiate meaning to facilitate second language learning.

Journal assessment: Using students' ongoing records of expressions, experiences and reflections on a given topic to determine student achievement and progress.

KWL: An instructional technique that provides a structure for recalling what students know about a topic, noting what students want to know, and finally listing what has been learned and is yet to be learned.

Language demand: Linguistic skills and academic language functions.

Learning cycle: An instructional technique that promotes inquiry-based learning by having students go through steps of exploration, concept introduction, and concept application.

Limited English Proficiency (LEP): People who have learned some English, but are not yet fluent—currently known as English Language Learners (ELL).

Measuring: A basic process skill. Using both standard and non-standard measures or estimates to describe the dimensions of an object or event.

Mainstream instruction: An approach in which second-language learners (ELLs) or students with exceptionalities (special needs students) are placed in the same class as native speakers of English with no handicaps.

Misconception: A wrong conception or understanding of what is in fact true.

National Science Education Standards (NSES): A set of guidelines for the science education in primary and secondary schools in the United States, as established by the National Research Council in 1996. These provide a set of goals for teachers to set for their students and for administrators to provide professional development.

Nature of Science (NOS): What science is, how it works, and how scientists contribute to scientific knowledge.

Objectivity: Judgment based on observable phenomena and uninfluenced by emotions or personal prejudices.

Observing: A basic process skill. Using the five senses to gather information about an object or event, its characteristics, properties, differences, similarities, and changes. Observations are recorded.

Output: Any linguistic utterance made by a person.

Performance indicators: Performance indicators are measurable indicators that demonstrate the achievement of an outcome. They enable decision-makers to assess progress towards the achievement of intended outputs.

Performance-based assessment: An assessment technique designed to determine a learner's knowledge, understanding, ability, skill and/or attitudes in a systematic manner. It typically includes exhibitions, investigations, demonstrations, written or oral responses, journals, and portfolios. Assessment of the performance is done using a scoring guide or rubric.

Portfolio assessment: Purposeful collection of student work that helps to determine student achievement and progress.

Predicting: A basic process skill. Forming an idea of an expected result—not a guess—but a belief about what will occur based on present knowledge and understandings, observations, and inferences.

Prior knowledge: Combination of the learner's pre-existing *attitudes, experiences,* and *knowledge.*

Problem-based learning (PBL): A student-centered instructional strategy in which students collaboratively work to find solutions to real-world problems and reflect on their experiences.

Project 2061: A long-term initiative of the American Association for the Advancement of Science to reform K–12 science education.

Project-based science: A student-centered instructional technique that emphasizes learning activities that are long-term, interdisciplinary, authentic, inquiry-based, and integrated with real-world issues.

Rubric: A scoring tool that lists criteria for evaluation and levels of fulfillment of those criteria.

Science process skills: Skills that are required to perform scientific inquiry.

Scientific inquiry: The process by which scientists ask questions, develop and carry out investigations, make predictions, gather evidence, and propose explanations.

Scientific literacy: The knowledge and understanding of key ideas of science, ability to apply these understandings to every day events, and understandings of nature of scientific knowledge as well as strengths and limitations of science.

Second language acquisition: The discipline that investigates how second languages are learned.

Sheltered instruction: An approach in which students develop knowledge in specific subject areas through the medium of English or another second language.

Structured (teacher-directed) inquiry: An inquiry-based teaching approach in which students are given a hands-on problem to investigate along with procedures and materials to use, but not informed about expected outcomes.

Summative assessment: Refers to the assessment of the learning and summarizes the development of learners at a particular time.

Teachers of English to speakers of other languages (TESOL): A professional organization for English language educators with a mission to ensure excellence in English language teaching to speakers of other languages.

Zone of proximal development (ZPD): A concept developed by the Russian psychologist and social constructivist Lev Vygotsky, which refers to the difference between what a learner can do without help of an adult or more knowledgeable peer and what he or she can do with help.

Notes

1.1 Orientation

1 Proposition 227 was part of a referendum in California to abolish bilingual education for ELLs in favor of more instruction in English. The *No Child Left Behind* legislation is a federal initiative to oversee teacher performance and student improvement in literacy and numeracy through such accountability measures as standardized testing in schools.

1.7 Not All Parents are the Same: Home–School Communication

1 Two research studies from the Center for Research on Education, Diversity & Excellence (CREDE) have recently been published through the Center for Applied Linguistics. The two books, arising out of a four-year and a three-year study, respectively, center on the solidification of home–school ELL communication. The first, entitled *Creating Access: Language and Academic Programs for Secondary School Newcomers*, describes the ins and outs of an effective education model—newcomer programs for immigrant students—and is designed to help district personnel create a newcomer program or enhance an existing program. The second book, called *Family Literacy Nights: Building the Circle of Supporters within and beyond School for Middle School English Language Learners*, discusses a project to improve students' education through a home–school collaboration called "Family Literacy Nights." The program brought parents of linguistically and culturally diverse students together with teachers and students, resulting in greater parental involvement and improved student learning. This report offers practitioners strategies for implementing similar programs.

2.3 Supporting Communication in Content Instruction for ELLs

1 *Made up of* is a phrasal verb. Phrasal verbs consist of a verb plus one or more prepositions. They are confusing for ELLs because the whole does not equal the sum of its parts. In other words, knowing what each word means individually won't tell you what the entire phrase means. *Made up of* means comprises, but knowing what *made, up,* and *of* mean individually won't get to the meaning of *made up of*. It's better to avoid phrasal verbs and use more formal verbs, which are easier for ELLs to understand or look up in bilingual dictionaries.

2 *Is like a* is a simile that may confuse ELLs —they may confuse the verb *to like* with the term *is like a*. The more formal term *is similar to* may be easier to understand or look up in bilingual dictionaries.

3 *Which is a cluster of protons and neutrons* is a relative clause, which is a grammatical form that is learned late in the process of becoming proficient in English. It also can be confusing to the ELL what the referent *which* is referring to. To simplify for ELLs, divide the sentence into two sentences: *In the center of the atom is the nucleus. The nucleus is a cluster of protons and neutrons.*

4 The most common meaning of *while* shows duration of time. For example, *I listened to the radio while I brushed my teeth.* In this sentence, *while* refers to an opposing or opposite concept. A more common way to state this would be to use *but* rather than *while*.

5 Here is another variation of the phrasal verb *makes up*. Of course, in this form the verb can also mean to reconcile.

6 The word *or* usually means either/or—a choice of one or the other, but it can also mean another way to say the same thing, such as "A harridan is a shrew, or an ornery woman." This can be very confusing for ELLs. A glossary or footnote could be an alternative way to show that mass does not equal weight for purposes of this example.

7 *Whirling* is a very uncommon term. Using a more common term or providing a glossary with a more common term such as *turning* can help.

8 The more common meaning of *fantastic* is *fabulous* or *wonderful* rather than *extreme*, as it means here.

9 This sentence does not use the most common sentence patterns in English (and in all languages of the world), subject/verb/object. Instead, it begins with a complex phrase that describes the subject, *electrons*. It could be rewritten as *Smaller and lighter particles called electrons spin at very fast speeds around the nucleus.*

10 This is another relative clause (as in sentence 2).

3.1 Teaching Science to ELLs at Secondary Grade Levels

1 The NRC established standards for science teaching, assessment in science education, for science content, science education programs, science education systems, and professional development for teachers of science. However, in this book we refer to the "standards for the science content."

3.7 Physical Science

1 Potential energy refers to the gravitational potential energy here.

References

Series Introduction

Ladson-Billings, G. (2001). *Crossing over to Canaan: The journey of new teachers in diverse classrooms*. San Francisco: Jossey-Bass.

Part 1

Baca, L., & Cervantes, H. (2004). *The bilingual special education interface*. Columbus, OH: Merrill.

Bailey, A. L., Butler, F. A., Borrego, M., LaFramenta, C., & Ong, C. (2002). Towards a characterization of academic language. *Language Testing Update, 31,* 45–52.

Baker, C. (2001). *Foundations of bilingual education and bilingualism* (third edition). Clevedon: Multilingual Matters.

Bassoff, T. C. (2004). Three steps toward a strong home–school connection. *Essential Teacher,* 1 (4). Retrieved July 17, 2007, from www.tesol.org/s_tesol/sec_document.asp?CID=659&DID=2586.

Boscolo, P., & Mason, L. (2001). Writing to learn, writing to transfer. In P. Tynjälä, L. Mason, and K. Lonka (Eds.), *Writing as a learning tool: Integrating theory and practice*. Dordrecht, the Netherlands: Kluwer Academic Publishers, pp. 83–104.

Brinton, D. (2003). Content-based instruction. In D. Nunan (Ed.), *Practical English language teaching*. New York: McGraw-Hill, pp. 199–224.

Carrasquillo, A. L., & Rodriguez, V. (2002). *Language minority students in the mainstream classroom* (2nd edn). Boston: Multilingual Matters.

Clark, D. (1999). *Learning domains or Bloom's taxonomy*. Retrieved August 3, 2007, from www.nwlink.com/~donclark/hrd/bloom.html.

Coady, M., Hamann, E. T., Harrington, M., Pacheco, M., Pho, S., & Yedlin, J. (2003). *Claiming opportunities:A handbook for improving education for English language learners through comprehensive school reform*. Providence, RI: Education Alliance at Brown University.

Collier, V. P. (1995). Acquiring a second language for school. *Directions in Language and Education*, 1 (4). Washington, DC: National Clearinghouse for Bilingual Education.

Collier, V., & Thomas, W. (1997). *School effectiveness for language minority students*. Washington, DC: National Clearinghouse for Bilingual Education. Retrieved December 2, 2006, from www.ncela.gwu/pubs/resource/effectiveness/index.htm.

Consent Decree. (1990). Retrieved January 17, 2007, from www.firn.edu/doe/aala/lulac.htm.

Crawford, J. (2004). *Educating English learners: Language diversity in the classroom* (fifth edition). Los Angeles: Bilingual Educational Services.

Cummins, J. (1979). Cognitive/academic language proficiency, linguistic interdependence, the optimum age question and some other matters. *Working Papers on Bilingualism, 19,* 121–129.

Cummins, J. (1980). The cross-lingual dimensions of language proficiency: Implications for bilingual education and the optimal age issue. *TESOL Quarterly, 14*(2), 175–187.

Cummins, J. (1986). Empowering minority students: A framework for intervention. *Harvard Educational Review,* 56(1), 18–36.

Cummins, J. (1992). Bilingual education and English immersion: The Ramírez report in theoretical perspective. *Bilingual Research Journal, 16,* 91–104.

Cummins, J. (2001). *Negotiating identities: Education for empowerment in a diverse society.* Los Angeles: California Association for Bilingual Education.

Dalton, J., & Smith, D. (1986). *Extending children's special abilities—strategies for primary classrooms.* Retrieved February 19, 2007, from www.teachers.ash.org.au/researchskills/dalton.htm.

Diaz-Rico, L., & Weed, K. Z. (2006). *The crosscultural, language and academic development handbook* (3rd edn). Boston: Pearson Education.

Echeverria, J., & McDonough, R. (1993). *Instructional conversations in special education settings: Issues and accommodations.* Educational Practice Report 7. National Center for Research on Cultural Diversity and Second Language Learning. Retrieved May 10, 2007, from www.ncela.gwu.edu/pubs/ncrcdsll/epr7.htm.

Ellis, R. (2005). *Instructed second language acquisition: A literature review.* Report to the Ministry of Education, New Zealand. Retrieved January 18, 2007, from www.educationcounts.edcentre.govt.nz/publications/downloads/instructed-second-language.pdf.

Gay, G. (2000). *Culturally responsive teaching: Theory, research, and practice.* New York: Teachers College Press.

Genesee, F. (Ed.) (1999). *Program alternatives for linguistically diverse students.* Santa Cruz, CA: Center for Research on Education, Diversity and Excellence. Retrieved January 8, 2007, from www.cal.org/crede/pubs/edpractice/Epr1.pdf.

Gold, N. (2006). *Successful bilingual schools: Six effective programs in California.* San Diego, CA: San Diego County Office of Education.

Gollnick, D. M., & Chinn, P. C. (2002). *Multicultural education in a pluralistic society* (sixth edition). New York: Merrill.

Hakuta, K., Butler, Y. G., & Witt, D. (2000). *How long does it take English learners to attain proficiency?* Santa Barbara: University of California Linguistic Research Institute Policy Report.

Hoover, J. J., & Collier, C. (1989). Methods and materials for bilingual education. In M. Baca and H. T. Cervantes (Eds.), *The bilingual special interface.* Columbus, OH: Merrill, pp. 231–255.

Kern, R. (2000). *Literacy and language teaching.* Oxford: Oxford University Press.

Kindler, A. (2002). *Survey of the states' limited English proficient students and available educational programs and services: 2000–2001 summary report.* Washington, DC: National Clearinghouse for English Language Acquisition.

Krashen, S. (1981). *Principles and practice in second language acquisition.* English Language Teaching series. London: Prentice-Hall International.

Long, M. (1996). The role of the linguistic environment in second language acquisition. In W. Ritchie and T. Bhatia (Eds.), *Handbook of second language acquisition.* San Diego: Academic Press, pp. 413–468.

Long, M. H. (2006). *Problems in SLA.* Mahwah, NJ: Lawrence Erlbaum Associates.

Lyster, R. (1998). Recasts, repetition and ambiguity in L2 classroom discourse. *Studies in Second Language Acquisition, 20,* 51–81.

Lyster, R. (2001). Negotiation of form, recasts, and explicit correction in relation to error types and learner repair in immersion classrooms. *Language Learning, 51* (Suppl. 1), 265–301.

Lyster, R. (2004). Differential effects of prompts and recasts in form-focused instruction. *Studies in Second Language Acquisition, 26,* 399–432.

Lyster, R. (2007). *Learning and teaching languages through content: A counterbalanced approach.* Amsterdam: John Benjamins.

Lyster, R., & Ranta, L. (1997). Corrective feedback and learner uptake: Negotiation of form in communicative classrooms. *Studies in Second Language Acquisition, 19,* 37–66.

Lyster, R., & Mori, H. (2006). Interactional feedback and instructional counterbalance. *Studies in Second Language Acquisition, 28,* 321–341.

Meltzer, J. (2001). *The adolescent literacy support framework.* Providence, RI: Northeast and Islands Regional Educational Laboratory at Brown University. Retrieved August 11, 2004, from http://knowledgeloom.org/adlit.

Meltzer, J., & Hamann, E. T. (2005). *Meeting the literacy development needs of adolescent English language learners through content-area learning. Part Two: Focus on classroom teaching strategies.* Providence, RI: Education Alliance at Brown University.

Oberg, K. (1954). *The social economy of the Tlingit Indians of Alaska.* Unpublished doctoral dissertation. University of Chicago.

Ortiz, A. (1984). Language and curriculum development for exceptional bilingual children. In Chinn, C. P. (Ed.), *Education of culturally and linguistically different exceptional children.* Reston, VA: Council for Exceptional Children–ERIC Clearinghouse on Handicapped and Gifted Children, pp. 77–100.

Ovando, C., & Collier, V. (1998). *Bilingual and ESL classrooms: Teaching in multicultural contexts.* Boston: McGraw-Hill.

Pienemann, M. (1988). Determining the influence of instruction on L2 speech processing. *AILA Review, 5,* 40–72.

Pienemann, M. (1989). Is language teachable? Psycholinguistic experiments and hypotheses. *Applied Linguistics, 10* (1), 52–79.

Pienemann, M. (2007). Processability theory. In B. van Patten and J. Williams (Eds.), *Theories in second language acquisition: An introduction.* Mahwah, NJ: Lawrence Erlbaum Associates, pp. 137–154.

Ragan, A. (2005). Teaching the academic language of textbooks: A preliminary framework for performing a textual analysis. *The ELL Outlook.* Retrieved 13 August, 2007, from www.coursecrafters.com/ELLOutlook/2005/nov_dec/ELLOutlookITIArticle1.htm.

Richards, H. V., Brown, A. F., & Forde, T. B. (2004). *Addressing diversity in schools: Culturally responsive pedagogy.* Tempe, AZ: National Center for Culturally Responsive Educational Systems. Retrieved 27 July, 2007, from www.nccrest.org/Briefs/Diversity_Brief.pdf.

Ruiz, N. T. (1989). An optimal learning environment for Rosemary. *Exceptional Children, 56* (2), 130–144.

Ruiz, N. T. (1995a). The social construction of ability and disability: I. Profile types of Latino children identified as language learning disabled. *Journal of Learning Disabilities, 28*(8), 476–490.

Ruiz, N. T. (1995b). The social construction of ability and disability: II. Optimal and at-risk lessons in a bilingual special education classroom. *Journal of Learning Disabilities, 28*(8): 491–502.

Scarcella, R. (2003). *Academic English: A conceptual framework.* Technical Report 2003-1. Irvine, CA: University of California Linguistic Minority Research Institute. Retrieved July 2, 2007, from www.ncela.gwu.edu/resabout/literacy/2_academic.htm.

Skehan, P. (1998). *A cognitive approach to language learning.* Oxford: Oxford University Press.

Swain, M. (1995). Three functions of output in second language learning. In G. Cook and B. Seidlhofer (Eds.), *Principle and practice in applied linguistics.* Oxford: Oxford University Press, pp. 125–144.

U.S. Census Bureau (2005). *Statistical abstract of the United States.* Retrieved February 24, 2008, from www.census.gov/prod/www/statistical-absract.html.

Valdez, G. (2000). Nonnative English speakers: Language bigotry in English mainstream classes. *Associations of Departments of English Bulletin, 124* (Winter): 12–17.

de Valenzuela, J. S., & Niccolai, S. L. (2004). Language development in culturally and linguistically diverse students with special education needs. In L. Baca and H. Cervantes (Eds.), *The bilingual special education interface* (fourth edition). Upper Saddle River, NJ: Merrill, pp. 125–161.

Zamel, V., & Spack, R. (1998). *Negotiating academic literacies: Teaching and learning across language and cultures.* Mahwah, NJ: Lawrence Erlbaum.

Zehler, A. (1994). *Working with English language learners: Strategies for elementary and middle school teachers.* NCBE Program Information Guide, No. 19. Retrieved May 25, 2007, from www.ncela.gwu.edu/pubs/pigs/pig19.htm.

Part 2

Abedi, J. (2004). The No Child Left Behind Act and English language learners: Assessment and accountability issues. *Educational Researcher, 33*(1), 4–14.

Abedi, J., & Dietel, R. (2004). Challenges in the No Child Left Behind Act for English language learners. *Phi Delta Kappan, 85*(10), 782–785.

Amaral, O., Garrison, L., & Klentschy, M. (2002). Helping English learners increase achievement through inquiry-based science instruction. *Bilingual Research Journal, 26*(2), 213–239.

Ballantyne, K. G., Sanderman, A. R., & Levy, J. (2008). *Educating English language learners: Building teacher capacity.* Washington, DC: National Clearinghouse for English Language Acquisition. http://www.ncela.gwu.edu/practice/mainstream_teachers.htm.

Ballenger, C. (1997). Social identities, moral narratives, scientific argumentation: Science talk in a bilingual classroom. *Language and Education, 11*, 1–14.

Bitgood, S. (1989). School field trips: An overview. *Visitor Behavior, 4*(2), 3–6.

Brophy, J. (2004). *Motivating students to learn* (2nd ed.). Mahwah, NJ: Erlbaum.

Chamot, A. U., & O'Malley, J. M. (1994). *The CALLA handbook: How to implement the Cognitive Academic Language Learning Approach.* Reading, MA: Addison-Wesley.

Committee on Undergraduate Science Education, National Research Council (1997). *Science teaching reconsidered: A handbook.* Washington, DC: National Academy Press.

Cuevas, P., Lee, O., Hart, J., & Deaktor, R. (2005). Improving science inquiry with elementary students of diverse backgrounds. *Journal of Research in Science Teaching, 42*(3), 337–357.

Cummins, J. (1999). BICS and CALP: Clarifying the distinction. (ERIC Document Reproduction Service No. ED438551.)

Dobb, F. (2004). *Essential elements of effective science instruction for English learners.* Los Angeles, CA: California Science Project. http://csmp.ucop.edu/downloads/csp/essential_elements_2.pdf.

Driver, R. (1983). *The pupil as scientist?* New York: Taylor & Francis, Inc.

Driver, R., & Oldham, V. (1986). A constructivist approach to curriculum development. *Studies in Science Education, 13*, 105–122.

Echevarria, J., Vogt, M. E., & Short, D. (2008). *Making content comprehensible for English learners: the SIOP® Model,* (3rd ed.), New York, NY: Allyn & Bacon.

Eick, C., Meadows, L., & Balkcom, R. (2005). Breaking into inquiry: Scaffolding supports beginning efforts to implement inquiry in the classroom. *The Science Teacher, 72*(7), 49.

Festinger, L., Schachter, S., & Back, K. W. (1950). *Social pressures in informal groups: A study of human factors in housing,* New York, NY: Harper.

Fillmore, L. W., & Snow, C. E. (2000). *What teachers need to know about language* (Report No. 99-C0–0008), Washington, DC: Center for Applied Linguistics. (ERIC Document Reproduction Service No. ED 444379.)

Fradd, S. H., Lee, O., Sutman, F. X., & Saxton, M. K. (2002). Materials development promoting science inquiry with English language learners: A case study. *Bilingual Research Journal, 25*(4), 479–501.

Gass, S. M. (1997). *Input, interaction, and the second language learner.* Hillsdale, NJ: Lawrence Erlbaum.

Goldenberg, C. (2008). Teaching English language learners: What the research does—and does not—say. *American Educator, 32*(1), 8–21, 44.

Haines, S. (2001). Signs of success. *The Science Teacher, 68*(2), 26–29.

Hart, J., & Lee, O. (2003). Teacher professional development to improve science and literacy achievement of English language learners. *Bilingual Research Journal, 27*(3), 475–501.

Haynes, J. (2007). Challenges for ELLs in Content Area Learning, Everything ESL. http://www.everythingesl.net/inservices/challenges_ells_content_area_l_65322.php.

Hsin-Kai, W. (2003). Linking the microscopic view of chemistry to real-life experiences: Intertextuality in a high school science classroom. *Science Education, 87*(6), 868–891.

Jarrett, D. (1999). *The inclusive classroom: Teaching mathematics and science to English-language learners. It's just good teaching.* Portland, OR: The Northwest Regional Education Laboratory.

Krashen, S. D. (1985). *The input hypothesis.* New York, NY: Longman.

Krashen, S. D., & Terrell, T. (1983). *The natural approach: Language acquisition in the classroom.* Hayward, CA: Alemany Press.

Ladson-Billings, G. (1994). *The dreamkeepers: Successful teachers of African American children.* San Francisco, CA: Jossey-Bass.

Ladson-Billings, G. (1995a). Toward a theory of culturally relevant pedagogy. *American Educational Research Journal, 32*(3), 465–491.

Ladson-Billings, G. (1995b). But that's just good teaching! The case for culturally relevant pedagogy. *Theory into Practice, 34*(3). 159–165.

Lee, O. (2002). Science inquiry for elementary students from diverse backgrounds. In W. G. Secada (Ed.), *Review of research in education* (Vol. 26, pp. 23–69), Washington, DC: American Educational Research Association.

Lee, O. (2003). Equity for culturally and linguistically diverse students in science education: A research agenda. *Teachers College Record, 105*(3), 465–489.

Lee, O (2004). Teacher change in beliefs and practices in science and literacy instruction. *Journal of Research in Science Teaching, 41*(1), 65–93.

Lee, O. (2005). Science education with English language learners: Synthesis and research agenda. *Review of Educational Research, 75*(4), 491–530.

Lee, O., & Fradd, S.H. (1996a). Interactional patterns of linguistically diverse students and teachers: Insights for promoting science learning. *Linguistics and Education: An International Research Journal, 8*, 269–297.

Lee, O., & Fradd, S. H. (1996b). Literacy skills in science performance among culturally and linguistically diverse students. *Science Education, 80*(6), 651–671.

Lee, O., & Fradd, S. H. (1998). Science for all, including students from non-English language backgrounds. *Educational Researcher, 27*(3), 12–21.

Lee, O., Fradd, S, & Sutman, F. X. (1995). Science knowledge and cognitive strategy use among culturally and linguistically diverse science students. *Journal of Research in Science Teaching, 32*, 797–816.

Long, M. (2006). Problems in second language acquisition. New York, NY: Routledge.

McCarthy, D. (2005). Newton's First Law: A learning cycle approach. *Science Scope, 28*(5), 46–49.

Merino, B., & Hammond, L. (2001). How do teachers facilitate writing for bilingual learners in "sheltered constructivist" science? *Electronic Journal in Science and Literacy, 1*(1). http://ejlts.ucdavis.edu.

Misiti, F. (2000). The pressure's on. *Science Scope, 24*(1), 34–37.

Morrison, J. A., & Lederman, N. G. (2003). Science teachers' diagnosis and understanding of students' preconceptions. *Science Education, 87*(6), 849–867.

National Research Council (1996). *National science education standards.* Washington, DC: National Academy Press.

National Research Council (2000). *Inquiry and the National Science Education Standards: A guide for teaching and learning.* Washington, DC: National Academy Press.

Noddings, N. (2005). Identifying and responding to needs in education. *Cambridge Journal of Education, 35*(2), 147–159.

O'Malley, J. J., & Chamot, A. U. (1990). *Learning strategies in second language acquisition.* Cambridge: Cambridge University Press.

Osborne, A. B. (1996). Practice into theory into practice: Culturally relevant pedagogy for students we have marginalized and normalized. *Anthropology and Education Quarterly, 27*(3), 285–314.

Osborne, R., & Freyberg, R. (1985). *Learning in science: The implications of children's science.* Portsmouth, NH: Heinemann.

Rodgers, D. L., & Withrow-Thorton, B. J. (2005). The effect of instructional media on learner motivation. *International Journal of Instructional Media, 32*(4), 333–342.

Rodriguez, I., & Bethel, L. J. (1983). An inquiry approach to science and language teaching. *Journal of Research in Science Teaching, 20*(4), 291–296.

Rosebery, A. S., Warren, B., & Conant, F. R. (1992). Appropriating scientific discourse: Findings from language minority classrooms. *Journal of the Learning Sciences, 21,* 61–94.

Rosenthal, J. W. (1995). *Teaching science to language minority students: Theory and practice.* Clevedon: Multilingual Matters.

Savinainen, A., Scott, P., & Viiri, J. (2005). Using a bridging representation and social interactions to foster conceptual change: Designing and evaluating an instructional sequence for Newton's Third Law. *Science Education, 89*(2), 175–195.

Scott, P., Dyson, T., & Gater, S. (1987). *A constructivist view of learning and teaching in science.* Leeds: Centre for Studies in Science and Mathematics Education.

Swain, M. (1985). Communicative competence: Some roles of comprehensible input and comprehensible output in its development. In Gass, S., & Madden, C. (Eds.) *Input in second language acquisition* (pp. 235–253). Rowley, MA: Newbury House.

Teachers of English to Speakers of Other Languages, (2006). *PreK–12 English language proficiency standards.* Alexandria, VA: TESOL.

Tobin, K., & McRobbie, C. J. (1996). Significance of limited English proficiency and cultural capital to the performance in science of Chinese-Australians. *Journal of Research in Science Teaching, 33*(3), 265–282.

Torres, H. N., & Zeidler, D. L. (2002). The effects of English language proficiency and scientific reasoning skills on the acquisition of science content knowledge by Hispanic English language learners and native English language speaking students. *Electronic Journal of Science Education, 6*(3). http://ejse.southwestern.edu/original%20site/manuscripts/v6n3/articles/art04_torres/torres.pdf.

Warren, B., Ballenger, C., Ogonowski, M., Rosebery, A., & Hudicourt-Barnes, J. (2001). Rethinking diversity in learning science: The logic of everyday language. *Journal of Research in Science Teaching, 38*(5), 529–552.

Part 3

Akerson, V. L., & Volrich, M. (2006). Teaching nature of science explicitly in a first-grade internship setting. *Journal of Research in Science Teaching 43*(4), 377–394.

Amaral, O., Garrison, L., & Klentschy, M. (2002). Helping English learners increase achievement through inquiry-based science instruction. *Bilingual Research Journal, 26*(2), 213–239.

American Association for the Advancement of Science (AAAS). (2001). *Atlas of science literacy.* Washington, DC: American Association for the Advancement of Science and National Science Teachers Association.

American Association for the Advancement of Science. (1993). *Benchmarks for scientific literacy.* New York, NY: Oxford University Press.

Athman, J., & Monroe, M. C. (2008). *Enhancing Natural Resource Programs with Field Trips.* Institute of Food and Agricultural Sciences, University of Florida. Retrieved from http://edis.ifas.ufl.edu/pdffiles/FR/FR13500.pdf.

Atkin, J. M., & Karplus, R. (1962). Discovery or invention? *The Science Teacher, 29*(5), 45.

Bitgood, S. (1989). School field trips: An overview. *Visitor Behavior, 4*(2), 3–6.

Burke, K. A., Hand, B. M., Poock, J. R., & Greenbowe, T. J. (2005). Using the science writing heuristic: training chemistry teaching assistants. *Journal of College Science Teaching, 35,* 36–41.

Bybee, R. (1997). *Achieving scientific literacy: From purposes to practices.* Portsmouth, NH: Heinemann Educational Books.

Bybee, R. (2000). Teaching science as inquiry. In J. Minstrel & E. H. Van Zee (Eds.) *Inquiring into inquiry learning and teaching in science.* Washington, DC: American Association for the Advancement of Science, pp. 20–46.

Cavagnetto, A., Hand, B., & Norton-Meier, L. (2009). The nature of elementary student science discourse in the context of the Science Writing Heuristic approach. *International Journal of Science Education, 31*(7), 1–24.

Coffey, H. (2008). *Culturally relevant teaching.* http://www.learnnc.org/lp/pages/4474.

Colburn, A. (2000). An inquiry primer. *Science Scope, 23*(6), 42–44.

Craviotto, E., Heras, A. I., & Espindola, J. (1999). Cultures of the fourth-grade bilingual classroom. *Primary Voices K–6, 7*(3), 25–36.

DeBoer, G. E. (1991). *A history of ideas in science education: Implications for practice*. New York, NY: Teachers College Press.

Dobb, F. (2004). *Essential elements of effective science instruction for English learners*. Los Angeles, CA: California Science Project. http://csmp.ucop.edu/downloads/csp/essential_elements_2.pdf.

Driver, R., Asoko, H., Leach, J. Mortimer, E., & Scott, P. (1994). Constructing scientific knowledge in the classroom. *Educational Researcher, 23*(7): 5–12.

Erben, T., Ban, R., & Castaneda, M. (2008). *Teaching English language learners through technology*. New York: Routledge.

Fang, Z. (2006). The language demands of science reading in middle school. *International Journal of Science Education, 28*, 491–520.

Finson, K. D., Beaver, J. B., & Cramond, B. L. (1995). Development and field test of a checklist for the draw-a-scientist test. *School Science and Mathematics, 95*, 195–205.

Flick, L. B. (1993). The meanings of hands-on science. *Journal of Science Teacher Education, 4*(1), 1–8.

Fouzder, N. B., & Markwick, A. J. (1999). A practical project to help bilingual students to develop their knowledge of science and English language. *School Science Review, 80(292)*, 65–74.

Garrett, P., & Shade, R. (2004). The laughter-learning link. *Science Scope, 27*(8), 27–29.

Gess-Newsome, J. (2002). The use and impact of explicit instruction about the nature of science and science inquiry in an elementary science methods course. *Science and Education, 11*, 55–67.

Halloun, I., & Hestenes, D. (1985). The initial knowledge state of college physics students. *American Journal of Physics, 53*(11), 1043–1055.

Hassard, J., & Dias, M. (2009). *The art of teaching science: Inquiry and innovation in middle school and high school*. New York, NY: Routledge.

Huitt, W., & Hummel, J. (2003). Piaget's theory of cognitive development. *Educational Psychology Interactive*. Valdosta, GA: Valdosta State University.

Jones, R., & Bangert, A. (2006). The CSI effect: Changing the face of science. *Science Scope, 30*(3), 38–42.

Kern, E., & Carpenter, J. (1984). Enhancement of student values, interests, and attitudes in earth science through a field-oriented approach. *Journal of Geological Education, 32*, 299–305.

Keys, C., Hand, B., Prain, V., & Collins, S. (1999). Using the Science Writing Heuristic as a tool for learning from laboratory investigations in secondary science. *Journal of Research in Science Teaching, 36*(10), 1065–1084.

Khishfe, R. (2008). The development of seventh graders' views of nature of science. *Journal of Research in Science Teaching, 45*(4), 470–496.

Khishfe, R., & Abd-El-Khalick, F. (2002). Influence of explicit and reflective versus implicit inquiry-oriented instruction on sixth graders' views of nature of science. *Journal of Research in Science Teaching, 39*: 551–578.

King, K. (2007). *Integrating the National Science Education Standards into classroom practice*. Upper Saddle River, NJ: Pearson.

Ladson-Billings, G. (1994). *The dreamkeepers: Successful teachers of African American children*. San Francisco, CA: Jossey-Bass.

Ladson-Billings, G. (1995a). Toward a theory of culturally relevant pedagogy. *American Educational Research Journal, 32*(3), 465–491.

Ladson-Billings, G. (1995b). But that's just good teaching! The case for culturally relevant pedagogy. *Theory into Practice, 34*(3), 159–165.

Lederman, N. G. (1998). The state of science education: Subject matter without context. *Electronic Journal of Science Education 3*: 1–12.

Lederman, N. G., & Abd-El-Khalick, F. (1998). Avoiding de-natured science: Activities that promote understandings of the nature of science. In W. F. McComas (Ed.) *The nature of science in science education*. Dordrecht, The Netherlands: Kluwer Academic Publishers, pp. 83–126.

Lee, O., & Avalos, M. A. (2002). Promoting science instruction and assessment for English language learners. *Electronic Journal of Science Education, 7*(2). http://wolfweb.unr.edu/homepage/crowther/ejse/lee.pdf.

Lee, O., & Fradd, S. H. (2001). Instructional congruence to promote science learning and literacy development for linguistically diverse students. In D. R. Lavoie & W. M. Roth (Eds.), *Models of science teacher preparation* (pp. 109–126). AA Dordrecht, Netherlands: Kluwer Academic Publishers.

Linik, J. R. (2004). Growing language through science. *Northwest Teacher, 5*(1), 6–9.

Moore, J. A. (1993). *Science as a way of knowing: The foundations of modern biology.* Cambridge, MA: Harvard University Press.

National Center for Education Statistics (NCES). (2003). *Overview of public elementary and secondary schools and districts: School year 2001–2002,* Washington, DC: Department of Education.

National Research Council (1996). *National science education standards.* Washington, DC: National Academy Press.

National Research Council (2001). *Classroom assessment and the national science education standards.* Washington, DC: National Academy Press.

Novick, S., & Nussbaum, J. (1978). Junior high school pupils' understanding of the Particulate Nature of Matter: an interview study. *Science Education 62*(3), 273–281.

Penick, J. E., Crow, L. W., & Bonnstetter, R. J. (1996). Questions are the answer. *The Science Teacher, 63*(1), 27–29.

Piaget, J. (1952). *The origins of intelligence in children,* New York, NY: International Universities Press.

Ramirez, J. D., & Douglas, D. (1988). *Language minority parents and the school: bridging the gap.* Sacramento, CA: California State Department of Education, Office of Bilingual Bicultural Education.

Richard-Amato, P. (1988). *Making it happen: Interaction in the second language classroom.* White Plains, NY: Longman.

Russell, H. R. (1998). *Ten-minute field trips.* Arlington, VA: NSTA Press.

Rutherford, J., & Ahlgren, A. (1989). *Science for all Americans.* Washington, DC: American Association for the Advancement of Science, *42*(1), 254–266.

Ryder, J., Leach, J., & Driver, R. (1999). Undergraduate science students' images of science. *Journal of Research in Science Teaching. 36,* 201–219.

Schwartz, R. S., Lederman, N. G., & Crawford, B. A. (2004). Developing views of nature of science in an authentic context: An explicit approach to bridging the gap between nature of science and scientific inquiry. *Science Education, 88,* 610–645.

St. John, J., Amram, F. M. B., & Henderson, S. K. (1996). *Hispanic scientists: Ellen Ochoa, Carlos A. Ramírez, Eloy Rodriguez, Lydia Villa-Komaroff, Maria Elena Zavala.* Mankato, MN: Capstone.

Torres, H. N., & Zeidler, D. L. (2002). The effects of English language proficiency and scientific reasoning skills on the acquisition of science content knowledge by Hispanic English language learners and native English language speaking students. *Electronic Journal of Science Education, 6*(3). http://ejse.southwestern.edu/original%20site/manuscripts/v6n3/articles/art04_torres/torres.pdf.

Watts, D. M., & Zylberstain, J. (1981). A survey of some ideas about force. *Physics Education, 16,* 360–365.

Index